= LDON/

WITHDRAWN

Continuum Studies in Contemporary North American Fiction

Series Editor: Sarah Graham, Lecturer in American Literature, University of Leicester, UK

This series offers up-to-date guides to the recent work of major contemporary North American authors. Written by leading scholars in the field, each book presents a range of original interpretations of three key texts published since 1990, showing how the same novel may be interpreted in a number of different ways. These informative, accessible volumes will appeal to advanced undergraduate and postgraduate students, facilitating discussion and supporting close analysis of the most important contemporary American and Canadian fiction.

Titles in the Series include:

Bret Easton Ellis: American Psycho, Glamorama, Lunar Park
Edited by Naomi Mandel

Cormac McCarthy: All the Pretty Horses, No Country for Old Men, The Road
Edited by Sara Spurgeon

Louise Erdrich: Tracks, The Last Report on the Miracles at Little No Horse, The Plague of Doves
Edited by Deborah L. Madsen

Margaret Atwood: The Robber Bride, The Blind Assassin, Oryx and Crake
Edited by J. Brooks Bouson

Philip Roth: American Pastoral, The Human Stain, The Plot Against America
Edited by Debra Shostak

Toni Morrison: Paradise, Love, A Mercy
Edited by Lucille P. Fultz

DON DELILLO

Mao II, Underworld, Falling Man

Edited by Stacey Olster

continuum

Continuum International Publishing Group
The Tower Building   80 Maiden Lane
11 York Road   Suite 704
London SE1 7NX   New York, NY 10038

www.continuumbooks.com

British Library Cataloguing-in-Publication Data
A catalogue record for this book is available from the British Library.

ISBN: 978-0-8264-4410-3 (paperback)
ISBN: 978-0-8264-4463-9 (hardcover)

Library of Congress Cataloging-in-Publication Data
A catalog record for this book is available from the Library of Congress.

Typeset by Newgen Imaging Systems Pvt Ltd, Chennai, India
Printed and bound in India by Replika Press Pvt Ltd

For all those who kept this falling woman
from touching ground, and never withdrew
their safety nets afterwards

Lauren Cassell

Barbara Edelstein

Gary Horbar

Walter Maddox

Mary Jane Massie

Beryl McCormick

Anne Moore

Burton Rochelson

Contents

Series Editor's Introduction   ix

Chapter 1   Introduction: Don DeLillo and the Dream Release   1
Stacey Olster

PART I   *Mao II (1991)*

Chapter 2   Delphic DeLillo: *Mao II* and Millennial Dread   19
David Cowart

Chapter 3   *Mao II* and the New World Order   34
Peter Knight

Chapter 4   *Mao II* and Mixed Media   49
Laura Barrett

PART II   *Underworld (1997)*

Chapter 5   *Underworld*, Memory, and the Recycling
of Cold War Narrative   69
Thomas Hill Schaub

Chapter 6   *Underworld* and the Architecture of
Urban Space   83
David L. Pike

Chapter 7   *Underworld*, Ethnicity, and Found
Object Art: Reason and Revelation   99
Josephine Gattuso Hendin

PART III   *Falling Man (2007)*

Chapter 8   Global Horizons in *Falling Man*   121
John Carlos Rowe

Chapter 9 Bodies in Rest and Motion in *Falling Man*   135
            Linda S. Kauffman

Chapter 10 Witnessing Trauma: *Falling Man* and
            Performance Art   152
            John N. Duvall

            Works Cited   169
            Further Reading   178
            Notes on Contributors   182
            Index   185

Series Editor's Introduction

Each study in this series presents ten original essays by recognized subject specialists on the recent fiction of a significant author working in the United States or Canada. The aim of the series is to consider important novels published since 1990 either by established writers or by emerging talents. By setting 1990 as its general boundary, the series indicates its commitment to engaging with genuinely contemporary work, with the result that the series is often able to present the first detailed critical assessment of certain texts.

In respect of authors who have already been recognized as essential to the canon of North American fiction, the series provides experts in their work with the opportunity to consider their latest novels in the dual context of the contemporary era and as part of a long career. For authors who have emerged more recently, the series offers critics the chance to assess the work that has brought authors to prominence, exploring novels that have garnered acclaim both because of their individual merits and because they are exemplary in their creative engagement with a complex period.

Including both American and Canadian authors in the term "North American" is in no sense reductive: studies of Canadian writers in this series do not treat them as effectively American, and assessment of all the chosen authors in terms of their national and regional identity, as well as their race and ethnicity, gender and sexuality, religion and political affiliation is essential in developing an understanding of each author's particular contribution to the representation of contemporary North American society.

The studies in this series make outstanding new contributions to the analysis of current fiction by presenting critical essays chosen for their originality, insight, and skill. Each volume begins with a substantial introduction to the author by the study's editor, which establishes the context for the chapters that will follow through a discussion of essential elements such as the writer's career, characteristic narrative strategies, themes, and preoccupations, making clear the author's importance and the significance of the novels chosen for discussion. The studies are all comprised of three parts, each one presenting three original essays on a a key recent work by the author, and every part is introduced by the volume's editor, explaining how the chapters to follow engage with the fiction and respond to existing interpretations. Each individual chapter takes a critical approach that may develop existing perceptions or challenge them, but always expands the ways in which the author's work may be read by offering a fresh approach.

It is a principle of the series that all the studies are written in a style that will be engaging and clear however complex the subject, with the aim of fostering further debate about the work of writers who all exemplify what is most exciting and valuable in contemporary North American fiction.

Sarah Graham

CHAPTER 1

Introduction: Don DeLillo and the Dream Release

Stacey Olster

The Red Scare which for years remained a journalistic luxury, a Hallowe'en false face for bored chauvinists, comes to resemble more and more the bad dream from which we cannot awaken, the bad dream of history.

Leslie A. Fiedler, "McCarthy and the Intellectuals" (1954)

The novel is the dream release, the suspension of reality that history needs to escape its own brutal confinements.

Don DeLillo, "The Power of History" (1997)

It is hardly coincidental that Leslie A. Fiedler, writing at the height of the Cold War, would invoke James Joyce's *Ulysses* (1922) when describing history as the bad dream from which we—which is to say, Americans—could not awaken. The intellectual climate at the time was filled with cries of modernist fracture, proof, as C. P. Snow stated from abroad, that "the Western societies are behaving as though they had reached an end-state of history" (16). Convinced that 6 August 1945 "marked the violent death of one stage of man's history," Norman Cousins titled his V-J Day editorial "Modern Man Is Obsolete" (5). Norman Podhoretz declared the "'modern' world of which Faulkner, Hemingway, and Dos Passos were the most penetrating interpreters" to have "froze[n] to death in 1948" (23). Eric F. Goldman cited "the shocks of 1949"—the communist conquest of China, the announcement of the Soviet atom bomb, and the trial of Alger Hiss—as "the last straw" that "shattered" all previous political alignments (117, 127). And reflecting this climate of apocalyptic despair, faced with what Norman Mailer termed the "knot of history"

(*Barbary* 203), American novelists of the Cold War period responded accordingly, offering works rooted in metaphors of impotence and paralysis (Mailer's *Barbary Shore* [1951] and *The Deer Park* [1955], John Barth's *The Floating Opera* [1956] and *The End of the Road* [1958]) and dependent on retreat as their operative principle (Ralph Ellison's *Invisible Man* [1952], Richard Wright's *The Outsider* [1953]).

Writing from the post–Cold War perspective of 1997, the year his re-creation of the Cold War era in *Underworld* (1997) would appear in print, Don DeLillo affirmed fiction that resisted being handmaiden to a history that did not, in fact, come to an end—at least not the kind of end predicted years earlier: as one of his early characters notes, "Obviously we can live with Communism; we've been doing it long enough" (*End Zone* 84). DeLillo proposed instead fiction that could serve as "a form of counterhistory" and language that "break[s] the faith of conventional re-creation" ("Power of History" 63). "Against the force of history, so powerful, visible and real," he wrote, "the novelist poses the idiosyncratic self" ("Power of History" 62). Indeed, spanning as it does the last three decades of the twentieth century and the first decade of the twenty-first, and consisting of fifteen novels to date, DeLillo's work provides a historical roadmap of the struggle of the individual self to retain a sense of autonomy within a world defined by crowds and consumerism, menace and mass media, totalitarianism and terrorism.

DeLillo, of course, is not the only American novelist to have chronicled this historical period and with such productivity—the names of Philip Roth, John Updike, and Gore Vidal immediately come to mind. But unlike those three authors, whose works often take the form of novelistic series that emphasize continuities (e.g., the Zuckerman books, the Rabbit tetralogy, the "American Chronicle" series respectively), DeLillo is more concerned with paradigm shifts. *Libra* (1988) depicts the assassination of John F. Kennedy as the moment that "broke the back of the American century" (181), its 5.6 seconds unraveling "the sense of a coherent reality most of us shared" and eventuating in a forced entry into "a world of randomness and ambiguity," as DeLillo wrote in a 1983 essay ("American Blood" 22). *Cosmopolis* (2003) portrays the millennium as the culmination of a decade in which "money has taken a turn" and "[a]ll wealth has become wealth for its own sake" (77). *Falling Man* (2007) opens with reference to "the world now" (3), defined by "figures in windows a thousand feet up, dropping into free space," and distinct from "the other life" before 9/11 (4, 131)—a novelized version of sentiments earlier expressed in a December 2001 essay, "In the Ruins of the Future," in which DeLillo declared the Cold War narrative as having "end[ed] in the rubble" and asserted the need for us to create a "counter-narrative" (34), no longer defined by two superpower nation-states but by one democratic, if flawed, United States and one "global theocratic state, unboundaried and floating and so obsolete it must depend on suicidal fervor to gain its aims" (40).

Not the least of the paradigm shifts to concern DeLillo has been the shift from modernism to postmodernism. On the one hand, DeLillo's presence on almost every twentieth- and twenty-first-century American literature syllabus today, both undergraduate and graduate, is in part due to the way that his portrayal of contemporary culture corresponds so well with the work of contemporary critical theorists. Typified by scholars such as Fredric Jameson, Guy Debord, Jean Baudrillard, and Linda Hutcheon, these theorists question whether a unique artistic style is possible in a world in which even aesthetic production has become a form of commodity production and technology, by way of the mass media, has replaced the history of that world with a set of consumable images, representations divorced from referents and subject to the political whims of their manufacturers. On the other hand, almost all of DeLillo's works concern themselves with Dedalian artistic surrogates— the documentary filmmaker David Bell in *Americana* (1971), the rock musician Bucky Wunderlick in *Great Jones Street* (1973), the CIA analyst Nicholas Branch in *Libra*, the novelist Bill Gray in *Mao II* (1991), the performance artist Lauren Hartke in *The Body Artist* (2001)—whose struggles to engage a media-infused culture without becoming absorbed by that culture, to seek that "dream release" from the "brutal confinements" of history, to recall DeLillo's own phrasing, have led critics to describe DeLillo as a modernist in postmodernist's clothing.

From Sea to Shining Sea

Just how much the paradigm shifts of the last half century signal a shift in DeLillo's own *oeuvre* can be seen by comparing his more recent depictions of America in an age of globalization with the portrayals of American nationhood that appear in his earlier works. Skeptical of all origins in an age of Baudrillardian simulacra, copies without originals, and aware of how little the *unum* represents the *pluribus*, DeLillo pays no more than lip service to the familiar Americanist tropes that his characters of the 1970s and 1980s nostalgically invoke. When David Bell opts to "[e]xplore America in the screaming night" in *Americana* by way of "the great golden West and the Indians and the big outdoor soul of America" (11, 125), he quickly discovers that the landscape is obscured by smoke and billboards and the country itself is linked mainly by telephone poles. When Jack Gladney waxes lyrical about sleeping bags, Western saddles, and bows and arrows that returning students bring to College-on-the-Hill—DeLillo's contemporary version of the theocratic

"Citty vpon a Hill"—in *White Noise* (1985), he is reminded that his autumnal ode to Manifest Destiny that bespeaks "a people, a nation," pertains only to those with enough cash to pay the school's high tuition bills (4).

But when DeLillo himself delves into the Bell family history that is meant to emblematize the nation's, much as Thomas Pynchon does in *Gravity's Rainbow* (1973) when tracing the history of the Slothrop family back to its 1630 arrival on the *Arbellla*, he returns with findings that, however different from those of Pynchon, are transhistorically binding. Pynchon's positing the Slothrops' paper business as the source of toilet paper, banknotes, and newsprint—"Shit, money, and the Word, the three American truths, powering the American mobility" (28)—presents America's subsequent transformation into capitalist giant not as a deviation from its foundational Puritan precepts but the apotheosis of them, since, as Sacvan Bercovitch has argued (46–47), the use of outer vocation as a sign of inner election enabled free enterprise to flourish in seventeenth-century New England. DeLillo's investigation of the Bell family history, by contrast, uncovers forebears of two antithetical impulses: an ascetic mother infused with a belief in magic and kite-souls, who traces her descent through ministers "practically all the way back to Jamestown" (*Americana* 147), and an ad man father known for "mov[ing] the merch" (92), who traces his line back to the father who once pitched "*McHenry—the Star-Spangled Pajamas*" (207) to the "great armchair dreamer," whose own consuming ancestors, in DeLillo's view, "came over on the Mayflower" (282).

Such a schizophrenic foundation played a pivotal role in Mailer's diatribes against America for years. Having deemed the "fissure in the national psyche widened to the danger point" as early as 1960 ("Super-man" 40), the result of a nation split between "the center of Christianity [that] was a mystery, a son of God," and "the center of the corporation [that] was a detestation of mystery, a worship of technology," he diagnosed, in 1968, the war in Vietnam as welcomed for offering "the only temporary cure possible" for its citizens' suppressed emotions (*Armies of the Night* 211–12). Aware, in much the same way, of the "menace of the history of quiet lives" from which a "scream seems imminent" (*Americana* 188), DeLillo, in the 1970s and 1980s, focused more on those domestic acts of "funny violence" that characterize the responses of individual American citizens—as occurs when parents order their daughter to shoot her dog as punishment for her own sexual activity and get arrested for cruelty to animals after the girl puts a bullet in her own head (*Americana* 374)—or, more frequently, those acts of violence that serve, as he put it, as "a kind of sardonic response to the promise of consumer fulfillment in America" (DeCurtis 57). Puerto Rican and

African American teens pelt a commuter train with rocks as it makes its way through Harlem and the South Bronx, and suburban passengers remain unfazed because they "knew it was coming sooner or later" (*Americana* 162). Marguerite Oswald gets fired from a saleswoman's job in New York because her deodorant does not work as well as advertised (*Libra* 38), and her impoverished son Lee, writing years later from the most recent of the small rooms in which he has been forced to live his entire life, orders two guns through mail order.

This is not to suggest that DeLillo's earlier portrayals of America ignore the world beyond its borders or forgo the binarism—in the case of the United States in particular, the Manichaeism, Exceptionalism, or what Michael Rogin has termed "American political demonology" (272–300)—that historically has been so crucial in the emergence of the modern nation-state. The Vietnam War continues to rage on television in *Americana*. Nuclear holocausts and the superpowers with the technological know-how to cause them form a constant subject of debate in *End Zone* (1972). Yet it is only as COMRUS, a name deliberately meant to "neutralize" emotions during a "totally simulated world situation" war-game that Gary Harkness, the book's narrator, plays with an Air Force ROTC major, that the Soviet Union ever appears in this second novel (220, 223). Exobiology professor Alan Zapalac, in fact, pointedly admits that his fears do not concern "our national enemies, our traditional cold-war or whatever-kind-of-war enemies," but rather the enemy that is "my own country" (159). The "eager violence of the heart" from which Coach Creed, "a landlocked Ahab" (54), fashions individual players into a Screaming Eagles football team thus has little to do with ideology and everything to do with bringing "men closer together" through a system of rules and regulations that convey "the illusion that order is possible," and "not just order but civilization" (34, 112). The "exemplary spectator[s]" who are privy to that illusion are transformed, by virtue of the shared spectacle, into "true, real and honest faces, Americans on a Saturday night" (111, 107).

Defining citizenship in this arbitrary manner flies directly in the face of those guardians of culture writing during the Cold War period who distinguished between a *people* or *folk*, bound by common interests, traditions, and values, and a *mass*, composed of individuals "not related *to each other* at all," as Dwight Macdonald argued, "but only to something distant, abstract, nonhuman," such as "a football game," to which they surrender their "human identity and quality" (69). Yet caught between the angst of modernist alienation and the vertigo that comes from "living in curved"—which is to say, unmappable postmodern—"space" (*Libra* 164), DeLillo's characters are often more than willing to merge their identities with that of the group, despite the totalitarianism in which all such unions have the potential to result. Gary Harkness seeks "the very middle of the rocking mass" during football scrimmages, despite the threats of swinging legs and flying fists, because he is aware that the "real danger" exists "at the periphery" where "individual attacks [could be] mounted" (*End Zone* 140). Jack Gladney screens Nazi convocations during class hours, despite his own terror of death, because he knows that "[t]o break off from the crowd is to risk death as an individual" and thus the crowds that "assembled in the name of death"— around Hitler in Germany, around himself in the lecture hall—"form a shield against their own dying" (*White Noise* 73).

The venue through which Americans are most frequently joined in these works of the 1970s and 1980s is American popular culture. The instructors of the American environments department in *White Noise* use the death of a movie star—James Dean—instead of a president— John Kennedy—as their historical touchstone because, within "the natural language of the culture" that they speak (9), it is the former that constitutes the event that most unites their generation. In so doing, of course, they merely duplicate what the characters in Ann Beattie's *Chilly Scenes of Winter* (1976) do when linking the end of their own formative decade—the 1960s—to the deaths of Janis Joplin, Brian Jones, Jim Morrison, and even Jim Morrison's widow. But when DeLillo's instructors also cite Woodstock, Altamont, and Monterey as other "seminal events" in their collective history (67), they cite events at which they need not have been physically present because each was made into a film, thus validating Debord's conception of the spectacle as not simply "a means of unification" but "a social relationship between people that is mediated by images" (12), specifically images generated by the electronic media. In contrast, then, to a novel like Robert Coover's *The Public Burning* (1977), in which being at Times Square on Friday, 19 June 1953, for the Hollywood extravaganza of Julius and Ethel Rosenberg's execution is a prerequisite for sharing in the "*untransacted destiny of the American people*" (615), all the Gladneys in *White Noise* need to do to renew their citizenship is gather in front of a television set with Chinese take-out and through this weekly "Friday assembly" link themselves to Americans all over the country tuned to the same channel (64).

The cost of such renewal is high, however, far higher than the cannibalizing of the mind later displayed in Pynchon's *Vineland* (1990) by those addicted to television, the "big fat computer [that] jus' had you for lunch" (337), or those Thanatoids who exist in a state "like death, only different," and, not coincidentally, "spen[d] at least part of every waking hour with an eye on the Tube" (170–71). Unlike Pynchon, who portrays television, film, and computer screens as equally complicit in the objectification of human beings as characters and equally subservient to a historically repressive state (Ronald Reagan both Screen Actors Guild and United States president, cable companies partitioning Northern California into zones "which in time became political units in their own right" [319]), DeLillo distinguishes between film, an art form, and television, a form of commerce (Moss 156). While the consolidation that both provide depends upon a shared set of references that colonize viewers' minds—the terrors of a near-airplane crash expressed by way of *Airport* and *Airplane!*, disasters only real to the extent that they appear on television (*White Noise* 90, 66)—the consolidation that television provides also depends upon viewers subscribing to a diminished set of aspirations that can fit within the contours of a small box. Neither Gatsbys seeking the green light at the end of Daisy's dock (much less Fitzgerald's "fresh, green breast of the new world" [182]) nor "Burt Lancaster[s] standing in the rain waiting for Deborah Kerr to open the door" (*Americana* 152), DeLillo's Americans settle for "two solid weeks of sex and adventure with a vacationing typist from Iowa City," tragically unaware that their desire is a function of the "limitation of dreams" to which advertising has conditioned them (282), and that "cluttered lust, long gone now," has no place in the "ascetic scheme" of today's "low motel" or among the images transmitted by the "electronic rabbit at the end of the bed" (220). The medium in *Libra* that dupes Lee Oswald into thinking that he, too, can be a star when he sees himself on screen in a Texas department store window turns out to be the smallest of small rooms in which he is entrapped once he is arrested for shooting Kennedy and is transformed by broadcasters into Lee Harvey Oswald, a name he cannot even recognize as his own (227, 416).

It is no wonder, then, that these works of the 1970s and 1980s provide DeLillo's artistic surrogates with few chances for meaningful polysemy and even fewer opportunities for distanced cultural critique. With "pee-pee-maw-maw" the last words he chooses to utter prior to being injected with a drug that causes loss of speech (256), the messianic return from that "unimprinted level where all sound is silken and nothing erodes in the mad weather of language" that Bucky Wunderlick plans at the end of *Great Jones Street* offers no more hope than the disappearance from which he seeks to "return with a new language" at the book's beginning (265, 3). With an orgy of piss and puke the last act in which he engages during the western odyssey that shapes *Americana*, the "montage of speed, guns, torture, rape, orgy and consumer packaging" from which David Bell has tried to "free" himself similarly comes full circle (35)— quite literally in the form of the nine-mile circular test track on which the climactic scene takes place. And with that montage, in turn, comprising the picture of America that DeLillo offers during the first half of his career, it is fully appropriate that in taking the assassination of John

F. Kennedy as its subject, the final novel of this period, *Libra*, itself comes full circle in returning to the place in which the first novel concludes: Dealey Plaza.

We Are The World

Mao II, *Underworld*, and *Falling Man* all take as their givens the end of the Cold War and the emergence of a globalized economy in which, as DeLillo writes, "[c]apital burns off the nuance in a culture" (*Underworld* 785). They also signal a shift in emphasis from some of the modernist/postmodernist concerns that mark his earlier fiction. Dovetailing more with the work of scholars such as Anthony Giddens, Immanuel Wallerstein, David Held, Michael Hardt, and Antonio Negri, to name but a few, who have examined the demise of nation-states in an age of huge conglomerates, these three novels interrogate all notions of national identity. "Home is a failed idea," DeLillo writes in *Mao II* (92), a point that is confirmed by the broken marriages in the later two books and, even more importantly, by the broken bonds between fathers and sons that point to ruptures in the patriarchal foundation on which the United States itself rests. If *Underworld* queries the difference of America from other countries by showing the constructed nature of all those Us/Them binaries that promote Exceptionalism (Thomson/Branca, Giants/Dodgers, USA/USSR), *Falling Man* questions the relevance of America when, in a world no longer defined by cores and peripheries, the only center that it occupies may be "the center of its own shit" (191).

Hints of such post-1990s concerns appear in DeLillo's earlier work, to be sure—*White Noise*, for instance, features a supermarket stocked with exotic products from twenty countries (169), an experimental drug funded by a multinational giant (299), and assorted characters whose features defy any single ethnic, racial, or national identification (208, 307). The work in which they figure most prominently is, not surprisingly, *The Names* (1982), DeLillo's one novel to take place outside the confines of the United States. Set in Greece during an interregnum period of multiple "befores"—"the summer before crowds attacked the U.S. embassies in Islamabad and Tripoli [21 November and 2 December 1979]" (67), "before Iraqi ground troops moved into Iran at four points along the border [thus before the war that began on 22 September 1980], before the oilfields burned and the sirens sounded through Baghdad" (233)—the novel ends with reference to "[b]ombings [that] will become commonplace" and terror for which "[n]o one claims credit" (330). The book also portrays America as poised between an older model of imperialism, defined by fixed boundaries (metropolis versus colony) and geographic conquest (the extension of European sovereignty), and the newer model of "Empire" proposed by Hardt and Negri, defined by smooth space in which power is as deterritorialized as it is all-encompassing and a world market that steadily absorbs the entire globe as its domain (xi-xvi). If a British Empire nostalgically recalled in terms of "[o]pportunity, adventure, sunsets, dusty death" (*Names* 7) is portrayed as anachronistic, a Henry Rawlinson granting a "humane face" to colonialism by way of deciphered cuneiform writing is revealed as oddly prophetic (80). For, as DeLillo notes, the urge to "[s]ubdue and codify" the spoken languages of Old Persian, Elamite, and Babylonian partook of the same impulse that subdued the land itself for profit (80)—the operating principle of the company for which Rawlinson worked for close to thirty years, the East India Company.

If DeLillo stops short at making that company the face of Bush's New World Order as Pynchon does in *Mason & Dixon* (1997)—locating it "ev'rywhere, and [in] Ev'rything" (69), with outposts that perform "the Doings of Global Trade in miniature" (159) making it "Something richer than many a Nation, yet with no Boundaries," and, "tho' never part of any Coalition, yet maintain[ing] its own great Army and Navy" (140)—it is because DeLillo already had prepared the ground to have the CIA play that role. First seen in *Running Dog* (1978) in the form of Radial Matrix, a legally incorporated proprietary of U.S. intelligence, whose rogue espionage ops dovetail with diversified rogue business ops overseas (74–76), it enters *The Names* in the form of the Northeast Group, another subsidiary of a multibillion-dollar "monster corporation," later exposed as the CIA, that is concerned only with "profit curve[s]" and that uses gains in consumer products to offset losses incurred when insured workers of multinationals are targeted for terrorist attack (242, 268). Anticipating all those organizations incorporated in one place, acting in others, and hidden by pyramids of paper—which turn the "monster" that is Frank Norris's *Octopus* (1901), its "tentacles of steel" at least linked to an identifiable head (51), into a fond memory—these subterranean groups expose how irrelevant all political heads of state now are. For all its mention of actual historical events in which U.S. presidents played a role, *The Names* does not cite a single U.S. president by name; for all its mention of actual U.S. presidents by name, *Underworld* attributes the greatest amount of power to the name J. Edgar Hoover, who finds his apotheosis in the completely deterritorialized Internet, distinguished by "no space or time," in which "[e]verything is connected" (825).

No longer is the violence in these later DeLillo works primarily an expression of consumer betrayal. The Texas Highway Killer of *Underworld*, driven by a need to "become part of the history of others" in order "to get out from under the pissant details of who he was" (266), and who "feel[s] real" only when talking live to a TV anchorwoman who replays a tape of one of his homicides (269), is the last of the frustrated performers for whom Lee Harvey Oswald serves as prototype (Arthur Bremer, James Earl Ray, and John Hinckley being some of the others) that appear in DeLillo's writing—by the end of the novel his name is a thing of the past (807). And Benno Levin, who plans to "make a public act of [his] life" by chronicling his shooting of billionaire Eric Packer in *Cosmopolis*, is even more doomed to obscurity because "stop[ping] the world" with ten thousand pages of longhand print means "living offline now" (149, 152). Rather, the violence that Americans fear as imminent in DeLillo's later works comes from a different source entirely, as James Axton, the narrator of *The Names*, presciently recognizes:

> I thought I sometimes detected in people who had lost property or fled, most frequently in Americans, some mild surprise that it hadn't happened sooner, that the men with the six-day beards hadn't come much earlier to burn them out, or uproot the plumbing, or walk off with the prayer rugs they'd bargained for in the souk and bought as investments—for the crimes of drinking whiskey, making money, jogging in shiny suits along the boulevards at dusk. Wasn't there a sense, we Americans felt, in which we had it coming? (41)

When an American banker does get attacked while jogging near the book's end, he experiences no shock, the only unknown having been how the attack would take place and in which country, only relief that "[i]t could have been worse" (326). When Axton realizes that the target just as easily could have been himself, he locates the attacker's motivation in the one word to have penetrated his own consciousness while facing a man with a gun: "*American*" (328).

Significantly, such targeting by way of nationality in no way contradicts DeLillo's portrayal of the world as a "system of connections in which you can't tell the difference between one thing and another, [...] because they are made by the same people in the same way and ultimately refer to the same thing" (*Underworld* 446), a world in which Times Square and Trafalgar Square and Tiananmen Square are interchangeable, as *Mao II* suggests. Nation-states may well be the "'mere' fictions" that authors have claimed (Giddens 26), and the United States with its billion-dollar deficits "sunk to the status of less developed country" in the eyes of its citizens (*Mao II* 5). Yet the "fiction of America" still persists, as Baudrillard argues, and it is "on this fictive basis that it dominates the world" (*America* 29). Or, as DeLillo succinctly states, "America is the world's living myth" (*Names* 114).

This is not to suggest, of course, that resisting an America that both symbolizes the world's Empire and is itself symbolized by strips of electronic data that track the flow of cyber-capital at speeds too fast for the mind to process—"microdecimal increments every sextillionth of a second" (*Cosmopolis* 106)—is a matter of mere representation. Even in a world whose leaders are driven by microchips instead of land masses, "we still have mass graves," as Nick Shay is reminded by a Russian counterpart at the end of *Underworld* (788). And not only for those killed in defiance of power, as the grave sites for the victims of Lockerbie and Oklahoma City attest. Nevertheless, the manner of resistance assumes a less than immediately obvious course. Hardt and Negri admit that the conceptual "*will to be against*" proposed in their book of 2000 is necessarily stymied by the practicalities of a task that "remains rather abstract" (210, 399) and that the arrival of the "postmodern posse" they eagerly await is an event for which they "do not have any models to offer" (411). Likewise, the terrorism portrayed in much of DeLillo's work—regardless of origin or alleged affiliation—is singularly lacking in direction or oppositional distinction. Emblematized by the late '60s affair between Moll Robbins and Gary "Dial-a-Bomb" Penner recalled in *Running Dog*, it is an "erotic commodity" (40, 168), barely different from all those consumer products that Moll has seen exploding in slow motion when the house in *Zabriskie Point* (1970) blows up. Reduced to "calculated madness," the "only worthwhile doctrine" to which those who plan to bomb the Stock Exchange in *Players* (1977) are committed (108), it is an expression of people who "come from nowhere," "d[o]n't even have a nationality," and have "no visible organization or leadership" and "no apparent plan" (121)—people barely different from those intelligence officers who also "don't have a prospectus" and "don't put out an annual report" (115), with whom they often "overlap" (116). And precisely because the overlap in question applies as much to foreign as domestic terrorists, DeLillo grants little credence to the claims of a liaison to a Beirut terrorist group in *Mao II* that "[i]n societies reduced to blur and glut, terror is the only meaningful act" because "[o]nly the terrorist stands outside" a "culture [that] hasn't figured out how to assimilate him" (157); local militias that fire at portraits of each other's leader and watch videos of their street fights on VCRs (227, 109–10) are evidence of not just how "many things Beirut has learned from the West," as the liaison is forced to concede (129), but how much *like* the West Beirut is.

Until September 11, that is. A "new communist element" and specifically not a "new fundamentalist element" (123), the Beirut terrorists in *Mao II* are not "making a race to go to God" and still do "business the old way" when the need arises: "You sell this, you trade that" (233, 235).

A member of Kommune 1 during the late '60s, and possibly the Red Brigades, the German Martin Ridnour in *Falling Man* still is, as Lianne Neudecker acknowledges, "one of ours," and not only for being "godless, Western, white" (195); a dealer who now "mov[e]s art" as relentlessly as Clinton Bell "moves merch" in *Americana*, the former terrorist is so completely assimilated as to be, in DeLillo's appropriation of a Beatles song, "here, there and everywhere" (113, 147). Yet no longer is he able, after the events of September 11, to flee "there to here, with darkest hardship pressing the edges of the frame," like the people whose passport photos are part of his collection, because the borders—both geographic and photographic—that once provided shelter inside from dangers outside are as much a part of the "sepia distance, lost in time," as the faces on the documents (142, 141). As such, 9/11 both actualizes and extends the Cold War dread shrilled by Lenny Bruce in *Underworld*: "*We're all gonna die!*" (506), with the significant difference that 9/11 reflects "two kinds of discipline, two kinds of fundamentalism," as DeLillo intimated as early as *The Names*, "talking across each other to the deaf and the blind" (193). What Ridnour poses as "[o]ne side ha[ving] the capital, the labor, the technology, the armies, the agencies, the cities, the laws, the police and the prisons" and the other "ha[ving] a few men willing to die" (*Falling Man* 46–47) is exactly what the jihadist Hammad notes in his own more succinct observations: "what they hold so precious we see as empty space" (177).

For DeLillo also to locate the "singularity" of 9/11 in its having "no purchase on the mercies of analogy or simile" ("In the Ruins" 39) is, in one sense, simply to reiterate the point made by Theodor Adorno ("Cultural Criticism and Society" [1949]) and, later, George Steiner (*Language and Silence* [1967]) with respect to the Holocaust. In another sense, however, it is to question his faith in the re-creative potential he has granted language throughout his career: glossolalia that can "[s]eal the old language and loose the new" in *The Names* (306, 336), street-corner patois and lower-case letters used for trademarked items that are meant "to work in opposition to the enormous technology of war" in *Underworld* ("Power of History" 63). Like Babette Gladney in *White Noise*, DeLillo, of course, realizes, "We have to use words. We can't just grunt" (233). But he also asserts, in his recent novels, that we don't have to use *only* words. Just as Karen Janney learns that she needs captions beneath photographs of famine, riot, and war to "locate the pictures" she sees in *Mao II* (174)—a work whose narrative sections are themselves prefaced by interpolated photographs—so must she learn that she also needs pictures to supply a context for words; with no such context, "Sendero Luminoso"—Spanish for "Shining Path"—remains "[b]eautiful-looking words" and not the name of a terrorist organization (175).

DeLillo's most recent works go even further, implying that the most effective aesthetic vehicles in conveying consciousness today—and the only ones that might be able to resist aesthetic commodification—are the works of performance artists: the eponymous artist of *Falling Man* whose headfirst falls are neither announced in advance nor designed to be recorded for posterity; the graffiti "writers" of *Underworld* who fashion an "art that can't stand still" (437, 441)—quite literally in the case of Moonman 157, who spray-paints moving subway trains and whose anthropomorphized letters "sweat" and "live and breathe and eat and sleep" and "dance and play the sax" (433). These are DeLillo's artistic surrogates—not Bill Gray, who dies an ignominious death on a ferry to Junieh in *Mao II*, still firm in his belief that "words stick even as lives fly apart" (170). In an age in which, as 9/11 exposed so clearly, lives fly apart both literally and figuratively, these most recent artistic surrogates of DeLillo suggest that words alone may just not be enough.

PART I

Mao II (1991)

Talking to David Remnick about the 1990s, Don DeLillo recalled a passage from Hermann Broch's *The Death of Virgil* (1945) in which the term "no longer and not yet" refers not only to the state of delirium that leaves the eponymous poet "no longer quite alive, and not yet dead," but also to the interim period between paganism and Christianity. As DeLillo went on to say, "I think of this 'no longer and not yet' in terms of no longer the Cold War and not yet whatever will follow" (Remnick 48). Published in 1991, set primarily in 1989, and looking ahead to the year 2000, *Mao II* opens with a mass wedding ceremony whose participants, by contrast, have no such doubts about the days ahead: the neighboring tenements and "miles of delirium" that surround Yankee Stadium only confirm the signs of "Last Days," chants for "End Time," and faith in a "messianic" Sun Myung Moon "come to lead them to the end of human history" (7, 16, 6).

Dubbed "millennial hysteria" by the book's protagonist, Bill Gray, whose xenophobia marks the event as foreign and whose temporal myopia prevents him from seeing past "a total implosion of the future" (80), the apocalyptic fervor displayed in Yankee Stadium is, in fact, meant by DeLillo to recall the grand narrative underlying Yankee history. Derived from a double-edged view of history, in which a sacred process fulfilled within secular time would conclude with a grand finale in which, as Increase Mather wrote, "*the mystery of God shall be finished*" and "*the kingdom shall become the Lord's all the world over*" (243), the notion of an apocalyptic finale held great attraction for early American writers who believed in the paradisiacal restoration that was to follow. If it became less attractive to fin de siècle writers, such as Henry Adams, who famously asserted, "in 1900, the continuity snapped" (457), it was because the new "supersensual" scientific forces that confounded both prelate and physicist refuted not just all grand narratives (486)—which Adams long recognized as having "no absolute truth," being "standard formulas" that man "invent[ed]" to "account to himself for himself somehow" (472)—but all attempts by people such as himself to fashion even what Jean-François Lyotard would later term *petits récits* (60). Viewing his "Dynamic Theory of History" as a failure to uncover "Unity" (472, 484), Adams lapsed into "*futilitarian* silence" (359), convinced that a nineteenth-century man weaned on eighteenth-century principles had no place in a twentieth-century "Nunc Age" defined by "hysteria," "alarm," and chaotic forces that "must at any cost be brought under control" (499).

With his current work-in-progress more than two decades in the making, DeLillo's Bill Gray cannot blame his own authorial silence only on what the twenty-first century seems to promise. Yet the fact that he enters the novel by way of mass-market paperbacks of his "modern classics" that shriek "*Buy me*" from bookstore shelves would suggest that the millennial period to come will be one in which aesthetic production has already become a form of commodity production (20, 19). With Adams's uncontrollable forces of physics replaced by the colonizing forces of late capitalism, signs in Beirut for a Western soft drink—Coke II—resemble character posters from China's Cultural Revolution (230), collapsing all cultural and national differences. And with the World Trade Center so familiar as to appear "harmless" and "[f]orgotten-looking" (40), a paradigm of sales, trade, and three-dimensional currency is giving way to an economics of "cyber-capital" and a "time beyond geography and touchable money and the people who stack and count it" (*Cosmopolis* 207, 36). "Years ago I used to think it was possible for a novelist to alter the inner life of the culture," Bill states early in the novel when lamenting "[w]hat writers used to do before we were all incorporated" and terrorists began "mak[ing] raids on human consciousness" in their stead (41); in Bill's case, however, that expiration date is signaled as much by his parsing of James Joyce as it is by the "insignificant cash" found on his corpse that the cleaner who rifles through his belongings discards at the book's end (217).

The three chapters that follow all examine *Mao II* from a post-millennial perspective. As such, they are able to interrogate all of these aforementioned premises and assess their current validity. David Cowart introduces this reassessment by situating DeLillo's novel within a tradition of apocalyptic literature, juxtaposing its historical prescience against its historical elisions, in order to distinguish what can be called postmodern prophecy. Beginning with the most significant event elided in the book, the fall of the Berlin Wall, Peter Knight explores the degree

to which DeLillo's novel actually confirms the post-apocalyptic paradise heralded by people like Francis Fukuyama, that New World Order
christened by George Bush Sr. In complicating earlier readings of the
novel in this manner, both chapters are able to contest the unremitting
bleakness that frequently informs critical discussions of it: to suggest
that the crowds that silence individual voices also might be the means
through which individuals of similar desires naturally orient themselves; to argue that a postmodern economy in which even people have
become commodities of exchange might be resisted by a voluntary act
of premodern sacrifice, however futile.

Significantly, both chapters also address questions of literary form in
their reassessments: the postponement of meaning and metahistorical
writing in the case of David Cowart, the relationship between metaphor
and metonymy in the case of Peter Knight. This leads logically to Laura
Barrett's investigation of the mixed media that form a crucial element of
the novel itself: the interpolated photographs, the debates about art and
aesthetics, the juxtaposition of novelist and photographer as central
figures. Refuting the view that characterizes images, as typified by those
of Andy Warhol, as weightless, and privileges words, as evidenced by
Bill's typewritten pages, as corporeal proof of subjectivity, this chapter
explores the adjustments to the modernist notion of the author/auteur
that must be made when the only lingua franca may be digital images
and the meaning of words is presented as contingent upon their
context. Looking at DeLillo's novel in conjunction with those of other
contemporary writers—Paul Auster, Jonathan Safran Foer, Mark Z.
Danielewski—that similarly integrate words and images, the chapter
proposes a model in which various modes of representation comple-
ment each other. In tracing this receptivity to DeLillo's skepticism of
any form of representation that does not acknowledge its limits or binds
itself to the reductiveness of mere literalism, the chapter anticipates his
later investigations into aesthetic forms beyond words and photographs—graffiti art, performance art—that are addressed in the other
two novels that are examined in this volume.

CHAPTER 2

Delphic DeLillo: *Mao II* and Millennial Dread

David Cowart

I think there is a sense of last things in my work that probably comes from a Catholic childhood.
  Don DeLillo to Vince Passaro, "Dangerous Don DeLillo" (1991)

He pledges his submission to God and meditates on the blood to come.
  Don DeLillo, "In the Ruins of the Future" (2001)

Religion, violence: the European came to the New World with a Bible in one hand, a weapon in the other. "All the new thinking," to paraphrase Robert Hass, was about spiritually justified coercion (l. 1). "In this"—one does little violence to the poet's original meaning—"it resembled all the old thinking" (Hass l. 2). Nor was religious violence visited only on the heathen. As in the Old World, smug believers in America scourged the heretic and hanged the witch, and such systemic violence, sanctioned by the Book, was always understood to be a miniature version of the great convulsion of the Last Days, when the Elect, who had dutifully converted or exterminated the heathen and the heterodox, would be spared the supreme wrath of God and delivered from the destruction of this fallen and corrupt world.

Small wonder, the robust tradition, in American letters, of apocalyptic imagining. From Michael Wigglesworth's *Day of Doom* (1662) to Nathanael West's *Day of the Locust* (1939) and Thomas Pynchon's *V.* (1963) and *Gravity's Rainbow* (1973), American literature offers up hearty servings of millennialist fare. With *Mao II*, Don DeLillo at once participates in this tradition and, like West and Pynchon, denies its pious premise. Set in 1989 and published in 1991, as the common era slouched toward its third millennium, DeLillo's novel seemed to add its own grim augury of both bang and whimper, its own chagrined testimonial as the anxiety—even among devout secularists—mounted toward hysteria. Scrutinizing 1989, DeLillo had his choice of disasters, portents, and historical benchmarks: the *Exxon Valdez* oil spill, the fatwa against Salman Rushdie, the assassination of Lebanese President René Moawad, the two hundredth anniversary of the French Revolution. Culling the year's events for the crowdscapes with which he punctuates his novel, DeLillo turns a handful of them into what appear to be harbingers of eschatological escalation. He notes, for example, the heavy death toll in April of that year, when thousands of soccer fans surged into high steel fences at Hillsborough Stadium in Sheffield, England. He notes, too, the appalling conclusion, in June, of the Tiananmen Square demonstrations in Beijing, as well as the death and burial, in the same month, of Iran's Ayatollah Ruhollah Khomeini, which sparked the frenzied lamentations of "crowds estimated at three million" (188). "The future," declares DeLillo in one of the most memorable sentences of the late twentieth century, "belongs to crowds" (16).

Crowds recur in the novel as carriers of the millennial virus, symptoms of which include the now anxious, now gleeful anticipation, on the part of the faithful, of "the Last Days" and "the bloodstorm to come" (7). This "millennial hysteria" (80) provides the ground bass of DeLillo's ideational counterpoint. The novel's crowd scenes present themselves for the most part on television screens, and Bill Gray, the protagonist, "has the idea that writers are being consumed by the emergence of news as an apocalyptic force" (72). Bill's somewhat creepy amanuensis, Scott Martineau, sees "footage" of "Chinese Christian cult" members striding into a river, "many swept downstream" (142–43). Brita Nilsson, who emerges as the novel's central figure after the anonymous death of Bill, visits Beirut on assignment and sees "a millennial image mill" (229), a violence-torn city symbolic of all the places where order has broken down and the worst are full of passionate intensity. Karen Janney, part of Bill's curious ménage, hears about, sees, and imagines the coming of what Moonie pidgin characterizes as "hurry-up time to all man" (146, 193). Like Eliot's Madame Sosostris in *The Waste Land* (1922) ("I see crowds of people" [l. 56]), Karen conjures at one moment "a picture of people running in the streets" (176), at another "a picture of people massing in a square" (185). She cannot shake the indoctrination she underwent in the Unification Church, which seems to realize itself chiefly in febrile chiliasm. The ceremony with which the novel opens, a wedding of cultists *en masse*, travesties the marriage of the Lamb in Revelation.

Although the event in Yankee Stadium is fictitious, DeLillo based it on an emergent phenomenon: "I saw a photograph of a wedding conducted by Reverend Moon of the Unification Church," DeLillo says, "and it was just lying around for months . . . a wedding in Seoul in a soft-drink warehouse, about 13,000 people. And when I looked at it again, I realized I wanted to understand this event, and the only way to understand it was to write about it. For me, writing is a concentrated form of thinking" (Passaro 76). In the opening pages of *Mao II*, then, DeLillo at once recalls and anticipates a number of mass marriages (or "blessings," as the cult prefers to call them) in America and abroad: in 1982, Moon officiated at the wedding of some 2,075 couples in Madison Square Garden; in 1998, 30,000 couples would marry at RFK Stadium in Washington, D.C.; in 2000, another 30,000 couples in Seoul; and in 2009, 45,000 more in Asan, South Korea. Some of these prodigious numbers, as the websites maintained by Steven Alan Hassan and Rick Ross indicate, reflect participation by satellite.

In the present essay I would like to consider *Mao II* from a post-millennial vantage and to gauge the extent to which it remains a valuable work of the imagination after the fading of its original timeliness. Does DeLillo's tenth novel (eleventh if one counts the anonymous collaboration *Amazons* [1980]) retain its power now that the Millennium has come and gone? Two decades and more having passed since 1989, that world-climacteric year, one can see with some clarity how much or how little this novel depends on topicality. Undistracted by that element, one places *Mao II* among the great and perspicacious meditations on futurity (the futurity that third-millennium readers paradoxically know at first hand and imagine as still flying before them). But even as he envisions a future inimical to individuality, a future that "belongs to crowds," DeLillo scrupulously interrogates every species of chiliasm for its quotient of superstition and its affinity with flawed or benighted politics. He has, one realizes, little patience with any historiography that might accommodate a doctrine of supernaturally ordained "last days." Declining to imagine any actual historical legitimacy in eschatological fable, he only observes and chronicles. He seeks, as Hamlet says, "to show [. . .] the very age and body of the time his form and pressure" (3. 2. 25–27). In doing so, to be sure, he scrutinizes a civilization that hovers at the brink of some hideous secular dissolution, but the reader may glimpse a better prospect: maybe, as a character in *Americana* (1971) says, "having set one foot into the mud, one foot and three toes" (128), the world will pull back from the swamp of spiritual and political totalitarianism. Maybe crowds will assemble to some better purpose than the embrace of ancient, sterile prophecy.

Thus prompted, one can discern, here and there in *Mao II*, a counter-tide to the currents of grave augury—not only with respect to history but with respect to literature as well. The text teems with equivoques—phrases that one understands in more than one sense, often with reversal of ostensible meaning: "[e]verybody's nowhere" (239), "[m]easure your head before ordering" (170, 201, 216), "hurry-up time" (146, 193). Even "[t]he future belongs to crowds" invites turning inside-out. At first, given the disturbing vision of Yankee Stadium aswarm with cult-addled human lemmings, it seems to announce that crowds will rule a dystopian future. Yet it can also be understood to have meanings that range from the less alarming—"such a future awaits those engaged in the present sacramental travesty"—to the nearly sanguine: "crowds naturally orient themselves to the collective aspiration that can only be realized in the future." In the end, the novel may in fact embrace that third construction. Although the future may not consider such collective aspiration binding, it may in some measure, DeLillo hints, alter course in response to the desire of certain individuals and the vision of certain artists.

Postmodern Prophecy

More commonly, the artist merely sees the future, and critics often, in fact, credit DeLillo with a kind of cultural precognition. One central character of the 1977 novel *Players*, for example, works at the World Trade Center; the other connives at attacks on the iconic institutions and places of the American economic dynamo. In *Running Dog* (1978), by the same token, the supposedly pornographic film shot in the *Führerbunker* prefigures the Hitler Diaries hoax of 1983. *White Noise* (1985), with its terrible Airborne Toxic Event, would have been in galleys when the Bhopal, India, disaster occurred at the end of 1984. The baseball grail in *Underworld* (1997) would also replicate itself—as the ball that Barry Bonds knocked into the stands to break Hank Aaron's longstanding home run record (according to John Wildermuth in the *San Francisco Chronicle*, it brought $752,467 at a 2007 auction [B1]).

Though less obvious as augury, the observations about and depictions of terrorism in *Mao II* ("midair explosions and crumbled buildings" [157]) look simultaneously backward to the late 1988 destruction of Pan Am Flight 103 over Lockerbie, Scotland, and forward to the 1998 embassy bombings in Dar es Salaam and Nairobi, the 2000 attack on the USS *Cole*, and of course the terrible attack on the twin towers on 11 September 2001 (here "the million-storey towers" of the World Trade Center fill the sky outside Brita Nilsson's apartment window [87], and one notes, in passing, the uncanniness of references, however casual, to these structures in texts antedating 9/11). Then and now, to be sure, the language of detonations and shredded bodies drowns out all other discourse in Baghdad, Kandahar, Peshawar, Jakarta, and the occupied territories. One may well nod glumly when an author declares that "[t]he future belongs to crowds" and a central character—himself an author—concedes to terrorists the power once reserved to writers. But in inviting reflection on the prophetic function of literature and its creators (whom Ezra Pound famously characterized as "the antennae of the race" ["Teacher's" 630]), such pronouncements have a way of exfoliating with unexpected qualifications and additional meanings.

For "prediction" is only the vulgar residue of prophecy. Biblical prophets did not predict—they cautioned, reproached, and upbraided to avert the consequences of spiritual backsliding. Cautionary, then, even in its biblical guise, prophecy avails itself of what rhetoricians call *kairos*—the opportune moment for utterance—to ward off an uncongenial future. When DeLillo declares, on the eve of the millennium, that the future belongs to crowds, he performs the classic rhetorical maneuver by which one proposes something objectionable so that it may be denied, avoided, or resisted. The chilling subjunctive in a letter DeLillo wrote to Jonathan Franzen some years after the publication of *Mao II* functions in much the same way: "If serious reading dwindles to near nothingness, it will probably mean that the thing we're talking about when we use the word 'identity' has reached an end" (Franzen 96). In the same letter he characterizes "writing" as "a form of personal freedom" that "frees us from the mass identity we see in the making all around us" (95). In the very act of writing—or reading—such a sentence, one resists that future.

Serious writing, like the utterances of the oracle at Delphi, features a subtlety that often postpones full recognition of meaning. "The poem must resist the intelligence," declares Wallace Stevens, "[a]lmost successfully" (ll. 1–2). Flannery O'Connor makes a similar point: "The fiction writer states as little as possible" (99). Literature, in other words, embraces a benign version of what in *Underworld* is called "*dietrologia*," which "means the science of what is behind something" (280), "the science of dark forces" (335). I rather think, then, that DeLillo intends, in the structuring of *Mao II*, a kind of massive historical ellipsis. Like the submerged part of the iceberg (in Hemingway's apt figure), meaning here turns out to have a great deal to do with something never named: the collapse, toward the end of 1989, of one of the world's great tyrannies. Like the Grail Knight at the Chapel Perilous, one has only to ask a simple question or two, and meaning will unveil: what kind of pattern, exactly, do the great crowd scenes in DeLillo's novel compose, and does the author omit any major examples? The reader who poses these questions arrives at a curious discovery or two: *there is no pattern*, and DeLillo makes no mention of the great crowd scenes with which the year 1989 ended. But why elide the Velvet Revolution, with half a million people in the streets of Prague or, before that, the breaching of the Berlin Wall? Did the future not belong to those crowds too?

Elizabeth K. Rosen has observed that critics pay too little attention to *postmodern* ideas of apocalypse (xxv). DeLillo's apocalypse is in fact as postmodern as the sunsets described in *White Noise* (227, 324–25). His postmodern point is that any pattern discerned in history is illusory—as when, looking into a microscope, one mistakes eyelash for paramecium. Readers of Pynchon will recognize the technique and the message here: to illustrate the speciousness of narratives about the past and its relevance to the present, the author has only to introduce bits and pieces of historical fact and speculation. With the more or less credulous reader in tow, a character such as Herbert Stencil (the latter-day Henry Adams of *V.*) shoulders the responsibilities of the historiographer to weave a narrative culminating in some unspeakable Descent of the Paraclete, as envisioned by his father, Sidney, in 1919. Whether generated by Stencil *père* or Stencil *fils*, such historiography makes of the past a mirror or gauge of the universal human hunger for coherence and significance—a hunger doubly sharp and doubly frustrated in a blood-drenched age. One knows from Yeats, who in "Meditations in Time of Civil War" (1923) also dissects the religion-tinged political violence of the twentieth century, that such hunger must go unsatisfied. "We had fed the heart on fantasies," says Yeats. "The heart's grown brutal from the fare" (vi: ll. 16–17).

DeLillo, like Pynchon (or Robert Coover, or Kurt Vonnegut, or John Barth), puts on an antic disposition when holding the mirror up to history. Sketching a number of portentous crowd scenes and mixing in the rhetoric of millennial dread, DeLillo invites a kind of edifying *méconnaissance* or misapprehension. One discerns a pattern, embraces it, becomes an historiographer—until, that is, one discovers the calculated deception, the mismatched components, the omissions. Disguised as an instance of the millennial hysteria it chronicles, then, *Mao II* is a lesson in what postmodern historiographer Hayden White would call metahistorical thinking. The events that brought 1989 to its extraordinary conclusion figure here as "metahistorical" in two senses: they are beyond (*meta*) the present narrative horizon, and they give the lie to the tendentious emplotment of history on the part of the Reverend Sun Myung Moon and others of his ilk, fixated on their own smug vision of ultimate spiritual and historical consummation.

History and Literary Indirection

Further to illustrate DeLillo's metahistorical points and literary originality, I should like to look a little more closely at one or two of the submerged features of this novelistic iceberg. Brita Nilsson's seemingly inconsequential story about the Great Wall of China, for example, strikes me as an invitation to reflect on other walls in history and literature—especially, of course, the wall whose destruction looms at the end of *Mao II*, but also the one commemorated in a famous poem by Robert Frost. Here, too, one discovers lessons in literary subtlety that bear on DeLillo's meanings.

Late in 1989, joyous crowds dismantled the wall that for some forty years had arrowed its way across Berlin, a Krushchev-Ulbricht Line recalling the similar cartographic intervention, in another century and on another continent, of Charles Mason and Jeremiah Dixon (their laying of a right line through the American wilderness, as Thomas Pynchon conceptualizes it, was also a terrible violation, fraught with proleptic "Bad History" [*Mason & Dixon* 615]). "Brutally interjectory, a censorious interruption of worldly colloquy, the Wall was modernity's defining caesura," observes Christian Moraru (56). It had its antecedents and literary congeners, and one wonders how the poet who wrote "[s]omething there is that doesn't love a wall" ("Mending Wall" ll. 1, 35) would have greeted the demolition of that great fence in Berlin. Frost, too, engages—indeed, delights—in literary indirection, which he called "ulteriority" or "saying one thing and meaning another, saying one thing in terms of another" ("Constant Symbol" 786). He sees the ironies of wall mending in a landscape inimical to such structures, but what really exercises him, as he describes this bucolic activity, is the recognition that slowly dawns as each man approaches his neighbor, stone in hand, to define a boundary: the territorial imperative, one realizes, is as "natural" as anything—frost, say, or Frost—that "doesn't love a wall." Nor does the ulteriority stop there, for another surprise attends on the conceit of the poem's speaker—a poet himself, perhaps—and his neighbor engaged in "just another kind of outdoor game, / One on a side" (ll. 21–22). The figure recalls Frost's famous remark repudiating free verse as tennis with the net down ("Conversations" 856). Whether obstacle, deception, or tennis net, form remains essential—the very condition of artistic achievement. As the speaker and his neighbor play their game, Frost plays another with his reader, who must, to gain a point or two, recognize the prosodic innovation that accompanies the surprise content. An example of what Frost called "sentence sounds," the iambic pentameter here blends deceptively with the rhythms of homely rural speech. The wall, then, is the poem, the necessary formal barrier between artist and audience. Such reflexivity represents a kind of prolegomenon to the postmodern, in which wall becomes word, the signifier that perpetually screens the real.

DeLillo, a novelist writing a novel about a novelist, deploys similar self-referential subtlety. In an era much given to discussing the Death of the Author (itself an example of critical crowdthink), DeLillo includes his own immensely original meditation on authorial mortality. Having adopted or transformed more than one Joycean conceit, DeLillo views the death of the author as a local instance of the death of God ("[i]n many ancient languages, God's name has four letters" [*Mao II* 69], declares the character whose names—"Bill" and "Gray"—both observe the divine orthographic norm). Local or cosmic, such a death requires considerable rethinking of human agency and human fate. It requires new thinking about creation—in all senses of that word.

From the sculptor Sullivan in *Americana* to the writer Fenig in *Great Jones Street* (1973) and the filmmakers Frank Volterra in *The Names* (1982) and Jim Finley in *Point Omega* (2010), DeLillo recurs often in his novels to artists and their work. In the later fictions, he frequently evokes unusual art forms and their visionary creators: one thinks of the performances of Lauren Hartke in *The Body Artist* (2001); the guerilla tableaux of David Janiak in *Falling Man* (2007); the B-52s carpeting the desert in *Underworld*; the Spencer Tunick-like cityscape of naked bodies in which Eric Michael Packer, in *Cosmopolis* (2003), participates; or the work of Alex Macklin in *Love-Lies-Bleeding* (2005), who "gave up easel painting," his son recalls, "to do land art in the West" (25). (As Macklin delights in the evocative names of desert plants, Bill Gray "liked to recite place names that carried the ghost music of remote terrain" [184].)

DeLillo includes two artists in *Mao II*, a photographer and the moribund novelist she eventually replaces as central character. In the end, Bill Gray leaves behind the manuscript of his endlessly revised third novel (*Bill III*, as it were) and a set of contact sheets bearing his image replicated and replicated like so many Warhol Maos—or like some visual mantra: "repeat it, repeat it, repeat it" (4). The insidious Scott Martineau recognizes these relics as commodities that will grow in value as long as he withholds them. DeLillo presents Brita Nilsson as an ambivalent figure as well: one admires her bravery in Beirut, but her abandonment of the Jill Krementz-like project of photographing authors may strike one as some postmodern *trahison des clercs* (cultural betrayal, that is, on the part of the intelligentsia). The change in her professional focus, in any event, seems to validate the disquieting transition bitterly described by one of the last novelists she photographs: "For some time now I've had the feeling that novelists and terrorists are playing a zero-sum game. [. . .] What terrorists gain, novelists lose. The degree to which they influence mass consciousness is the extent of our decline as shapers of sensibility and thought. The danger they represent equals our own failure to be dangerous" (156–57).

One sees DeLillo's ambivalence in remarks he made to a German interviewer about his own

> acute visual sense. I am not an opponent of the proliferation of pictures in our culture, I am just trying to understand its impact. I like photography, I like to look at photographs and paintings. However, the difference between the world of pictures and the world of printed matter is extraordinary and hard to define. A picture is like the masses: a multitude of impressions. A book on the other hand, with its linear advance of words and characters seems to be connected to individual identity. I think of a child learning to read, building up an identity, word by word and story by story, the book in its hand. Somehow pictures always lead to people as masses. Books belong to individuals. (Desalm, "Masses")

In other words, DeLillo would find the photographs taken by a real-life Brita Nilsson compelling, and he treats her with respect. I think it important, however, that she witnesses but does not join in photographing the brave little Beirut wedding in the novel's closing pages. That ceremony of innocence is *not* drowned: it suggests the survival, in even the worst circumstances, of an alternative to the immolation of individuality depicted in the mass nuptials with which DeLillo's story opens.

Brita, too, reflects on wall-epistemology, and she sketches an engaging aesthetic parable in a story that she briefly recalls for her dinner companions. Brita describes "a man and woman who are walking the length of the Great Wall of China, approaching each other from opposite directions" (70). She identifies them as "artists," their convergence some vast "art piece" in which, again, readers may discern a modest instance of the grand and unorthodox creations to which DeLillo so often directs the attention of his readers (70). The artists of Brita's story ride an historic interface, as Pynchon might say, between civilization and barbarism. Yin and yang, anima and animus, sperm and egg, the artists draw toward each other to fructify, to *create*. At once denying, neutralizing, and transcending the barrier they walk, their convergence transforms it into an artistic medium, a cultural membrane. The Great Wall becomes the channel of coming together, not the instrument of keeping apart, and one recognizes Brita's wall-walking artists as up-to-date versions of Ts'ai Yen, the Chinese poet whose story Maxine Hong Kingston tells in *The Woman Warrior* (1976). The poet's suffering and exile among the barbarians are the very conditions of her artistic achievement. But as artist she flourishes on both sides of the wall. Brita's artists effect or enact a similar reconciliation.

One discerns a Matthew Arnold component to this parable, withal. In *Culture and Anarchy* (1869), Arnold labels those ignorant of art Barbarians (as opposed to Philistines, those indifferent to the art available to them). But postmodern art obliges revision of all the Arnoldian criteria, for it does not exclude the aesthetic expression of barbarians and cultural outsiders—nor does it imagine it inferior to that of ostensibly more refined sensibilities. Andy Warhol, one of the inventors of Pop Art, got his start designing window displays for department stores. Wholly uncivilized in the eyes of the contemporaneous art establishment, he became one of the architects of postmodernism. When he went to China in 1982 (six years after the death of Mao), it was the reverse of the Ts'ai Yen story: the barbarian sojourned among the Han—and came away newly inspired.

Within months of Brita's describing her cryptic fantasy, the Berlin Wall would no longer separate one European polity from another. Indeed, even Beirut's notorious Green Line would pass into welcome desuetude with the conclusion, in 1990, of Lebanon's fifteen-year civil war. But even as he stages—or allows—recognition of some brighter prospect for humanity in the wake of communism's overthrow, DeLillo remains history's great skeptic, and just as he suggests that only the most credulous take all the apocalyptic anticipation seriously, so does he resist the secular optimism of those who misunderstood Francis Fukuyama, who in a much discussed essay of 1989 noted the widespread success of democracy and the globalized economy and argued the "end of history" as a consequence of what seemed the irreversible "victory of economic and political liberalism" (3). Fukuyama emphasized that his thesis bore chiefly on the great nations that had capitulated to or at least accommodated the liberal vision. They alone became "posthistorical." Elsewhere, the old antipathies of nation and race and clan would go on generating "history" for years to come. In the popular mind, however, Fukuyama had made a much more sweeping pronouncement, and he was alternately scoffed at or cheered. Superficial readers of Fukuyama in effect said to Clio, "Have a nice day," and she answered (as a famous curmudgeon urges us all to counter that banal wish): "Thank you, but I have other plans" (Fussell 202).

"*Mao II* dramatizes," as Peter Boxall observes, "the arrival of the millennial moment, the end of history, the permanent future," and "the final exhaustion of the conflict between east and west that has determined the political life of a generation" (161). DeLillo engages, with no small irony, what Boxall describes as "the perception that history is already over," the perception "that the future is already here, revealed to us in all its stark completion" (158). Registering his incredulity toward the metanarratives of both Western jingoists and the ridiculous Asian messiah "come to lead them to the end of human history" (6), DeLillo again proves himself ahead of the historical curve that would bring another Balkan conflict, two wars in Iraq, another in Afghanistan, and of course 9/11.

Postures of Disbelief

In large measure, ironically, these have been religious wars, the secular states against many-tentacled Islamism. DeLillo conjures this implacable, ignorant enemy in "In the Ruins of the Future," the essay he wrote after 9/11:

> [T]hink of people in countless thousands massing in anger and vowing revenge. Enlarged photos of martyrs and holy men dangle from balconies, and the largest images are those of a terrorist leader.
>   Two forces in the world, past and future. With the end of communism, the ideas and principles of modern democracy were seen clearly to prevail, whatever the inequalities of the system itself. This is still the case. But now there is a global theocratic state, unboundaried and floating and so obsolete it must depend on suicidal fervor to gain its aims. (40)

Long before the emergence of a popular resistance to the theocratic regime in Iran, DeLillo reaffirms, with Fukuyama, the triumph of "the ideas and principles of modern democracy." Such level-headed recognitions temper the horror of the hydra that calls itself Islamic Jihad in Egypt, Lebanon, and the occupied territories; the Abu Nidal Organization in Iraq; the Abu Sayyaf Group in the Philippines; Jemaah Islamiah in Southeast Asia; and, in many places, simply al-Qaeda.

One must emphasize that DeLillo is not much friendlier to homegrown Western religiosity. Readers have always recognized DeLillo's tough-mindedness about what Pound called history's "march of events" (*Hugh* i: l. 17)—the quotation marks signal the poet's contempt for journalistic cliché—but they have not always seen his tough-mindedness about religion. Critics (I include myself) have flirted with the idea of a spiritual DeLillo, a DeLillo who might veil his own propensities in the faith that a Nick Shay (in *Underworld*) or Lianne Glenn (in *Falling Man*) cannot quite shake, a DeLillo who tells interviewer Andrew Billen, "I feel a drive towards some kind of transcendence, perhaps religious but not in traditional ways" (26). Such a sentiment remains a far cry from belief. At most, it allows what Amy Hungerford calls the "honoring of mystery" (374). Yet critics such as Hungerford (or John A. McClure) do not, after all, characterize DeLillo as believer or even closet believer, and readers must avoid imputing a kind of supernaturalism—if not crypto-piety—where none actually exists. Yes, as Joseph Dewey observes, he "was raised amid the pageantries of pre-Vatican Two Catholicism and attended a Catholic prep school" before studying with "the Jesuits of Fordham" ("DeLillo's Apocalyptic" 53), but much the same can be said of Joyce—whose *non serviam* still echoes (indeed, DeLillo has invoked the Irish master's "[s]ilence, exile, cunning" credo [LeClair, "Interview" 20]). Like so many in the modern and contemporary era, DeLillo articulates a modicum of nostalgia for the certainties enjoyed by so many for so long, but nowhere in his work does he really gainsay the "rockbound doubt" expressed by James Axton in *The Names* (92). (McClure notes that Axton "chooses not to challenge" another character's "assertion that there is no God, an assertion [. . .] DeLillo himself seems mostly to accept" [*Partial Faiths* 68].) "Disbelief," reflects *Falling Man*'s Lianne Glenn, "was the line of travel that led to clarity of thought and purpose" (65). Occasional recourse to a spiritualized lexicon does not, then, signal any real flirtation with supernaturalism. The narrator's irony gives the lie to the wan faith clung to by a Sister Edgar or a Nick Shay or the puerile narrator—he identifies himself only as "Robby"—of DeLillo's 2009 story "Midnight in Dostoevsky." No apologist for the supreme metanarrative, DeLillo treats Sister Edgar and her fellow believers in *Underworld* with sympathy (his tone modulates from the ironic to the elegiac), but he does not present them as fellow passengers on some ark of conviction.

One cannot resist a brief excursus on "Midnight in Dostoevsky," whose narrator declares that he and a classmate "believed in God" (70). The story Robby tells, however, hints at a vast web of adult, "Dostoevskian" darkness and disillusionment awaiting collegiate ephebes: one day they will know all too well what troubles old men in their solitary walks—or drives the enigmatic teacher, Ilgauskas, to read "Dostoevsky day and night" (73). DeLillo subtly orients Robby's narrative to an uncelebrated Christmas, that caesura in the academic year. "We called ourselves the Left Behind" (73), Robby says of those with nowhere to go over the winter break. A joke appropriate to a fiction published a decade into the third millennium, twenty years after perfervid 1989, the phrase speaks to a burnt-out chiliasm and invites a smile at the expense of the immensely popular—and silly—series of apocalyptic fictions by Tim LaHaye and his occasional collaborators. Perhaps, too, the appearance of this story at the end of November 2009 makes it a shadow commemoration of events in Berlin and Prague twenty years previously—events that did not, after all, mark the end of history (in Dostoevsky's native Russia, in fact, the cultural and political midnight would continue for a considerable period).

The phrase "[l]ike midnight in Dostoevsky" comes from a Frank O'Hara prose poem, "Meditations in an Emergency" (1954), that has a special meaning for New Yorkers (words from O'Hara's poem, along with some by Whitman, adorn the railings of Battery Park, once shadowed by the twin towers, from whence one looks west, across the Hudson to New Jersey, or south, across Upper New York Bay to the Statue of Liberty). The story exhibits a certain affinity with "In the Ruins of the Future," the essay DeLillo published after the 9/11 attacks. Both grapple—as *Mao II* does—with forms of dread that refuse every attempt at understanding. But if the ancient recognition of *lacrimae rerum* has a contemporary or postmodern meaning, such texts help their readers toward insight. The connection to O'Hara's poem, which features a witty analysis of homosexual identity and intimations of the martyrdom 1950s gays underwent daily at the hands of the straight world, suggests a current of unacknowledged homoerotic anxiety in the relationship between Robby, the evidently heterosexual narrator of DeLillo's story, and the friend with whom he finds himself violently at odds in the end. In the line that DeLillo appropriates for his title, O'Hara apostrophizes the obscure martyr in a Zurbarán painting: "St. Serapion, I wrap myself in the robes of your whiteness which is like midnight in Dostoevsky" (39). This painting, which hangs in the Wadsworth Atheneum Museum in Hartford, Connecticut, offers a remarkable picture of martyrdom: the saint is unconscious, in repose, the ropes around his wrists not immediately noticed by the viewer. But the saint's robe, of a startling whiteness, belies the violence to which he has been or will be subjected. Like midnight, such whiteness makes seeing difficult; like Dostoevsky's midnight, the image cloaks a universe of existential, solitary suffering.

In *Mao II*, too, the world struggles toward some dawn beyond its Dostoevskian midnight. But DeLillo brackets faith in the sphere of demented politics or psychopathology. Religion figures here only as cult activity (the Moonies represent the fevered residue of a moribund eschatology) or the vaguely comic wish or expectation of a Brita Nilsson, "the woman who talked about needing people to believe for her" (191), the woman who declares: "I don't like not believing. I'm not at peace with it. I take comfort when others believe" (69). Brita resembles the protagonist of *White Noise* in this regard, but where Sister Hermann Marie disabuses Jack Gladney, *Mao II* offers, for whatever comfort she may provide, Karen Janney: "If it's believers you want, Karen is your person. Unconditional belief. The messiah is here on earth" (69). Repeated, the assertion underscores Karen's pathetic credulity: "The messiah is here on earth and he is a chunky man in a business suit from the Republic of Korea" (186). Not exactly the Parousia—the Christ in glory—of patristic prophecy.

One recurs to a much-quoted yet somewhat ambiguous passage in which a liturgical metaphor illustrates an aesthetic—and wholly secular—point: "The novel used to feed our search for meaning. Quoting Bill. It was the great secular transcendence. The Latin mass of language, character, occasional new truth" (72). The great *secular* transcendence, the novel has been displaced, as has the Latin mass, by discourse better calculated to communicate with the person on the street: "the major work" or "new tragic narrative" that "involves midair explosions and crumbled buildings" (157). Also much quoted, Bill's remarks about the disheartening power differential between novelists and terrorists figure in a conversation about the twisted role of belief in our time. Presently to meet George Haddad, unctuous apologist for terrorism, Bill observes Greek priests in the streets of Athens as "great black ships of faith and superstition" (154). Again, when Haddad declares that "faith" drove Mao's Cultural Revolution, the religious idea is traduced in events political, historical, and emphatically secular: "[l]uminous, sometimes stupid, sometimes cruel" (158), such faith serves enormity sooner than beatitude. These are the terms in which a reader should assess DeLillo's view of millennial energy, which may foster only the kind of blind passion seen in Mao's China: "the old wild-eyed vision, total destruction and total order" (158).

"The future belongs to crowds." The sentence chills readers with its implicit obituary for the individual. But DeLillo means for his readers to recognize the exaggeration (to recall Twain's still trenchant irony) in reports of this death. Indeed, calling 1989 "the best year in European history," Timothy Garton Ash salutes individual agency without misconstruing Fukuyama, and without recourse to supernatural ("apocalyptic") assumptions: "With Mikhail S. Gorbachev's breathtaking renunciation of the use of force (a luminous example of the importance of the individual in history), a nuclear-armed empire—which had seemed to many Europeans as enduring and impregnable as the Alps, not least because it possessed those weapons of total annihilation—just softly and suddenly vanished" (par. 4). The Soviet leader thus praised puts in one appearance in *Mao II*. The painting that Brita sees and evidently dislikes, *Gorby I* (134), appears to satirize both Soviet leader and reigning Popmeister Andy Warhol, whose style is so aggressively burlesqued. Thinking the picture derivative, Brita renders a harsh artistic judgment, but sentiments such as those expressed by Ash (and others) effectively validate the Soviet premier's legitimacy as Slavic saint, a figure of Russian Orthodox veneration. Happily, he becomes an icon (in both the traditional and contemporary senses of the word) without having to suffer the fate of St. Serapion.

By way of conclusion, I offer a brief recapitulation of the argument here. *Mao II* includes memorable representations (often through the eyes of its frustrated chiliast, Karen Janney) of the Tiananmen Square massacre, the funeral of the Ayatollah Khomeini, the Sheffield soccer stadium disaster, and, in the emergent phenomenon of Moonie weddings, the burgeoning of global cults. But DeLillo adduces these events (and omits others) to generate resistance, on the part of readers, to the seductive logic of millennial expectation. Indeed, appearing in the last decade of the last century of the last millennium, DeLillo's *Mao II* critiques a chiliasm that, in retrospect, seems terribly, shockingly naïve in an advanced civilization. DeLillo's good sense, along with his extraordinary gift for the long view, delivers his readers from an oppressive historical conceit. If they look in vain for representation of the millennial nuptials of the Lamb, they may still rejoice in the marriage, here, of imagination and history.

In the end, DeLillo knows better than to make the message in *Mao II* explicit. But he allows his readers to see that art may yet, in the new millennium, prove as surprising as history. No doubt one errs to see DeLillo's self-portrait in Bill Gray, but the fictional novelist must at times speak for his creator. One such moment occurs in the colloquy with George Haddad, whose febrile abstractions—"total politics, total authority, total being" (158)—echo those of Pyotr Stepanovich Verkhovensky, the cracked revolutionary in Dostoevsky's *The Possessed* (1872) who so relishes the prospect of "total obedience and total depersonalization" (399). The novelist, however, Dostoevsky or DeLillo, knows that "autocracy fails," that "total control wrecks the spirit" (DeLillo, *Mao II* 159). Quoting Bill.

CHAPTER 3

Mao II and the New World Order

Peter Knight

In an address to Congress on 11 September 1990—eleven years before a more momentous eleventh of September—President George Bush Sr. famously sketched out the contours of a "new world order" (par. 7). In the middle of the Persian Gulf War, the U.S. president argued that the future would be shaped not by the old ideological struggle of superpowers that had marked the Cold War but by international cooperation. "Until now," Bush asserted in a later speech, "the world we've known has been a world divided—a world of barbed wire and concrete block, conflict and cold war" (1991; par. 23), but he was confident that the world was about to enter the "new era—freer from the threat of terror, stronger in the pursuit of justice, and more secure in the quest for peace" that he had predicted the previous autumn (par. 7). Critics, however, wondered whether the "new world order" was in fact merely business as usual, with America now as the sole remaining superpower able to spread its economic and military influence across the globe with little hindrance, a more cynical view of the triumphalist account of the "end of history" (read: the triumph of neoliberal capitalist democracy) proclaimed in Francis Fukuyama's influential analysis.

Don DeLillo's *Mao II* (1991) was published nine months after Bush's September speech, and it grapples repeatedly—if somewhat obliquely, since the fall of the Berlin Wall appears only subliminally (Boxall 157–62)—with the question of what kind of "new world order" was being created in the aftermath of the Cold War. The novel presents a series of propositions that the emerging future at the end of the Cold War is not the peaceful vision of world cooperation espoused by Bush, but a depressing acceleration of the death of the individual with the rise of media-saturated terrorism and globalization. This chapter will analyze how in *Mao II* the seemingly opposing forces of globalization and terrorism are shown in both theme *and* form to blur into one another.

The Future Belongs to Crowds

In the armature of its plot and through the dialogue of its characters, *Mao II* debates a series of propositions. The first proposition explored insistently by the novel is that "[t]he future belongs to crowds" (16). From the "undifferentiated mass" (3) of a collective Moonie wedding in Yankee Stadium to the hysterical crowds at the Ayatollah Khomeini's funeral, and from crushed soccer fans at Hillsborough Stadium to Chinese protesters in Tiananmen Square, the depictions of crowds in *Mao II*—both in the text and the photographs that divide the book's sections—are in tune with the depressing conclusion expressed by the central character, novelist Bill Gray, that the power of individual thought and identity is dangerously eroded when immersed in the mass mind. The replicated couples in Yankee Stadium, we are told, "chant for one language, one word, for the time when names are lost" (16). Bill's literary helpmeet, Scott, echoes him in fearing the blandness of "the future [that] makes room for the nonachiever, the nonaggressor, the trudger, the nonindividual" (70).

The crowd is no longer necessarily the actual crowd of mass sporting occasions or public rituals, but now includes the virtual crowd of a television audience, isolated yet fused into an unthinking mass mind of passive spectatorship, a fragmented indoors crowd watching the massed ranks of outdoor crowds. DeLillo's contention in *Mao II*, as in *Underworld* (1997), is that numbed and anonymous ranks of TV viewers have replaced the joyous crowds of sports fans coming together for a shared moment that—before the age of the instant replay—was unrepeatable. Scott's girlfriend, Karen, likes to watch television with the sound turned down, letting the endless, desensitizing repeats of violent events, such as the Hillsborough disaster, wash over her. In the case of Khomeini's funeral, "Karen could not imagine who else was watching this. It could not be real if others watched"; she imagines wistfully that the television viewing crowd is a shadowy mirror image of the real crowd: "If other people watched, if millions watched, if these millions matched the number on the Iranian plain, doesn't it mean we share something with the mourners, know an anguish, feel something pass between us, hear the sigh of some historic grief?" (191).

The second proposition explored by the novel is that the increasing mass reproduction of images in the postmodern mediascape tends toward the same erosion of uniqueness that the mass mind of the crowd inflicts on the individuality of its participants. At first sight a photo might seem the perfect, unmediated encapsulation of an unrepeatable moment, but, as DeLillo put it in an interview, "[t]he photographic image is a kind of crowd in itself" (Nadotti 88), an endlessly reproducible commodity that diminishes the unique quality of the singular moment. For Bill, the intensity of an original work of art or the singularity of an event is slowly diminished every time it is reproduced as a fake "aura" of the original: "Nature has given way to aura. A man cuts himself shaving and someone is signed up to write the biography of the cut. All the material in every life is channeled into the glow" (44). The power of artists and writers likewise ebbs away as they become sucked up into the machinery of publicity and commodification: "The more books they publish, the weaker we [writers] become. The secret force that drives the industry is the compulsion to make writers harmless" (47). As soon as he's been photographed by Brita Nilsson, the first person to capture his image in thirty years, Bill feels that "I'm a picture now, flat as birdshit on a Buick" (54).

The only answer to the fact that "[a]rt floats by all the time, part of the common bloat" of media saturation is to refuse to participate: "the withheld work of art is the only eloquence left" (67). On the surface, then, the novel's polarities are clear: one pole is occupied by Bill, the modernist writer who, in search of singularity, retreats to upstate New York with his twenty-three-years-in-the-making novel; the other is represented by Andy Warhol, who embraced the cult of artistic celebrity through reproduction and lampooned modernism's disdain for the market by making artworks that replicated the superficiality and repetition of commodity culture. And its basic story is that of a reclusive writer who slides toward death once he has agreed to participate in the juggernaut of publicity, first with Brita the photographer and then in the publicity stunt aimed to rescue Jean-Claude Julien, the Swiss writer held hostage in Beirut.

These twin propositions on the dangers of the crowd and the image are familiar from both defenses of high modernism and theories of postmodernism. In the 1950s and 1960s the New York intellectuals articulated a fear that the soporific blandness of mass culture (dubbed "masscult" by Dwight Macdonald) was in danger of producing exactly the same kind of zombified masses as the totalitarian states of Hitler's Germany and Stalin's Russia. Only the idiosyncratic individualism of difficult modernist art, the argument went, could save the nation from the mass mind of consumer capitalism. (It comes as little surprise that "the major influences" on DeLillo "have been European movies, and jazz, and Abstract Expressionism" [Passaro 38].)

Theorists of postmodernism such as Jean Baudrillard and Fredric Jameson have taken this argument further, suggesting that, after Warhol, art itself has become thoroughly commodified, removing the hope of some sacred place outside the market from which to mount a critical resistance to its endless cooptation and incorporation. Allied to this argument about the "exhaustion" of the avant-garde project is the now familiar complaint that globalization reduces local difference, producing a "planing away of particulars," as a character puts it in *Underworld* (786), with the same products and logos reproduced everywhere. In a scene, for example, that recalls Jameson's reading of the spatial confusion he feels in a downtown hotel in Los Angeles as an analogy for our collective cognitive disorientation in the face of the unfathomable complexity of global capitalism (44), Scott meets Brita in a revolving bar in Manhattan and experiences a sense of dislocation in the time-space compression of globalization: "The signs for Mita, Midori, Kirin, Magno, Suntory—words that were part of some synthetic mass language, the esperanto of jet lag" (23). Likewise, when Bill arrives in London he has no interest in tourism as it is already familiar to him, London coming to resemble its clichéd media version: "A glimpse of Trafalgar Square from a taxi, three routine seconds of memory, aura, repetition, [...] a dream locus, a doubleness that famous places share, making them seem remote and unreceptive but at the same time intimately familiar, an experience you've been carrying forever" (120).

The third proposition examined by *Mao II* is that the novelist has now been superseded by the conjoined forces of terrorism and catastrophe journalism. If, according to Scott (who, as is his custom, is merely "[q]uoting Bill" in a moment of apocalyptic pessimism), the "novel used to feed our search for meaning," providing the "great secular transcendence," now "[w]e don't need the novel" because instead "we turn to the news" as it provides an "emotional experience not available elsewhere," with its endless "reports and predictions and warnings" of catastrophe (72). Similarly, as Bill realizes, the power of the novelist to influence society has been overtaken by the far more immediate and spectacular actions of the terrorist.

> "There's a curious knot that binds novelists and terrorists. In the West we become famous effigies as our books lose the power to shape and influence. Do you [Brita] ask your writers how they feel about this? Years ago I used to think it was possible for a novelist to alter the inner life of the culture. Now bomb-makers and gunmen have taken that territory. They make raids on human consciousness. What writers used to do before we were all incorporated." (41)

If writers once shared an affinity with terrorists, then, since Warhol, only the terrorist can succeed in puncturing the bubble of media saturation, as George Haddad, the political theorist who is a close ally of the Beirut terrorist group, explains:

"In societies reduced to blur and glut, terror is the only meaningful act. There's too much everything, more things and messages
and meanings than we can use in ten thousand lifetimes. [. . .]
Who do we take seriously? Only the lethal believer, the person
who kills and dies for faith. Everything else is absorbed. The artist
is absorbed, the madman in the street is absorbed and processed
and incorporated. Give him a dollar, put him in a TV commercial.
Only the terrorist stands outside. The culture hasn't figured out
how to assimilate him." (157)

Haddad here anticipates Baudrillard's question in the wake of 9/11:
"When the world has been so thoroughly monopolized, when power
has been so formidably consolidated by the technocratic machine and
the dogma of globalization, what means of turning the tables remains
besides terrorism?" Terrorism, Baudrillard concludes, "is the act that
restores an irreducible singularity to the heart of a generalized system of
exchange" ("L'Esprit" 14).

It's Just Like Beirut

Stacked up on one side of the equation in the novel are the destructive
forces of the crowd, the repeated image, and the homogenizing forces
of globalization, while on the other are the vulnerable qualities of writing, individuality, singularity, and uniqueness. The argument of the
novel could be summed up as: crowd = repetition = image = globalization = death of the individual. For all the clarity of the central propositions set out by the narrator, the characters, and even DeLillo himself
in interviews, *Mao II* nevertheless gives readers reason to reconsider
those central axioms. For example, the deindividualizing force of the
crowd is repeatedly figured as foreign (Mao's Chinese followers, the
Iranian funeral mob), but the novel also suggests, as Richard Hardack
has argued in great detail (378–87), that the logic of repetition is central to the American mode of mass production (Sun Myung Moon is
described as a "chunky man in a business suit" [186] who once "lived in
a hut made of U.S. Army ration tins" [6]). The whole of idea of the
Moonie wedding might strike Karen's parents as alien, but it takes
place pointedly within Yankee Stadium, transposed into "American
light" (6) by DeLillo from a photo of a wedding in Korea that was one
of the original inspirations behind the novel (see Passaro 76).

Likewise, if *Mao II* considers the possibility that the terrorist is like a
novelist, it also provides ammunition to the contrary argument that
terrorism produces the same diminution of sacrosanct individuality as

both the crowd and the repeated image. We learn, for example, that the "boys who work near Abu Rashid have no face or speech. Their features are identical. They are his features. They don't need their own features or voices. They are surrendering these things to something powerful and great" (234). As Bill's former publisher, Charlie Everson, speculates, the terrorists who derail the press event in London to help free the Swiss hostage are media savvy enough to understand that "this man's release depends completely on the coverage. His freedom is tied to the public announcement of his freedom. You can't have the first without the second. This is one of many things Beirut has learned from the West" (129). As much as terrorism might be seen as a last-ditch resistance to the "blur and glut" of the postmodern mediascape, it nevertheless relies on the oxygen of publicity. Far from living in the here-and-now of terrorist violence, the Beirut militias "were looking at videos of the war in the streets. They wanted to see themselves in their scuffed khakis, the vivid streetwise troop, that's us, firing nervous bursts at the militia down the block" (109–10; for more on this argument, see Osteen, *American Magic* 206–07). In a similar vein, although the romantic image of the bomb-throwing anarchist might have affinities with the lone writer, the Maoist terrorists in *Mao II* parrot the formula that "All men one man" (235). Even Bill is not convinced by Haddad's account of the terrorist as a lone hero: "It's pure myth, the terrorist as solitary outlaw. These groups are backed by repressive governments. They're perfect little totalitarian states" (158).

Contributing to this undermining of the strict logic of the central propositions, the novel is structured through a host of suggestive parallels, substitutions, echoes, and affinities. One theme running through *Mao II* (and other DeLillo novels such as *Underworld* and *Cosmopolis* [2003]) is that New York, the zenith of postmodern Western technologically advanced capitalism, looks remarkably like a third-world city at times. New York *is* Beirut, *Mao II* implies, with its garbage bags stacked in alleyways and its tent city of the homeless in Tompkins Square Park making it look more like the third world than the first: "There were water-main breaks and steam-pipe explosions, asbestos flying everywhere, mud propelled from caved-in pavement, and people stood around saying, 'It's just like Beirut, it looks like Beirut'" (146; see also 173). In contrast to a version of the New World Order in which globalization is merely Americanization, *Mao II* shows the fusing of first and third world, with the United States as much the victim as the champion of neoliberal capital's "race to the bottom" in the global marketplace. As the postmodern Marxist theorists Michael Hardt and Antonio Negri note in their study of how old-school Western imperialism has been replaced by a newer, deterritorialized version of "Empire" that undermines the power of the nation-state, "the spatial divisions of the three Worlds (First, Second, and Third) have been scrambled so that we continually find the First World in the Third, the Third in the First, and the Second almost nowhere at all" (xiii). Karen, for example, becomes fascinated with the taxis in New York, "yellow cabs driven by fantastically named men from Haiti, Iran, Sri Lanka, the Yemen" (148). In the shantytown in Tompkins Square Park that strikes her as a "refugee camp or the rattiest edge of some dusty township," she hears "a language everywhere that sounded like multilingual English" (149). Or when Bill ventures into the city for the first time in years, he doesn't quite know how to react to or describe "[t]he rush of things" that can only be compared to "your first day in Jalalabad" (94). For Karen's mother watching the Moonie mass wedding, the homeless wandering through the stadium ("people who seem to be wearing everything they own") are "city nomads more strange to her than herdsmen in the Sahel" (4). Her husband, Rodge, ponders on the irony that now America is the target of missionaries like the Moonies "that don't look American," and speculates that "[m]aybe they think we've sunk to the status of less developed country" (5).

Although comparing New York to Beirut potentially repeats the erasure of difference and the masking of the underlying power structures enacted in globalization's "vertigo of intermingled places" (178), it is part of a larger movement within the novel to undermine the distinction between the familiar and the foreign. If New York is becoming increasingly like Beirut in its inclusion of third-world peoples and third-world poverty within its shiny exterior, then the flip side is that Beirut begins to seem remarkably like New York. It is the postmodern city par excellence, as West and East merge into one another as globalization produces an erasure of singularity. It comes as no surprise, then, that Brita thinks of Beirut as "a millennial image mill," with its "pictures of martyrs, clerics, fighting men, holidays in Tahiti" (229). In an odd collision of seemingly incommensurate worlds, she finds a bottle of Midori melon liqueur in the apartment she is using in Beirut: "She can hardly believe there is such a thing. She has seen it advertised at airports and convention centers" (238), and it is a name that crops up twice in the list of exotic product names that float out of the advertising ether in Manhattan. But ultimately it should come as no surprise to find it in Beirut, "[e]verybody's nowhere" (239), the whole globalized world of image, violence, and repetition compressed into the rubble of the city. In the end, "[o]ur only language is Beirut" (239). In the city the very signifiers of foreignness and familiarity are fused together: the graffiti in "gorgeous" Arabic script, for example, are tags for "Suicide Sam the Car Bomb Man" and the "Blood Skulls of Hollywood U.S.A." (229). This uncanny fusion of first and third world finds its symbolic culmination in the huge posters all over the city for Coke II:

> [Brita] has the crazy idea that these advertising placards herald the presence of the Maoist group. Because the lettering is so intensely red. [. . .] The placards are stacked ten high in some places, up past the second storey, and they crowd each other, they edge over and proclaim, thousands of Arabic words weaving between the letters and Roman numerals of the Coke II logo. (230)

Spiritual Kinship

Although at first sight these structuring equations in the novel seem straightforward, the doublings and echoes in the novel put into question the very idea of equivalence. Nowhere is this more clearly evident than in the figure of Bill Gray. It is significant, for example, that the map of Bill's great unfinished novel has "arrows and scribbles and pictographs, the lines that connected dissimilar elements" (140), a commentary on the organizational structure of DeLillo's own novel. Some of the parallels in *Mao II* operate on a large scale, but other duplications operate on a smaller scale, sometimes even through the merest verbal echo. On her way to visit Bill in his writer's refuge for the first time, for example, Brita compares him to a terrorist: "I feel as if I'm being taken to see some terrorist chief at his secret retreat in the mountains" (27), an idea that Scott assures her Bill will relish. If he is seen as a terrorist, he is also figured as a hostage in his farmhouse hideaway. But in the second half of the novel he seems to be on a mission to become a literal hostage. Haddad likes the idea of Bill meeting the leader, Abu Rashid, in person because "[i]t appeals to my sense of correspondence, of spiritual kinship" (156). For Haddad, the meeting of the novelist and the terrorist—"[t]wo underground figures" (156)—has a symmetry that goes beyond the mere utility of their meeting. In a similar fashion, textual echoes and reversals suggest not so much a logical relatedness as a figurative merging of separate characters: we learn, for example, that the tortured prisoner spits up blood, just as Bill does after his car accident; and Karen sees a man living in the shacks in Tomkins Square Park "on his knees coughing up blood" (149). A homeless man in a New York bookstore claims to be a writer, while Bill the writer ends up dying as a homeless man on the boat to Beirut. In a moment of seeming singularity Bill stares at the hair in his typewriter (136), only for that moment to be echoed later when Scott lovingly tries to clean the fluff and hair out of Bill's typewriter (141), and finally with Bill reflecting that his was "a life consisting chiefly of hair" (199).

In interviews DeLillo has noted that he was originally inspired by a newspaper photo of the notoriously reclusive novelist J. D. Salinger, frightened and angrily lunging out at the photographer sent to discover him (Passaro 76). Bill Gray is obviously based on Salinger, but at the same time Bill is also a substitute for Salman Rushdie, whose condition of having to hide in safe houses following the publication of *The Satanic Verses* (1988) DeLillo compared to being a hostage (Passaro 77). (DeLillo also later published a pamphlet with Paul Auster condemning the fatwa against Rushdie, and participated in a media event designed to draw attention to the latter's plight.) If Bill is like Rushdie because he is like a hostage, then the Swiss poet is also a stand-in for the British author because he is literally a hostage. Many readers of the novel have also assumed that Bill is a double of DeLillo himself, and this is easy to believe given that in interviews given at the time of the novel's publication DeLillo echoed many of Bill's pronouncements about crowds, terrorism, and the novel (sometimes quite literally "quoting Bill," as Scott and Karen would say), coupled with the fact that DeLillo confessed that "I used to say to friends, 'I want to change my name to Bill Gray and disappear'" (Passaro 38). But the equation of DeLillo and Gray doesn't always match up (see also Osteen, *American Magic* 192–93). If, as DeLillo has suggested, *Mao II* is a novel about the "polar extremes" of the "arch individualist" and the "mass mind" (Passaro 76), then, for all that Bill represents the modernist artist heroically resisting the logic of the crowd, we also have to recognize that he has much in common with the charismatic leader of a cult: Scott and Karen are each in their own way attracted to Bill as a talismanic figure and give up their lives to his messianic mission. (Bill's disappearance, we are told, "made Scott think of great leaders who regenerate their power by dropping out of sight and then staging messianic returns" [141].) The scenes with Bill and his daughter, not entirely necessary for advancing the plot, reveal how Bill's pursuit of his modernist artistic path of "silence, exile, and cunning" has often been merely a pretext to excuse his alcoholism and cruelty to his family. Moreover, "Bill Gray" is itself an assumed name, a second identity played out by Willard Skansey, the lonely boy from the Midwest who invented himself as a writer (for more on this argument, see Joseph Dewey, *Beyond Grief* 102–06).

General Equivalence

In effect this repeated building up and undermining of equivalence in the novel forces the reader to ask questions about the relationship between metaphor (the comparison of two things that are unalike) and metonymy (an equation or relation between two things that are substitutable). Is a novelist like a terrorist, or is a novelist actually a kind of terrorist? Is the postmodern mediascape of mass reproduced images merely like a crowd, or is it fundamentally the same as a crowd? Is therefore a metaphor in danger of producing the same troubling erasure of difference and a loss of singularity as, say, the participants in a Moonie wedding who serve as interchangeable parts in a machine, or terrorists oblivious to the individuality of their victims? Does the economy of metaphor (finding a language that can substitute one unrelated thing for another in a single transaction) work in the same way and with the same potentially damaging consequences as the real economy of capitalist exchange based, in Marx's terminology, on money as a "general equivalent"? Is the novelist, who, like the terrorist, violently interrupts the familiar with the foreign thereby eroding the difference between the two, merely echoing the underlying system of exchange that underpins the globalized economy?

The central plot of the novel, it must be remembered, revolves around the ethics of exchange and equivalence, gift and sacrifice. Bill agrees to come out of seclusion in order to help the cause of a fellow writer who has been forced into seclusion. He is suspicious about the nature of this transaction conducted in the currency of publicity, seeing behind Charlie Everson's altruistic gesture merely a win-win trade-off: "Your new group gets press, their new group gets press, the young man is sprung from his basement room, the journalists get a story, so what's the harm" (98). George Haddad likewise reveals that the Beirut terrorist group with which he has connections had been considering staging a spectacular kidnapping of Bill at the London press conference, in an attempt to trade up for a more famous writer: "One man released in Beirut, another taken in London" (155). In the eyes of the terrorists, each victim is equally anonymous and expendable, but one has more market value in a culture of publicity. As the plot develops, Bill hatches a vaguely formed plan in effect to exchange himself for the Swiss poet. Bill asks Haddad what Rashid will want in return if he goes to Beirut and completes the "spiritual union" between novelist and terrorist, and the answer is that "[h]e'll want you to take the other man's place" (164). The chief of the anti-terrorist police in London insists that Bill return home rather than proceed on to Athens, hinting that "you would be worth a great deal more to the group in Beirut than the hostage they're now holding" (132).

Looked at one way, this is the end point of the logic of global capitalism that turns everything, even people, into fungible commodities, erasing any difference and local particularity among them. The novel highlights the ambiguities of exchange, exploring both sides in the question of whether there is always a price to be paid, always a trade-off in any engagement between two people—even whether all encounters, no matter how intimate and "mysterious," can ultimately be cashed out into an underlying economic impulse. As Bill and Brita flirt and spar during the photo shoot at the farmhouse, for example, Bill wonders out loud about what is really going on between them: "We're alone in a room involved in this mysterious exchange. What am I giving up to you? And what are you investing me with, or stealing from me?" (43). The final indignity for Jean-Claude Julien, we learn in passing at the end of the novel, is that he is sold by his kidnappers to a rival group, as if people had become mere objects to be bought and sold. Although Rashid boasts that they are trying to achieve a "new future" through terror, "chang[ing] history minute by minute" (235), he also recognizes that they still have to do business the old way, perhaps the only way: "We have no foreign sponsors. Sometimes we do business the old way. You sell this, you trade that. Always there are deals in the works. So with hostages. Like drugs, like weapons, like jewelry, like a Rolex or a BMW. We sold him to the fundamentalists" (235). It seems that, whatever the ideological stance of the Maoist terrorists or their Islamic fundamentalist opponents within Beirut, all sides are ultimately trapped in the inescapable network of global capitalism in which everything has its price. In *Mao II* this is the New World Order that is emerging in the wake of the Cold War and its fierce territorial and ideological struggle.

Looked at another way, however, Bill's quest to give himself up willingly for the hostage is not a replication of the damaging logic of commodity exchange but a heroic (if ultimately futile) attempt to resist it. Although Bill understands the cynical, horse-trading nature of the transactions needed to free the hostage, he also seems willing to give himself up for the hostage for free, evoking not a world-weary postmodern economy of media events but a premodern economy of sacrifice, a gift that creates webs of obligation and connectedness but which undermines the logic of transaction by not insisting in advance on something in return. Bill's death is also, of course, a tragic waste of life, caused by a random car accident in Athens. It is a lonely and ignominious end, in which his body is pickpocketed for his last few possessions, his identity reduced to a passport ("a name and number" [217]) that has more value as a tradable currency in the shifting sands of Beirut than even the actual money left in his wallet. But his death is also narrated with a sense of peace and quiescence, as if it is a final escape from a life of calculation.

Surge of the Noontime Crowd

Although, as we have seen, the novel presents a forceful attack on the erosion of the self by the deindividualizing force of the crowd and the society of the spectacle, it also repeatedly explores the attractions of escaping the self of Western possessive individualism. As Scott notes, Bill had earlier failed to grasp the consolations offered by the anonymity of city life: "Bill doesn't understand how people need to blend in, lose themselves in something larger" (89). But Bill begins his deathward journey by giving Scott the slip in New York and escaping into the "surge of the noontime crowd" (103), a welcome merging of the individual into the masses, a sense of the verve of the city that DeLillo's writing has always cherished. John Carlos Rowe has argued that the modern novel of terrorism places at its center the problem of the alienated self, typically resolving that problem with an act of self-sacrifice or suicide that affirms the survival of that self (*"Mao II"* 23–24). But Bill's death is unlike that of the suicide bomber for whom the spectacular sacrifice of the alienated self is both a reaffirmation of the self and an attempted resistance to the "generalized system of exchange" (Baudrillard, "L'Esprit" 14). Instead it is figured in muted, poetic tones as an unnoticed and insistently unspectacular passing out of the trap of vanity, a slow draining away of the insistent voice of the self, and a final refusal to live up to the media image of himself.

Bill conceives of his duty to the Swiss hostage not merely as lending media authority to the campaign to release him or even of trading places with him (whether as a deal or a gift), but as engaging in an intense act of imagination that tries to reach out to him, to imagine what it is like to be a hostage, deprived of liberty, deprived of sensory input, and deprived of even the means to construct a narrative sense of self through writing. In the passages that describe Bill's imagination of Jean-Claude, the prose that is focalized through Bill's consciousness takes on the constricted rhythm and narrowed diction of the hostage, so that it is hard to say whether it is Bill's inner voice or that of the hostage that we are reading. It is thus not enough for Bill simply to be concerned about a writer being taken hostage by terrorists, or even to exchange his body for the hostage's. He needs rather to *become* the hostage through merging into his language, to effect an equivalence at a much deeper level than the glib observation that the reclusive writer is *like* a hostage. His task is first to "[r]ead his poems again," to begin to "[s]ee his face and hands in words," and finally to "[f]ind the places where you converge with him" (160). This is arguably DeLillo's task in the novel as a whole, to merge into the consciousness of the otherwise alien and unimaginable others such as the cult victim or the terrorist leader: "This is how we reply to power and beat back our fear. By extending the pitch of consciousness and human possibility" (200). This possibility of transcending the constrictions of the self through merging into the communal sea of language that is not strictly personal undermines the novel's manifest championing of the distinctive voice of the individual in the face of the brainwashing power of the crowd. For all Bill's dogged insistence on the unique individual creativity of the writer, the novel also suggests that the self is as much a product of writing as its cherished origin: "I've always seen myself in sentences. I begin to recognize myself, word by word, as I work through a sentence. The language of my books has shaped me as a man" (48). For all that Bill's journey toward Beirut is a journey toward death and silence, it is also a moving out of his bunkered self into the communal, imaginative space of language.

In common with the rest of DeLillo's work, there is a recurrent fascination with the possibility of finding transcendence not in the traditional modernist refuges of art, nature, or the unconscious, but *within* the seemingly inescapable iron cage of postmodernity, as John A. McClure has argued (*Late Imperial* 118–51). Karen is presented as a damaged and diminished individual whose inner voice is barely her own, her mind taken over first by the cult and then by her deprogrammers. She is "thin-boundaried," making her a passive receptor of the TV images of disaster that flow through her: "She took it all in, she believed in it all, pain, ecstasy, dog food, all the seraphic matter" (119). Yet this thin-boundariedness also makes possible her empathy with the homeless in New York, the crowds in Tompkins Square Park, who would remain otherwise invisible as individuals. If the novel is a concerted lament that the future belongs to crowds, then it also betrays a fascination with the mystical possibilities of the transformational communion of crowds. The Moonies, for instance, are presented as a money-obsessed cult that seems more American than foreign, cynically exploiting the faithful who live in a cramped van "chanting their monetary goal" (13) and "coming not to show us the way and the light" but, as Karen's mother sardonically suggests, to "make sharp investments" (5). But the mass ceremonies choreographed by Reverend Moon also seem to embody a yearning for religious belief in a post-secular society that is both scary and enticing in its apocalyptic fervor: "They are gripped by the force of a longing. [...] They chant for world-shattering rapture, for the truth of prophecies and astonishments" (16), a realm of mysticism that is lost to the bland world of suburban American consumerism. Significantly, it is the "families snapping anxiously, [...] trying to neutralize the event" that begin to "drain it of eeriness and power" (6), the suburban American parents left wondering, "When the Old God leaves the world, what happens to all the unexpended faith?" (7). The unifying chant at the Moonie wedding "transports them with its power," Reverend Moon leading them "out past religion and history" (15), a transcendence of the here and now that is both frightening and exhilarating. Likewise, Bill sees in the enforced communal rituals of the Chinese Cultural Revolution under Mao merely "Bad sex. Rote, rote, rote," but George Haddad challenges him to rethink: "Don't you see the beauty in this? Isn't there beauty and power in the repetition of certain words and phrases? You go into a room to read a book. These people came out of their rooms. They became a book-waving crowd" (162). And at the end of the novel, amid the ruins of Beirut and led by a "free-lance tank" left over from the Cold War, Brita observes the wedding party that "look[s] transcendent, free of limits and unsurprised to be here" (240).

Everybody's Nowhere

If the fall of the Berlin Wall paved the way for the global spread of American-led neoliberal capitalism, then it also laid the foundations for a terrorist opposition to that seemingly inexorable "end of history." In the wake of the attacks of 11 September 2001, some commentators— including DeLillo himself in an article in *Harper's*—wondered whether now "the world narrative belongs to terrorists," interrupting the "power of American culture to penetrate every wall, home, life, and mind" ("In the Ruins" 33). Other pundits, however, saw the attacks on New York and Washington as part of a larger "clash of civilizations," in which fundamentalist terrorism is pitted against the free market principles of democracy and globalization. Although *Mao II* contains elements of a reading of terrorism as the last-ditch struggle against the "blur and glut" of global consumer capitalism, it also sketches out an alternative analysis in which both globalization and terrorism are part of the same process of deterritorialization. If, according to DeLillo, the "utopian glow of cyber-capitalism" in the 1990s meant that "markets are uncontrolled and investment potential has no limits," so too "now there is a global theocratic state, unboundaried and floating and so obsolete it must depend on suicidal fervor to gain its aims" ("In the Ruins" 33, 40). In their account of the emergence of a deracinated sovereignty of globalist institutions and law, Hardt and Negri adopt a Foucauldian perspective to argue that it is the placelessness of power that is the significant development: "In contrast to imperialism, Empire establishes no territorial center of power and does not rely on fixed boundaries or barriers. It is a *decentered and deterritorializing* apparatus of rule that progressively incorporates the entire global realm within its open, expanding frontiers" (xii). In *Mao II*, it is Jean-Claude Julien, the poet who works, fittingly, for the United Nations, who comes to understand that "[h]e had tumbled into the new culture, the system of world terror," becoming "a digital mosaic in the processing grid, lines of ghostly type on microfilm. [...] He was lost in the wavebands, one more code for the computer mesh" (112). The terrorists in the novel are part of a "system of world terror" that is not so much in ideological opposition to the postmodern media world as part of its very logic. Beirut is ground zero for this deterritorialized system of terror, a city that, as we have seen, is figured as "everybody's nowhere."

CHAPTER 4

Mao II and Mixed Media

Laura Barrett

[B]efore everything, there's language. Before history and politics, there's language.
    Don DeLillo to Adam Begley, *"The Art of Fiction" (1993)*

I think more than writers, the major influences on me have been European movies, and jazz, and Abstract Expressionism.
    Don DeLillo to Vince Passaro, *"Dangerous Don DeLillo" (1991)*

There's a palpable tension between words and images in even the earliest works by Don DeLillo. In *Americana* (1971), David Bell, a television network executive whose personality is largely determined by the films of his youth, finds himself in competition with Bobby Brand, a friend who claims to be writing a novel. Before Brand has finished describing his work, David announces his idea for a "messy autobio-graphical-type film, [. . .] a long unmanageable movie full of fragments of everything" (215). David's film turns out to be less cinematic than linguistic, "a sort of ultimate schizogram, an exercise in diametrics which attempts to unmake meaning" (357), and, while Brand never writes a book, David completes one that he describes in visual terms: "Cézannesque in the timeless light it emits, a simple object, the box-shaped equivalent of the reels which sit in my small air-conditioned storage vault" (356). Ultimately, he describes his art as "merely a literary venture, an attempt to find pattern and motive, to make of something wild a squeamish thesis on the essence of the nation's soul. To formulate. To seek links. But the wind burned across the creekbeds, barely moving the soil, and there was nothing to announce to myself in the way of historic revelation" (359–60).

David's isolation on an island, his closest companions his novel, "pages neatly stacked, hundreds of them" (356), and his film, safely sequestered in an air-conditioned vault, presage Bill Gray's seclusion in *Mao II* (1991), and the former's disappointment with his lack of "historic revelation" resonates in Bill's bitterness and frustration with his latest project, a book twenty-plus years in the making. Indeed, *Mao II*'s publication twenty years after *Americana* is significant since these are the years that Bill has been in hiding, attempting to avoid two decades of increasing media influence, an influence exploited by celebrities and terrorists, politicians and serial killers. These are the years during which novelists have lost the power "to alter the inner life of the culture" (41).

While a central focus of *Mao II* is an anxiety about the waning importance of writers in an age of terrorism, another is certainly the author's decline in the wake of visual culture, forging a connection between terrorism and image-production affirmed by Bill's observation that "[t]here were the camera-toters and the gun-wavers and [he] saw barely a glimmer of difference" (197). Those combined threats, moreover, are also implicated in the erosion of individuality so central to American identity, an erosion literally illustrated in the seriality implied by the work's title, as well as by repeated images of Chairman Mao on the first edition's cover. Almost perversely, those images supplant alphabetical letters that we would expect to see in the seemingly arbitrary arrangement of squares that resembles a crossword puzzle or a scrabble board. In their stead, we have two words that announce, in a typeface dwarfed by the images and the title, the nature of the work: A NOVEL. Reiteration, reproduction, and multiplicity are built into the very structure of the novel, identified by the photographs that initiate each section, images whose grayness and lack of clarity announce their own belatedness in the cycle of mechanical reproduction and which heighten the connection between images and crowds, a connection DeLillo made explicit in an interview with Maria Nadotti:

> There's something menacing and violent about a mass of people which makes us think of the end of individuality, whether they are gathered around a military leader or around a holy man.
> The photographic image is a kind of crowd in itself, a jumble of impressions [. . .]. There's something in the image that seems to collide with the very idea of individual identity. (87–88)

Inversely, it is easy to assume that DeLillo, an author whose own reclusiveness has been overstated, privileges individuality and writing, but in the same interview he also said, "I don't think that a writer can allow himself the luxury of separating himself from the crowd [. . .].

It is indispensible to be fully involved in contemporary life, to be part of the crowd, of the clash of voices" (88). We know from the prologue of *Underworld* (1997) that crowds offer camaraderie and heterogeneity as well as mayhem and uniformity, and images, like the most photographed barn in America, Bruegel's *The Triumph of Death*, and Zapruder's footage of the Kennedy assassination, are no less complex in DeLillo's work. More than other DeLillo novels, then, *Mao II* challenges the reader to consider words and images as conspirators in the construction of American culture, often promoting and occasionally resisting the national agenda of production and reproduction, consumption and disposal.

The Impact of Images

Mao II follows the trajectory of a novelist grown weary with his self-imposed exile who enters into an underworld of terrorism as an antidote to the futility of writing. A modernist living in a hyper-mediated world, Bill Gray performs the role of the solitary author, but his avoidance of media effects seemingly contradictory results. The absence of public appearances or even photographs lends Bill an aura: "Bill gets bigger as his distance from the scene deepens" (52). His refusal to embrace celebrity results in his surrender to it, and he becomes more famous as an icon than as a writer. In an attempt to free himself from his imprisonment, Bill hires a photographer, Brita Nilsson, "[t]o break down the monolith [he has] built" (44), to allow him to see himself as others might see him, resulting in exposure and surrender: "I've become someone's material. Yours, Brita. [. . .] Already I see myself differently" (43–44). While the photographs are meant as a renaissance, a reentry into the social order, they are described with the language of violence: "Something about the occasion makes me think I'm at my own wake. Sitting for a picture is morbid business. [. . . T]hese pictures are the announcement of my dying" (42, 43). Brita's prolonged "operation" increasingly resembles an execution as Bill's "bright-eyed fear" assumes "the starkness of a last prayer" as Brita "shot and shot" (44, 49). By the conclusion of the photo session, Bill confesses that he "no longer see [s himself] in the language" of his current book: "I'm sitting on a book that's dead" (48). A dead man sitting on a dead book, Bill agrees to help his agent effect the release of a hostage—a young poet—from a terrorist group in Beirut despite the warning that as soon as he exchanges places with the poet, the terrorists will kill him and photograph his corpse. Before he can assist in the release, however, he dies on a ferry to Junieh, where his wallet with his identification is stolen, so that it can be sold to the militia in Beirut. His fate, it seems, is to be reduced to an image.

In an age of media saturation, it appears the pen is no longer mightier than the sword. In fact, *Mao II*'s Bill Gray argues that "[w]hat terrorists gain, novelists lose. The degree to which they influence mass consciousness is the extent of our decline as shapers of sensibility and thought" (157). Bill's desire for the power of the terrorist is demonstrated by the reclusive nature of his existence in an upstate New York "bunker" (32), which mandates that the rare visitor be escorted at night through "dirt roads and gravel roads and old logging trails," an excursion that prompts Brita to express the feeling that she's "being taken to see some terrorist chief at his secret retreat in the mountains" (27). His refusal to be "incorporated" by the machinery of capitalism relegates Bill to a state of near invisibility, evident in his conversation with a couple of British vets who try to locate him in the marketplace of writers:

> "But mightn't we have read something you've written?" the woman said. "Perhaps at an airport, where the names don't register sharply." [...]
> "Right. Are any of your books also movies?" the second vet said. [...]
> "They're just books, I'm afraid." [...]
> "But presumably as an author you make appearances," the woman said.
> "You mean on television?" the second vet said. (205, 206)

As the café conversation suggests, images not only reduce art to small, framed doses; they become prior to the subject itself. Brita warns Bill that once his picture is seen, people will expect him to reflect it, and Bill's factotum, Scott, suggests that the image will somehow transform Bill's conception of himself:

> Scott thought the photograph might make him look older. Not older in the picture but older as himself, after the fact of the picture. The picture would be a means of transformation. [. . .] Pictures with our likeness make us choose. We travel into or away from our photographs. (141)

The photographs designed to announce Bill's reentrance into society instead replace the man himself.

The novel suggests that we've all been replaced by images. As Scott notes, "We've learned to see ourselves as if from space, as if from satellite cameras, all the time, all the same," a sentiment which attests to the impact of fifty years of photographs of earth taken from space but also hints at a self-consciousness that arises from ubiquitous surveillance (89). Art browsers in Manhattan

> knew exactly how they appeared to those who were walking or driving by [. . .]. They appeared to float outside the world [. . .] privileged and inviolate, transcendent souls lighted against the falling night [. . .], as if they believed they might still be here a thousand nights from now, weightless and unperspiring, stirring the small awe of passersby. (133–34)

The human body, paradoxically, seems to be disappearing because it is a constant object of scrutiny. Ironically, during the Unification Church's mass marriage in Yankee Stadium that opens the book, Rodge scans the multitudes for a glimpse of his daughter, Karen, "adjust[ing] the eyepiece lever and zoom[ing] to max power" (4). He attempts to contain the madness, the chaos, and incredibility of the situation by photographing it, but, ironically, the very instrument used to contain the event is implicated in it. Ostensibly a weapon against the diminished self, the loss of individuality, the increase of conformity, repetition, and mass, the camera merely duplicates the work initiated by the cult: "They're here but also there, already in the albums and slide projectors, filling picture frames with their microcosmic bodies, the minikin selves they are trying to become" (10). Rodge ponders the absurdity of a mass wedding—"They take a time-honored event and repeat it, repeat it, repeat it until something new enters the world" (4)—without recognizing his statement's applicability to mechanical reproduction. Nor does he recognize the redundancy of frantic parents, united in their traveler's checks, credit cards, subway maps, and "precision glasses" (15). The "repetition and despair" that he sees on the field is paralleled in the grandstand (15): "The brides and grooms exchange rings and vows and many people in the grandstand are taking pictures, standing in the aisles and crowding the rails, whole families snapping anxiously, trying to shape a response or organize a memory, trying to neutralize the event, drain it of eeriness and power" (6). The crowd in the grandstand reduces the event to its miniature no less successfully than their children on the field, children like Karen, who has learned to see the world as reflections of the images she encounters so that what "strikes" her about her mail-order husband, a man she meets through a photograph, what "makes him real to her," is "his hair, which is shiny and fine and ink-black, with a Sunday-comics look" (8).

Perhaps nowhere is the vacuity of repetition more obvious than in the novel's evocation of Andy Warhol, an artist whose cult of personality hinged on absence and vacancy. Scott is mesmerized by "the Warhols" (20), a metonymic that reminds us of the loss of the subject in contemporary society. Warhol's work, those "repeated news images of car crashes and movie stars," illustrates the erasure of singularity and the leveling of experience (20). His art conflates people and things, so that violence and celebrity are equivalent, Marilyn Monroe and Campbell's Soup cans both available for consumption, both conveying the same level of complexity and levity. One silk screen, Crowd (1963), which depicts a "vast mesh of people [. . .] being riven by some fleeting media catastrophe" (21), recalls "The Burning of Los Angeles," Todd Hackett's painting in Nathanael West's The Day of the Locust (1939), a painting realized in the last scene of West's novel. Described as "unwitting of history," "indifferent to the effect" it has on viewers (21), Warhol's art, however, seems far removed from the ethical considerations that plagued West and more akin to television, which manages to de-historicize and depersonalize even the most grotesque atrocities, as evinced by Karen's description of the Hillsborough Stadium soccer tragedy: "[I]t is like a religious painting, the scene could be a fresco in a tourist church, it is composed and balanced and filled with people suffering," a "crowded twisted vision of a rush to death as only a master of the age could paint it" (33, 34).

Karen's response to televised tragedies exemplifies the loss of distinction between reality and representation:

> There were times she became lost in the dusty light, observing some survivor of a national news disaster, there's the lonely fuselage smoking in a field, and she was able to study the face and shade into it at the same time, even sneak a half second ahead [. . .]. (117)

Shading into the image, Karen simultaneously observes the scene and participates in it. The repetition inherent in mechanical reproduction, embodied in this passage by Karen's ability to predict the next scene, to "sneak a half second ahead, inferring the strange dazed grin," is illustrated at the narrative level by recurring phrases: "They show men standing off to the side somewhere, watching sort of half interested"; "They show men calmly watching"; "They show men calmly looking on," all three lines suggesting the weightlessness of spectacle to onlookers at the scene and in front of the television screen (33, 34). The repetition of "they" emphasizes the anonymous authorship frequently associated with images, an anonymity that exacerbates the objectification of the subject and augments the paranoia of a population constantly under surveillance and engaged in voyeurism. The image, not unlike Reverend Sun Myung Moon's effect on his followers, "lifts [us] out of ordinary strips of time and space" and "lead[s us] to the end of human history" (9, 6).

Warhol's images, "floating nearly free of [their] photographic source" (21), are weightless, liberated from space and time, and in that regard reflect the surrounding streets of New York City where Scott watches "blocks of time and space [that] had come loose and drifted" as he sits with Brita in a revolving bar in a midtown hotel (23). Bill describes the city as an urban art form that objectifies people and rejects language: "The rush of things, of shuffled sights," "the deep stream of reflections, heads floating in windows, towers liquefied on taxi doors, bodies shivery and elongate, all of it interesting to Bill in the way it blocked comment" (94). Everything about contemporary society seems to block comment, including those devices designed to facilitate communication. When Bill leaves a long, rambling message on Brita's answering machine, she hears it, not after the fact but during his monologue. She eavesdrops on her own private message, rendering even more astute Bill's observation that "[t]his is a new kind of loneliness you're getting me into" precisely because he is not, as he thinks, "playing to an empty room" (91). As Bill notes, "The machine makes everything a message, which narrows the range of discourse [. . .]. People are no longer home or not home. They're either picking up or not picking up" (92). Not surprisingly, the message ends with neither any reciprocal communication from Brita nor a formal conclusion; "[t]he machine cut[s] him off" (93), a particularly ironic ending since Bill, who is not allowed to terminate the conversation, begins his message by pointing out the lack of closure in their previous meeting: "You left without saying goodbye" (91).

The Weightlessness of Words

Ostensibly in contrast to glossy photographs, weightless television, and the reconstituted voices of answering machines are words, complicated, heavy, fraught. Language initially seems to be a weapon against dislocation. Indeed, it seems to be the bastion of individualism in a world increasingly prone to duplication. The poet held hostage, Jean-Claude Julien, feels that writing will solidify his fading identity: "Written words could tell him who he was. [. . .] The only way to be in the world was to write himself there" (204). Such writing is a palpable act for DeLillo's characters as well as for the author himself whose instrument of choice is a typewriter, described by Bill Gray as "the hand tool of memory and patient thought, the mark-making thing that contained his life experience" (160) because he believes that typeface is the last refuge of solidity, of materiality, the sharp clack of the typewriter keys suggesting a more immediate world than the soft thud of a computer keypad; it is, he argues, "the only way he knew to think deeply in a subject" (160). For Bill, the act of writing is corporeal, literally a splattering of one's self on the page—"the scant drip, the ooze of speckled matter, the blood sneeze, the daily pale secretion, the bits of human tissue sticking to the page" (28). The bodily metaphor goes even deeper for Bill who, as he admits, "write[s] to survive now, to keep my heart beating" (48).

In fact, language in much of DeLillo's work is literally at the center of humanity. Anatole Bloomberg in *End Zone* (1972) attempts to "forge a new consciousness" by "straightening out [his] grammar, getting rid of the old slang and the old speech rhythms" (186, 187), and Nick Shay in *Underworld* is instructed by a Jesuit priest that knowledge must begin with nomenclature: "You didn't see the thing because you don't know how to look. And you don't know how to look because you don't know the names" (540). In *The Names* (1982), James Axton understands that "[c]onversation is life, language is the deepest being" (52). Bill Gray, too, places an enormous faith in the ethical power of language: "The language of my books has shaped me as a man. There's a moral force in a sentence when it comes out right" (48), a sentiment uttered by DeLillo years earlier in an interview with Thomas LeClair: "I think after a while a writer can begin to know himself through his language. [. . . I]t's possible for a writer to shape himself as a human being through the language he uses" ("Interview" 23).

At its most productive, language is democratic, providing connections among people, evoking "the shared past of people who had loved each other, who lived so close they'd memorized each other's warts and cowlicks and addled pauses" (170). Even a sentence associated with consumerism, a phrase as seemingly "nonsensical" and vacuous as "Measure your head before ordering," contains a "mystery and power" that ultimately reminds us "that words stick even as lives fly apart" (170). That mystery and power seems to be at the heart of what Jean-Claude describes as "the uninventable poetry, inside the pain, of what people say" (216). Scott's cryptic, coded letters to Bill reveal to him "that the world was a place where travelers in language could know the same things" (58). Similarly, Brita and Scott's conversation serves as a bond and sanctuary during the long drive to Bill's hideaway: "Two near strangers in night confinement inside the laboring drone of the small car, coming out of long silences to speak abruptly, out of long thoughts and memory chains and waking dreams and every kind of mindlife, the narrative that races just behind the eyes, their words sounding clean and shaped in the empty night" (27). Language, for DeLillo, offers a route from personal to public, from reverie to dialogue, from solipsism to connection.

Just as language connects strangers, captions fix photographs to particular places and times. As Karen pores through Brita's books of photographs, she sees myriad images of poverty, suffering, and death, all of which are meaningless without words: "The picture was bare without the words, alone in open space. [. . .] The words helped her locate the pictures. She needed the captions to fill the space. The pictures could overwhelm her without the little lines of type" (174). Indeed, despite her image consumption, Karen is often perplexed by visual culture, resulting in her blunt but astute response to Brita's confession that her current project is motivated less by photography than by writers. "Then," Karen inquires, "why don't you stay home and read?" (56).

For all its transparent innocence, revelatory promise, and salutary effects, however, fiction can be oppressive, even dangerous. Brita finds herself "silent," wanting to run from the "thick binders [in Bill's house] filled with words," "all the words on all the pages" (75). But even before her escape, she comments on the "secret language" of writers that makes her feel like "an outsider, not able to converse in the private language" (37). As it turns out, language is often opaque, even inaccessible, and certainly not immune to the epidemic of weightlessness in late twentieth-century America, resulting in the "band of glowing letters" that encircles One Times Square (185). Neon signs advertise words— "Mita, Midori, Kirin, Magno, Suntory"—"that were part of some synthetic mass language, the esperanto of jet lag" (23), while airplanes and automobiles give rise to "intense and shallow" conversations between strangers, disjointed dialogues generated by the "stutter reality of the broken white line and the picture in the window" (29). Communication has been replaced by words that flow freely in the ether of cyberspace or casually evaporate in the utterance of ritualistic incantations: "Must sacrifice together. Build with hands God's home on earth" (8). Rodge laments the "broken English" of cults (13)—"They speak a half language, a set of ready-made terms and empty repetitions. All things, the sum of the knowable, everything true, it all comes down to a few simple formulas copied and memorized and passed on. And here is a drama of mechanical routine played out with living figures" (7)—but neglects to grasp that his clichéd half-sentences are the hollow lingo of another species of cult, one defined by strategy, speed, and progress: "The sooner we get started on this" (11); "I fully intend" (12). Not surprisingly, the clipped phrasing of sects, antithetical to narrative, subjectivity, and knowledge, permeates the conversations in DeLillo's novel: "All that driving," Karen observes, "you must be really" (32); "But the fact is," Charlie said (133).

This increasing weightlessness of language is perhaps nowhere more apparent than in "word processing," a phrase that equates writing with factory production: "There's a new model that Panasonic makes and I absolutely swear by it," George Haddad comments. "It's completely liberating. You don't deal with heavy settled artifacts. You transform freely, fling words back and forth" (164). The particular model, a Panasonic, underscores the ubiquity of information in the computer age, which, like Warhol's art, levels distinctions and judgments, making all data equal and resulting in the world of excess data without comparable meaning experienced by Oedipa Maas in *The Crying of Lot 49* (1966). What George understands as a boon for writers, however, Jean-Claude Julien experiences as a bane: "He was a digital mosaic in the processing grid, lines of ghostly type on microfilm. [...] He was lost in the wavebands, one more code for the computer mesh" (112). Words, it seems, have followed the lead of images in the past century—shedding a physicality that, for the characters in *Mao II*, also suggests the loss of subjectivity.

No longer the savior that it was for modernists, language cannot serve as a panacea for the postmodern ills that plague us. As subjective, unnatural, and culturally determined as visual representations, language is a code to be disentangled, evinced by DeLillo's characters who are attuned to the secret language of buildings and the innuendo of road signs. As Brita notes, "everything is coded" (90). The word "baseball" sums up "a hundred happy abstractions, themes that flare to life in the crowd shout and diamond symmetry, in the details of a dusty life," but "[t]he word has resonance [only] if you're American" (8–9). As George insists, in the face of Bill's worship of words, language is class-bound as well as cultural: "There are different ways in which words are sacred. The precious line of poetry often sits in ignorance of conditions surrounding it" (161).

The contingency of meaning endemic to all media sounds sinister when Brita observes that photographs supplant their subjects and remarks that Bill will need to conform to his picture once it has been taken (43); however, as *Mao II* makes clear, such contextuality is not unique to photography. We even discover that the release of Bill's new book will alter the public perception of his past ones, indicating that words themselves are subject to reexamination in a new context. When Brita first sees Bill, she cannot "fit the voice and body to the books": "She'd expected someone lean and drawn, with eyes like hex signs on an Amish barn. But Bill was slowly beginning to make sense to her, to look reasonably like his work" (39). It's not surprising that Scott claims to have recognized Bill in a parking lot because a "great man's face shows the beauty of his work" since he sees the world in light of representations (61). A famous Garry Winogrand photograph reminds him of Bill and, inversely, "when [he] read[s] Bill," Scott thinks of "photographs of tract houses at the edge of the desert" (51), an admission that allies rather than opposes photography and writing, echoing Winogrand's own statement that "a photo is a literary narrative" (qtd. in Rabb 1). Scott, moreover, describes his encounter with Karen in White Cloud, Kansas, as a "scene that felt familiar" with its "low mean sky" and "old tin canopies leaning off the café," a backdrop for a girl trying to peel the sticky wrapper from a piece of candy (76). The familiarity of the scene finally dawns on Scott: "It was like something out of Bill Gray [. . .]. The funny girl on the tumbledown street with an undecidable threat in the air, stormlit skies or just some alienating word that opens up a sentence to baleful influence" (77). What Scott doesn't recognize is that the familiarity of the scene is evocative not just because it is reminiscent of Bill Gray's fiction but that the moment "like something out of Bill Gray" is literally something out of Eve Arnold. As Brita notes, the scene from White Cloud, Kansas, is a famous photograph—down to the sign with the mysterious word "Ha-Hus-Kah" that, for Scott, is a "Bill Gray touch," a "Bill Gray place" (83). The "doubled landscape of [Scott's] original journey in search of Bill and his return with a character out of Bill's fiction" (80), "[t]he same room repeat[ing] itself in a crosscountry chain" (81), simultaneously recall and reenact the reproduction of photography. What the novel suggests, then, is not that photography or fiction replaces reality but that humans seek models to follow, regardless of the medium they choose, an observation supported by Bill's remark about a stranger in a restaurant: "It was as if the man had fitted himself to a predetermined space, to an idea of something that was waiting to happen" (126), not unlike Bill's own impersonation of the isolated writer.

A Meditation on Mediation

Published shortly after *Mao II*, Paul Auster's *Leviathan* (1992), which is dedicated to DeLillo, presents an uncannily similar conjunction of writing, photography, and terrorism. Auster's Benjamin Sachs is, like Bill Gray, a writer of allegedly immense talent and limited productivity who withdraws from humanity. When his "state of perfect innocence," founded upon a belief that "[w]ords and things matched up" (55), is abruptly halted, Ben repudiates writing: "I don't want to spend the rest of my life rolling pieces of blank paper into a typewriter. I want to stand up from my desk and do something" (137). What he does includes an alliance with Maria, a photographer who follows Sachs around because "he wanted to know what it felt like to be watched" (144).

Sometime after his photographic therapy, Sachs's literary career ends when he is confronted in a used book shop by "a mountain of books," "millions of words piled on top of each other, a whole universe of discarded literature—the books that people no longer wanted, that had been sold, that had outlived their usefulness" (254). Face to face, literally, with his own novel, *The New Colossus*, he decides that terrorism is a more useful act than writing. Bombing Statue of Liberty replicas, he reasons, "would bring all the broken pieces of myself together. For the first time in my life, I would be whole" (256), an ironic assertion given that he inadvertently blows himself up during one of his missions. Terrorism picks up where photography leaves off as a means of self-integration for Ben. Likening terrorism to writing and photography, Ben speaks of his crimes "with the assurance of an artist who knows he has just created his most important work" (260).

For both Ben Sachs and Bill Gray, terrorism gives rise to an understanding that fiction must wrangle with the world if it is to be relevant, even though, ironically, it is terrorism's unifying, totalizing vision that makes it antithetical to art. As Bill notes:

When you inflict punishment on someone who is not guilty, when you fill rooms with innocent victims, you begin to empty the world of meaning and erect a separate mental state, the mind consuming what's outside itself, replacing real things with plots and fictions. One fiction taking the world narrowly into itself, the other fiction pushing out toward the social order, trying to unfold into it. He could have told George a writer creates a character as a way to reveal consciousness, increase the flow of meaning. (200)

A writer who "extend[s]" the "pitch of consciousness and human possibility" offers an antidote to the solipsism of the terrorist and of the writer who sits in a room, unable or unwilling to engage with the world (200). Perhaps surprisingly, Karen, the character most vulnerable to a world of images and crowds, adamantly opposes Brita's session with Bill because it undoes the "careful balance" of Bill's sequestered life and creates a "fissure" (57). Visual representation, however, is less the problem than the dismantling of a myth for Karen, a character whose vulnerability to the appeal of totalizing visions is evident in her membership in the Unification Church. That fissure or crack inaugurated by the photography session undermines Bill's entropic world, as does a picture that Bill notices in his hotel room—of "fishing nets stowed in canvas baskets and it had sex, memories, cravings, names of old friends, principal rivers of the world"—which allows Bill to see "everything that existed outside the room he was sitting in" (198).

For DeLillo, communication is an open-ended process, engendering the misinformation so prevalent in the Gladney family's conversations in *White Noise* (1985) and requiring the sophisticated and vigilant monitoring that fails James Axton in *The Names*. Art is ambiguous, entailing, as Bill notes, "dissent, self-argument," a "democratic shout," "[o]ne thing unlike another, one voice unlike the next. Ambiguities, contradictions, whispers, hints" (159). Scott notes that "[i]t was dangerous to speak because he didn't know which way a sentence might tend to go, toward one thing or the logical opposite. He could go either way, one reaction as easy as the other. He was not completely connected to what he said and this put an odd and dicey calm in his remarks" (219). At its best, photography, too, is ambiguous, as evinced by Brita's work, which she describes as a "work-in-progress. Not so permanent and finished" (26).

One such ambiguous image is the last reproduced photograph in the novel, inaugurating the section entitled "In Beirut." In the midst of concrete and iron railings are three boys, two of whom appear to be giving a peace sign while a third stares with intensity at some incident beyond the frame. A similar scene is described earlier in the novel as Scott chats with Brita about the importance of the image. Scott notices figures moving around a "tower under construction" in New York City before identifying them as "three or four kids playing on the girders, making the building seem a ruin, an abandonment" (23). These two moments, one narrative, one photographic, evoke the novel's rampant parallels—weddings in New York and Beirut, Bill's and Brita's entries into the world of terrorism—and reinforce the connections between disparate media. Both media are open-ended, and the image, which we often assume is proscriptive, can expand rather than limit interpretation. If the novel's prologue describing a mass wedding in Yankee Stadium, photographed by a spectator, offers its actual and fictional images as metaphors of "repetition and despair," then the epilogue depicting the noisy passing of a wedding party in Beirut as viewed (without a lens) by a professional photographer, prefaced by the images of three renegade boys playing amid the girders, suggests the complexity of the medium and its artists.

In this and other novels, DeLillo demonstrates that dogmatism and parochialism are not the exclusive province of images. In *End Zone*, Professor Zapalac expresses his fear of a country that could coin the word "militarize" (165), and Gary Harkness laments euphemisms meant to contain tragedies: "[T]here's no way to express thirty million dead. No words. So certain men are recruited to reinvent the language" (85). As Joseph Dewey points out, *Mao II* forces us to reckon with Mao's Little Red Book, "the written word [. . .] deployed to enforce totalitarian uniformity, crush individuality, and justify recasting the individual into two-dimensional facsimiles that dress and think alike" (*Beyond Grief* 104). While the reproduced photographs in the novel underscore the connection between images and crowds and remind us how easily photographs are used for propaganda or shorthand summary, "visual images," as Adam Begley notes, "have no monopoly on coercive power. The printed word, an effective propaganda tool in its day, retains some residual potency" ("Don DeLillo" 486).

When used in the service of art, fiction and photography, however, are both capable of moving beyond literal meaning. Referring to "ambiguous moments of possible transcendence [that] are frequently linked to artistic production," John N. Duvall asserts that DeLillo "wants us to imagine that, beyond the realm of media simulation, there is still a possibility for the artist to effect change" ("Power of History" 4). *Mao II* suggests that the artist is as likely to be a photographer as a writer. Brita may want to convince herself that her project is a "form of knowledge and memory" (25), less "technique and personal style" than documentary, but she admits to "doing certain things to get certain effects" (26). "[E]stablish[ing] rhythms and themes" (221), Brita is an author behind the lens: "So often in her work the human shambles was remade by the energy of her seeing, by the pure will that the camera uncovered in her, the will to see deeply" (37). Mark Osteen thus describes Brita as a "more viable model for artistic engagement," who "uses her craft to create a counternarrative to the dominant ones" ("DeLillo's Dedalian" 138, 144).

The novel repeatedly affirms that no medium has a patent on truth or bears sole responsibility for the weightlessness of modern experience. Nor, for that matter, is any single medium capable of restoring order, a sentiment common to writers in the past half century. Joan Didion begins "The White Album," the first essay in her eponymous collection (1979), by claiming that "We tell ourselves stories in order to live. [. . .] We live entirely, especially if we are writers, by the imposition of a narrative line upon disparate images" (11), but the essay chronicles a world in which "the script" of her life fails and ultimately laments that "writing has not yet helped me to see what it means" (12, 48). Jonathan Safran Foer's *Extremely Loud and Incredibly Close* (2005) includes photographs, film stills, pages filled with numbers, and reproductions of art supply-store memo pads covered in multi-colored scrawls, all attesting to the difficulty of representing loss and grief. One character whose biographical index reduces people to one word ("Henry Kissinger: war!," "Ornette Coleman: music!") keenly observes that no amount of ink spilled in the task of capturing a life would be sufficient: "You could write a book about Manuel Escobar! And that would leave things out, too! You could write ten books! You could never stop writing!" (157). A series of impossibly unreliable narrators producing "[e]ndless snarls of words, sometimes twisting into meaning, sometimes into nothing at all" (xvii), alongside descriptions of videotapes proffered by a blind man combine to make Mark Z. Danielewski's *House of Leaves* (2000) a eulogy for representation. Much less bleak is Auster's *The Invention of Solitude* (1982), a memoir that resists the assumption of photographic transparency and truthfulness, focusing instead on the metaphoric possibilities of both images and prose.

DeLillo is less critical of modes of representation than of its uses. He has, after all, admitted that comic books were his earliest reading material and that "European movies, and jazz, and Abstract Expressionism" constituted his major influences (Passaro 38). He attributes his narrative style to Godard, Antonioni, Fellini, and Bergman as much as to Joyce and Beckett (DeCurtis 59). Regardless of the medium, DeLillo is skeptical of representation that doesn't recognize its limits or challenge its reader, of reductive images, of literal language. Indeed, the most dangerous characters in DeLillo's work are often those who feel compelled to bind words to things. In *The Names*, he imagines a cult so driven by the need to connect language to the world that its members devise a system of human sacrifice in which a link is made between the names of the victims and the towns in which they are murdered. In *White Noise*, Dylar, a drug designed to quash one's fear of death, results in an inability to understand language as symbolic, so that the phrase "[h]ail of bullets" causes the listener to drop to the floor and seek a space to hide (311).

In contrast to a desire for more precise language is DeLillo's almost perverse fascination with words absent of meaning, with language as enchantment. *White Noise*'s synthetic trinities—"MasterCard, Visa, American Express"; "Dacron, Orlon, Lycra Spandex"; "Krylon, Rust-Oleum, Red Devil" (100, 52, 159)—clearly represent the infiltration of American consumerism into the unconscious, but they also evoke an attempt to redeem those terms from marketing and advertising. Describing, in an interview, the incantatory quality of the phrase *Toyota Celica*, DeLillo said: "There's something nearly mystical about certain words and phrases that float through our lives. [. . .] If you concentrate on the sound, if you disassociate the words from the object[s] they denote, and if you say the words over and over, they become a sort of higher Esperanto" (Begley, "Art of Fiction" 291). He also expressed an implausible affinity for the architecture of language, the materiality of words disconnected from meaning: "I construct sentences. There's a rhythm I hear that drives me through a sentence. And the words typed on the white page have a sculptural quality. [. . .] The rhythm of a sentence will accommodate a certain number of syllables. One syllable too many, I look for another word" (283). Indeed, for DeLillo, rhythm, tempo, and appearance supercede significance: "I'll consider altering the meaning of a sentence to keep the rhythm, the syllable beat. I'm completely willing to let language press meaning upon me" (283), a sentiment that approaches fiction as poetry, that privileges the aural and oral components of language. It is a sentiment that could almost be the philosophy of *The Names*'s cult, in which meaning derives from the accidental nature of words, but with a notable difference: while the cult members assume they are making language more concrete, DeLillo suggests that meaning lurks in error, allusion, and abstraction, as in Tap Axton's epilogic story, "The Prairie," that culminates *The Names*. His "spirited misspellings," as his father notes, "made [the words] new again, made me see how they worked, what they really were. They were ancient things, secret, reshapable" (313).

Similarly, for DeLillo the photograph's power inheres not in its documentary ability but in its metaphoric possibilities, not in what it ostensibly depicts but what an oblique reading reveals. In *Mao II*, Brita's photographs of Bill "were glimpses of Brita thinking, a little anatomy of mind and eye" (221). Vicki Goldberg argues that photography's veracity lies not in its representational but in its evocative potential:

> One way or another, the photographic medium is busy destabilizing the very nature of existence. A medium intent on such subversion just might have more power as fiction than fact. [...] Maybe photographs are not lying even when they skitter along the thin edge between real life and theater. Rather, they uncover the secret stories, mythic constructions and uncertainties that constitute our lives. (34)

In Auster's *The Invention of Solitude*, A. discovers his father through a series of representations—newspaper clippings, fairy tales, poetry, and photographs, but the most useful images turn out to be fraudulent—a trick photograph from Atlantic City and a doctored image from a family album. DeLillo, like his friend Auster, understands that truth is often found in the least likely places; a photograph may find its power in metaphor and language its strength in seeming nonsense. Amy Hungerford argues persuasively that the babbling and glossalalia so prevalent in DeLillo's work is an attempt to sacralize the word, to make visible in language the "immanence of transcendent meaning in the material of daily life" (346); however, if Karen's "fractured" idiom is a language "commensurate" to imagination and mystery, an "'unwritable and interior' language that transcends the language of logic and convention" (362, 363), if it is, as Hungerford claims, the language "that Bill seems to seek but cannot find," then literature is reduced to a sympathetic incoherence, a disoriented refraction (363). Instead, DeLillo presents a world in which the argot of cultists and capitalists, artists and terrorists provides pieces of the puzzle. No single language, no single perspective, no single image completes the picture since, as Scott realizes, language, like all media, is dangerous, as likely to go "toward one thing" as "the logical opposite," as likely to serve propagandistic purposes as revolutionary aims, as likely to be quotidian as sublime.

PART II

Underworld (1997)

The pipe-smoking man who introduces himself to Bucky Wunderlick as "Morehouse Professor of Latent History" in *Great Jones Street* (1973) describes his work at the Osmond Institute as prompted by a desire "to avoid a narrow purview" and concerned with "events that almost took place, events that definitely took place but remained unseen and unremarked on, [...] and events that probably took place but were definitely not chronicled" (75). Such devotion to the unrecorded and the unofficial anticipates the "secret history" of the Kennedy assassination that DeLillo later will have Nicholas Branch hired to write in *Libra* (1988), of course (15), as well as DeLillo's own interrogation of the Warren Commission findings in that same text. It also underlies any number of earlier historical novels intent on providing counternarratives of the American past and the less-than-authoritative sources on which those works rely: the "protests scrawled on the margins in pencil" in the "publiclibrary full of old newspapers and dogeared historybooks," the "kidding stories," "hired man's yarns," and "tall tales" (vii), in which John Dos Passos locates the *U.S.A.* in his trilogy (1930, 1932, 1936); the sexually charged *Secret Historie of the Voiage Up the Bay of Chesapeake* that John Barth ascribes to John Smith in *The Sot-Weed Factor* (1960); the jumbled doctoral dissertation of the disturbed narrator that E. L. Doctorow presents as *The Book of Daniel* (1971).

Reflecting their writers' concern with "bringing the past to life as the prehistory of the present" in the manner proposed by Georg Lukács when defining the genre (53), these narratives differ from those of the Morehouse Professor in offering few illusions of their practical impact. "Latent history never tells us where we stand in the sweep of events," asserts the professor (himself a fraud, as it turns out) in *Great Jones Street*, "but rather how we can get out of the way" (76). By the time of

DeLillo's *Underworld* (1997), however, getting out of the way is hardly an option. The reverse chronology of its structure, recognized by DeLillo in hindsight as evoking the countdown to a nuclear test (Howard 122), reveals that within an underlying system of power in which everything is connected—orange juice and Agent Orange (463, 465), rubber kitchen gloves and plutonium-protection gloves (519–20, 419), major league baseballs and atom-bomb cores the size of baseballs (172)—and connected "at levels outside your comprehension" (465), we long ago were tossed into the trash.

Predicating that system on "death from the sky," as incarnated by the Bomb (458), and recalling the "screaming [that] comes across the sky" that famously opens another novel structured around a movement to zero (3), DeLillo tips his hat to Thomas Pynchon and the economic connections of *Gravity's Rainbow* (1973) that bypass all political alliances, from the prewar selling of Tyrone Slothrop to IG Farben "like a side of beef" to the postwar marketing of concentration camps as tourist attractions (286, 453). But if Pynchon leaves open the possibility, however small, that the "stately Finger" pointing to IG Farben as "*the very model of nations*" may be the product of paranoid characters who think that Providence is always giving them the finger (566), DeLillo, nearly a quarter-century later, has no doubts. With the portrayal of its opening binaries—Thomson/Branca, Giants/Dodgers, USA/USSR—that "bring each other to deep completion" collapsed by all those posed photos of Thomson and Branca "joined at the hip for life" that punctuate the novel (51, 465), the "connection between Us and Them" that J. Edgar Hoover intimates at the start extends well beyond the suspicions of a single figure by midpoint: "Because everything connects in the end, or only seems to, or seems to only because it does" (465). In contrast to Rabbit Angstrom, then, who views the Cold War as that which "gave you a reason to get up in the morning" and, in *Rabbit at Rest* (1990), mourns its end in terms of an impersonal economics—specifically, "Japan, and technology, and the profit motive"—replacing politics and standing armies as the adjudicators of power (Updike 353, 272), the characters in *Underworld* who view the Cold War as a "[p]oint of reference" both "honest" and "dependable," and understand just how linked economics and politics have always been, experience its end in terms of abject terror: "when the tension and rivalry come to an end, that's when your worst nightmares begin" (170). More than just a question of "[t]hings hav[ing] no limits now" (76), as one such character notes in 1992, it is the exposure of things perhaps never having had limits. When one man involved in underground weapons work tells another, "You can never underestimate the willingness of the state to act out its own massive fantasies" (421), he states nothing that his fellow "bombhead" has not already learned from his service in Vietnam, "where everything he'd ever disbelieved or failed to imagine turned out, in the end, to be true" (418).

The chapter by Thomas Hill Schaub that opens the critical discussions of *Underworld* that follow introduces DeLillo's novel, with its inverted narrative that moves backward from 1992 to 1951, as a counternarrative to the Cold War narrative that typically moves forward toward inexorable doom. Viewed in this light, the book's invocation, and repetition, of Cold War tropes—the Lenny Bruce improvisations, the satire on plastic, the sexualized discourse of nuclear missiles and bombs—contribute to a phenomenological reading of the book as approximating the workings of memory, driven by a longing for the past that, in theory, need not be limited to any one specific period. The next two essays suggest just how extended the book's notion of that past—cultural as well as historical—is. Opening his discussion of urban space by referring to a group of coeval artists—working in fiction, film, and sculpture—in whose work the underground plays a major role, David L. Pike goes on to explore DeLillo's underworlds with respect to the tradition of "lower depths writing" that harks back to the first responses to industrialized cities, to the portrayal of cities as dens of iniquity, and finally to the underworlds of classical literature, notably Dante's *Commedia*. Opening her discussion of ethnicity by citing the ancient Mediterranean religious traditions that inform the Bronx Little Italy in which DeLillo's book is rooted, Josephine Gattuso Hendin goes on to depict its postwar celebration of American diversity as joining the radical Protestantism of Emerson with the agonistic spirituality of Aquinas.

Such joining of spiritual and secular reflects the union of high and low that all three chapters address, from the physical structures in which such elements are literally embodied (walls, tunnels, buildings) to the art works in which High Modernism and mass culture coalesce (films, murals, castoffs). Such unions prompt Thomas Hill Schaub to view DeLillo's book as—to recall one of its governing metaphors—a "waste collection," a recycling of cultural associations and artifacts that are already part of its reader's memory. David L. Pike, by contrast, emphasizes the novel's concern with the materiality of waste, defining its act of collecting as inspired by DeLillo's desire to restore the "thingness to things" otherwise discarded or obsolete. Viewed as contributing to the found object art that Italians term *arte povera*, however, such things may require no restoration at all since, according to Josephine Gattuso Hendin's reading of Aquinas, all art is formed by rearranging materials originally created by God. With the distinction between "artist" and "outsider artist" thus collapsed, these three chapters on *Underworld* anticipate the portrayal of the performance artist in *Falling Man* (2007) a decade later.

CHAPTER 5

Underworld, Memory, and the Recycling of Cold War Narrative

Thomas Hill Schaub

Cold War narratives in their simplest formulation were narratives—in witch hunts, in the courtroom and Congress, in fiction, in newspapers, movies, and music—that framed contemporary world history as a contest between two superpowers, the Christian theocracy of U.S. capitalism and the godless communism of the USSR. The key words in these narratives were "the enemy within," "mutual assured destruction," "conspiracy," "containment," "conformity," "paranoia," and "chance," among others. To be sure, there were many cultural narratives and myriad story-lines, but dominant among them was that of a culture suffused throughout by the struggle between communism and capitalism. Considerable effort has gone into showing how systematic and widespread the effects of that struggle were.

Especially in the years of most intense confrontation, from the realization in 1949 that the Russians had the bomb until after the 1962 Cuban Missile Crisis, the Cold War narrative was teleological and apocalyptic. In books such as Nevil Shute's *On the Beach* (1957), made into a movie two years later, the end of the nuclear standoff is imagined as the end of human life. In the Henry Fonda film *Fail Safe* (1964), based on a 1962 novel by Eugene Burdick and Harvey Wheeler, the President allows Russia to bomb New York in compensation for our having destroyed Moscow. Even the lesser skirmishes among spies, from the James Bond novels of Ian Fleming to *The Spy Who Came in from the Cold* (1963) by John le Carré, take place on a temporal continuum leading to direct confrontation. As these books show, the literary imagination often focused less upon victory over the enemy than upon the victimization of the citizenry by the bureaucracies of state power on both sides. Joseph Heller's *Catch-22* (1961) and Stanley Kubrick's *Dr. Strangelove* (1964) showed us there was as much to fear from one's own side as there was from the adversary. In this second-stage Cold War culture of the early 1960s, as Stephen J. Whitfield has shown, the intensity and paranoia of the Cold War period gave way to more domestic preoccupations (237–38). Both Heller's novel and Kubrick's film are symptomatic of this change in tone, as were spoofs like the television series *Get Smart* (first broadcast on 18 September 1965).

Nevertheless, worries about nuclear warfare and debates about the need for a nuclear freeze continued well into the Reagan administration and remain with us today. In the introduction to *Slow Learner* (1984), Thomas Pynchon recalls the period when he was writing his short fiction:

> [T]he Bomb is in there too. It was bad enough in '59 and is much worse now, as the level of danger has continued to grow. There was never anything subliminal about it, then or now. Except for that succession of the criminally insane who have enjoyed power since 1945, including the power to do something about it, most of the rest of us poor sheep have always been stuck with simple, standard fear. I think we all have tried to deal with this slow escalation of helplessness and terror in the few ways open to us, from not thinking about it to going crazy from it. Somewhere on this spectrum of impotence is writing fiction about it [. . .]. (18–19)

As it concerned the bomb, the Cold War narrative remained teleological and apocalyptic: at the end of Pynchon's novel *Gravity's Rainbow* (1973), the nuclear-tipped missile (and the long social and political history that has gone into its creation and launch), "falling nearly a mile per second, absolutely and forever without sound, reaches its last unmeasurable gap above" the audience below (760). This is history as missile, chickens coming home to roost.

In contrast to this ending, the narrative structure of Don DeLillo's *Underworld* (1997) differs sharply from that of the Cold War narrative. *Underworld* is without question a novel about the Cold War period, and of the years subsequent to 1989, when the Berlin Wall came down, and Eastern Europe went about the often bloody business of re-establishing nation-states and settling ethnic scores, while capitalism's detail men looked for investment opportunities previously foreclosed. The novel appeared four years before 2001, in a period that now seems to have been an interim moment between Cold War narrative and the Narrative of Terror. This is the period when Rabbit Angstrom, in John Updike's *Rabbit at Rest* (1990), wonders, "Without the cold war, what's the point of being an American?" (442–43).

Although about the Cold War period, however, *Underworld* is not a Cold War narrative. Rather than creating an apocalyptic plot that moves inexorably toward holocaust, or a narrative of characters whose lives are dominated by fear of its possibility, DeLillo's novel establishes little or no tension, evinces little forward momentum to speak of, and in place of plot offers the gradual revelation of a static structure. DeLillo takes the air out of Cold War narrative with several temporal structures: the movement backward in time from "Spring-Summer 1992" to "Fall 1951–Summer 1952"; the Manx Martin sequence that remains within a twenty-four-hour period in 1951, but is distributed evenly in three segments throughout the inverted time of the 1992–1951 inside narrative; and the trajectory forward inscribed by the prologue and epilogue, from "The Triumph of Death" in October 1951 to "Das Kapital" in the early 1990s. Further, the inverted sequences of the inner narrative come to rest within the time period of the novel's prologue (1951); and the epilogue, in which Nick Shay and Brian Glassic visit a nuclear facility in Kazakhstan, rejoins the time period of the "Long Tall Sally" section (1992), the first episode of the inverted narrative. Pondering Marvin Lundy's effort to establish the line of ownership for Bobby Thomson's home-run ball, the narrator describes a narrative structure that could serve as shorthand for the workings of the novel itself: "Strange how he was compiling a record of the object's recent forward motion while simultaneously tracking it backwards to the distant past" (318).

Going Backwards: Time

The backward movement of what I'm calling the inside narrative (1992–1951) suggests a number of self-evident analogues, especially to the activity of memory, and to a kind of psychoanalytic and cultural archaeology. As archaeology, the movement backward is also a movement down, under, and within—each suggestive of an underworld to be revealed. Just as repetition is a narrative strategy to create circularity and stasis, so the inverted time of this narrative would seem to be a version of the search for origins. Clearly, the novel is determined to bring the reader to that period in Nick Shay's life when he loses his father and kills George Manza, but in no sense does *Underworld* aspire to the satisfactions of the romance genre. The accidental shooting of the waiter and the father's disappearance are determinative events; they do launch a history, at least a psychological history that Nick is still contending with in the first section of the novel. But DeLillo makes no effort to develop suspense or to set up the moment of discovery as one of resolution. The end of the inner narrative reveals nothing the reader hasn't known for hundreds of pages (118–19, 299–300; see Knight 831). Instead of fostering narrative desire, DeLillo seems devoted to establishing a narrative dwelling that imitates the prolonged present of meditation on the past.

Crucial to that meditation in the inverted inner narrative is an element of play that duplicates the structure of children's games, and the time of childhood for which Nick longs. In one instance, as the Shay family drives home from visiting a ruin south of Phoenix, the children sing "Ninety-Nine Bottles of Beer," "counting backwards all the way to one" (345). As other readers have noted, games like this one often have other analogues within the novel. Here one can't help thinking of the countdown sequence made famous by nuclear testing and the subsequent moon and space station launches, not to mention its replication in television and movies. Joining them together is the concept of "game" widely dispersed throughout the novel, and inaugurated in the prologue by the famous Giants-Dodgers playoff game and the news of the Soviet Union's nuclear test. Father Paulus remarks upon the ability of children to "sidestep time, as it were, and the ravages of progress," to conclude, "I think they operate in another time scheme altogether" (673). In one sense, then, *Underworld* is a kind of children's game that seeks to defeat time, or at the very least aspires to do so through the mechanism of sequences that go forward in time, while the series of the sequences run backward.

Albert Bronzini's delight in George the Waiter's memories of childhood brings another dimension of the novel's structure to the fore: "How children adapt to available surfaces, [. . .]. How they take the pockmarked world and turn a delicate inversion, making something brainy and rule-bound and smooth, and then spend the rest of their lives trying to repeat the process" (664). The emphasis in this passage falls upon repetition and the loss of some ability or latitude in the past, made thematically explicit in Nick's longing for "the days of disarray" (806). If "[l]onging on a large scale is what makes history" (11), then longing for the past—at least in this novel—is the engine driving the narrative backward in time, retreating from a future that seems to hold no allure. In one of his poignant reflections, Nick sees the past and future bound up in the objects of his home, "objects that bind us to some betokening" but also breathe "a kind of sadness" (808), especially when caught in language and named: "There is something somber about the things we've collected and own, the household effects, there is something about the word itself, *effects*" (808). Effects are the objects left over, the consequences of the consumed life, or possessions that become waste. Objects remind their owners of what is past and passing and to come; for Nick there is something oracular about them, presaging a future he doesn't welcome. He feels himself to be in the "firm grip" of a "different direction, not back but forward" (808); he longs for the "days when he was alive on the earth," the days when his own life constituted a "breach of peace" (810).

These pages reveal much that motivates the inverted narrative structure of *Underworld*. Longing seems central not merely to Nick Shay's middle age, but to DeLillo's imagination. In a sense, longing replaces (and enervates) desire, giving rise to many of the novel's feints and jabs, especially in the recurrent suspicion of secrets kept or withheld and the opposite insistence upon the value of the ordinary and the everyday. Just as frequently, the categories of the secret and the disclosed are collapsed into one: Marvin Lundy tells Brian Glassic the "biggest secrets are the ones spread open before us" (185); Klara Sax realizes "how rare it was to see what stands before you" (379); Eric Demming tells Matt Shay, "Nobody's supposed to know this. It's something that's more or less out in the open but at the same time" (405). On the one hand is the desire to penetrate a secret like a latter-day Ahab and, on the other, recognition of the sacred dwelling in the open on the profane surfaces of ordinary life, pockmarked or smooth. In collapsing the value of the withheld and the valuing of the everyday, DeLillo's longing produces a faded version of Joycean illumination—*quidditas* without epiphany. "The soul of the commonest object," Stephen tells Cranly, explicating Aquinas in *Stephen Hero* (1944), "the structure of which is so adjusted, seems to us radiant. The object achieves its epiphany" (Joyce 213). Nick Shay is no Stephen Dedalus, but Father Paulus schools him in Aquinas nonetheless: "How everyday things lie hidden," he tells Nick. "Because we don't know what they're called" (541).

The effort to divine radiant meaning through naming may be the central animating aspiration of the novel. As David Cowart has written persuasively, "realism may be secondary to some visionary quality in his [DeLillo's] text, a language-based rectification of the ills that Nick Shay and all in his generation are heir to" (182). This may explain why so many of the paragraphs in *Underworld* are devoted to the prolonged scrutiny of objects, as if sufficient dwelling upon them would redeem them in language, force them to yield their mystery. One example serves to disclose the novel's ambition: Nick with the baseball in his hand. "You have to know the feel of a baseball in your hand, going back a while, connecting many things, before you can understand why a man would sit in a chair at four in the morning holding such an object" (131). Befitting the novel's talismanic object, DeLillo devotes twenty-five lines of type—perhaps the longest paragraph in the novel—to describing Nick's observation of the baseball: "How the hand works memories out of the baseball," Nick thinks, "that have nothing to do with games of the usual sort" (132). Working memories out yields a kind of history, connections real and imagined, repeated riffs on objects and feelings that draw out and slow down narrative time. This tendency is also part of the novel's focus upon the whatness or objecthood of the past. The riff on the baseball offers a microcosm of *Underworld* as an improvisation on the theme of waste, insofar as the novel constitutes the remaining "effects" of memory, here accumulating like a landfill. The novel as dump.

Indeed, *Underworld* seems rooted in an idea of history as an object worthy of recollection in language. DeLillo "discharge[s] the debt to memory" (64) as if Dr. Lindblad of the juvenile correction center had told him, rather than Nick, that he is "required to try to make sense of" his history (512), but the book as a totality seems to echo Nick's mother, Rosemary: "What mattered were the mysteries, not the language in which you said them" (757). There are times, the narrator says, when "faith needs a sign," times "when you want to stop working at faith and just be washed in a blowing wind that tells you everything" (757). Alluding to the rushing wind of Pentecostal revelation, DeLillo antici-pates the "persistent wind" (818) on the night of the miracle ginned up by the need for belief in "*Keystroke 1*" (817–24), the penultimate section of the novel: "A dozen women clutch their heads, they whoop and sob, a spirit, a godsbreath passing through the crowd" (821). For a few moments, they hear what Thomas Pynchon terms "the Word, the cry that might abolish the night" (*Lot 49* 87).

David Cowart has written so well of longing in the "physics of language." Of Nick's story, he writes, "With its attention to mystical words and the 'theological' significance of naming, *Underworld* is in large measure a story of spiritual travail" (186). Yet this story must be told in reverse precisely because Nick, like Gatsby and his acolyte, Nick Carraway, wants to recover the past. His spiritual travail—or, rather, the spiritual travail of the novel itself—derives from remembering back-ward rather than forward, as Kierkegaard theorized the problem: the "real repetition is remembered forwards. Hence it is that repetition, if it be possible, makes a man happy; while memory makes him unhappy" (xxxi). Remembering forward for Nick—and the novel, I am arguing—requires a belief that redemption lies in the future, a belief that seems as impossible for DeLillo as it is for Gracie in the refectory, urging Sister Edgar not to join the crowd waiting to see Esmeralda's face emerge through the picture of pouring orange juice. The novel is pervaded by "the sadness and clarity of time" (229).

Repetitions: Space

Except for Albert Bronzini's astonishment at the symmetrical headlines in which DeLillo locates the origin of his novel (668), mention of the Cold War and the bomb completely disappears as the novel retreats to its most cherished period: 1951–1952 (661–781). Including the prologue and the Manx Martin pages, DeLillo devotes 219 pages to evoking these months in language. Counting the pages from "Better Things for Better Living through Chemistry" ("Selected Fragments Public and Private in the 1950s and 1960s")—which include a good deal of Cold War hysteria and the inspired Lenny Bruce improvisations—the total comes to close to half the novel: 356 pages. This era is clearly the privileged location of the novel.

Given this fact, one of the remarkable accomplishments of *Underworld* is DeLillo's ability to sustain a compelling focus upon relatively inert material over the length of such a long novel. This inert quality derives in part from the distribution of the 1951–1952 time period and the recurrence of the Thomson home-run ball throughout the whole—most obviously in the Manx Martin sections, but also in the sections devoted to Marvin Lundy and Nick Shay. This distribution has the effect of undermining even the inverted time of the inside narrative, creating that dwelling quality of memory as it moves around in the spaces of collapsed time. The persistence of the baseball, like an underneath thread that surfaces now and then in the weave, is only the most celebrated of the remembered objects whose repetition helps to create the novel's architecture of static space. Repetitions of various kinds constitute the novel's stuffing, and account for one of the reader's most common experiences—let's call it a narrative *déjà vu*. Some of the most significant of these repetitions, at least for Nick Shay, are the memories of his father leaving (86–87, 106–07, 118–19, 121–22, 139–40, 764–65) and of having shot George Manza (132, 299–300, 778–81). These repetitions make perfect sense within the world of the story itself for they reproduce the activity of memory, the persistence of the past in the present thoughts of the main character, but DeLillo's repetitions (within those thoughts) of exact words and phrases also call attention to the textuality and purposeful structuring of the novel.

That is to say the effect of memory is an effect of the novel as a mnemonic structure as well as a feature of Nick Shay's interiority. Robert McMinn describes this aspect of the novel: "DeLillo's aim here is to narrate events, then renarrate them, [...] to juxtapose events, to double and mirror them, until we have seen or been reminded of the same thing many times" (39). Speaking through Bronzini, the narrator may be said to explain this spatial dimension of *Underworld*: "How memory conspires with objects of human craft, pressing time flat, inciting a tender reminiscence" (233). Consider the moment that Nick holds the baseball and thinks about "how it fits the palm so reassuringly" (131) and the passage on the following page in which he recalls the moment before shooting Manza: "I hefted the weapon and pointed it" (132). This paratactic repetition may provoke reflections upon baseballs and guns, waste and weaponry, but the example also identifies a key aspect of narrative structure. The sex scenes between Nick and Klara Sax, and between Nick and Donna, provide even better examples of repetition because in them repetition doesn't seem to mean anything, and, told in the third person, they cannot be dismissed as Shay's memories. In their first encounter, Klara "went back to the room and gave him [Nick] the mattress" (732), an action repeated seventeen pages later: "[s]he threw down the mattress" (749). Describing their feverish sex, the narrator tell us, "They were everywhere on each other, noisy and damp" (733), language that echoes Nick and Donna, some four hundred pages earlier, "patched together grappling and straining" (300). Reflecting upon his time with Donna, a member of a swingers' club meeting at the same conference center as a group of waste managers, Nick summarizes his recollections so far: "These were movie scenes" (292)—that is, the actual settings and events were like scenes in movies. But he also remembers those scenes in such a way that first and third persons are spliced together so as to allow memory to act like a film editor: "And now the scene in the room, my room, where she took off her jeans" (293). DeLillo's narrative voice moves in and out here, the dropped-in phrase "my room" the only reminder that these are supposed to be Nick's thoughts. In between them, Nick echoes Bronzini on the flattening of time: "The long lens insinuates a certain compression, a half-lurking anxiety that serves not only the moment but the day and week *and age*" (292–93, my italics).

Such flattening effects occur throughout the novel. In some instances repetition suggests a key to an idea or concept; in others it creates a structural affect. In this same set of pages, Nick recalls the fourteenth-century *The Cloud of Unknowing* as having "made [him] think of God as a force that withholds himself from us because that is the root of his power" (295). Six pages later, Nick thinks to himself, "You withhold the deepest things from those who are closest" (301)—in this case that he once shot a man. And, much later, the force of Nick's father comes exactly from his having disappeared, withheld himself from his wife and children: "The failure it brought down on us does not diminish" (809). Nick imagines his father's disappearance as a descent into the realm of Pluto, the god of the underworld—"The earth opened up and he stepped inside" (808)—echoing an earlier articulation of the same thought: "[T]hey dropped him into the lower world" (119). The effect of such repetition—the withholding of God, of Nick, and of Nick's father in the realm of Pluto—is to collapse distinction and difference under the spatial inertia of an idea, a word.

DeLillo nests Nick's memory of his infidelity with Donna (290–301) inside Nick's conversations with Jesse Detwiler and Big Sims at a conference of waste managers in Mojave Springs. From the perspective of the waste manager, everything is garbage, Sims tells Shay (283); and Shay persistently links his father's disappearance with waste. "The Cloud of Unknowing" section begins with Nick's tour of Sabato Rodia's sculpture of waste, Watts Towers, intermingled with thoughts of his father: "the deep disturbance, was that my own ghost father was living in the walls" (277). This is a recurring association for Nick: "We built pyramids of waste above and below the earth. [. . .] The word plutonium comes from Pluto, god of the dead and ruler of the underworld. They took him out to the marshes and wasted him as we say today, or used to say until it got changed to something else" (106). This association travels, as it were, surfacing in Brian Glassic's visit to the Fresh Kills landfill on Staten Island: "He imagined he was watching the construction of the Great Pyramid at Giza" (184).

Passages such as this one suggest the character of the novel as waste collection, a reprise of words, phrases, and associations that are already part of the reader's memorabilia. We know where the word "plutonium" comes from, and who Pluto is. Pynchon first wrote of a landfill in his story "Low-lands" (1960), though the landfill in that story is on Long Island. Joseph W. Slade was the first to connect Pynchon's use of landfill as a metaphor of history to Henry Adams's *The Degradation of the Democratic Dogma* (1919; 54–55). Waste itself was so pervasive a metaphor among works of the modernists—fundamentally in T. S. Eliot's *The Waste Land* (1922), but also in F. Scott Fitzgerald's *The Great Gatsby* (1925) and Ernest Hemingway's "Big Two-Hearted River" (1925)—that it had become a cliché that Pynchon must parody in order to recover the figure for serious purposes in *The Crying of Lot 49* (1966). In this way, DeLillo's entire novel, or much of it, is a reprise of characteristic vocabularies and ideas from a period and culture falling away from us, like a lure in water. Numerous readers have commented usefully upon the thematics of waste in the novel, reading "waste for traces of our social practices and collective desires" (O'Donnell 110) and assessing the book as a "study of waste and its containment" (Duvall, *Don DeLillo's* 46). But David Cowart comes closest to my interest in the formal dimension of the novel as waste, what he terms DeLillo's "inspired recycling as a localized or self-bounded illustration of the principle of intertextuality" (198), for he shows how DeLillo recycles quests and themes from his own earlier fictions as well as conventions and styles drawn from modernism to postmodernism, including allusions to the work of Joyce, Eliot, James T. Farrell, and Philip Roth (198–202).

Cowart points out, as I have been doing, that there are passages within the novel that are themselves recycled or repeated, noting those in which Shay thinks about his family's conscientious recycling (89, 119, 803–04, 806–07), and suggesting, persuasively to this reader, that these recurrent thoughts both frame and partially mask "a half-conscious hunger for the larger recycling of spiritual waste" (187). In drawing the connection between a repetition of passages and Nick Shay's spiritual equilibrium, however, Cowart makes a thematic point about waste that reinforces the novel's own preoccupations with recycling and waste, including Nick Shay's fear that "[w]hat we excrete comes back to consume us" (791; qtd. in *Physics* 187). Viewing recycling as a form of repetition, which it surely is, returns us to formal questions about narrative structure and makeup, and their use in creating a kind of midden of Cold War artifacts.

For a further implication presents itself: not only is the novel a meditation upon waste, conveyed in an architecture of repetition and recycling of structures of waste, of memory itself as a containment structure of waste; the novel itself is such a structure, and DeLillo a waste engineer at the controls of a front loader piling up pervasive Cold War tropes, discourses, and associations. How else account for the repetition of such familiar ideas as entropy—a pivotal concept in both Norbert Wiener's *The Human Use of Human Beings* (1950) and Pynchon's "Entropy" (1960)—or the underground and underworld—ubiquitous figures central to Ralph Ellison's *Invisible Man* (1952), Mario Puzo's *The Godfather* (1969), the Weathermen (a 1969 offshoot of Students for a Democratic Society), and the rock band the Velvet Underground (1965–1973)? How else explain the worry that social history is outdoing the artistic imagination, the fear of "forces in the culture that could out-imagine them" felt by those watching the Zapruder film in 1974 (495), which echoes Philip Roth's 1961 description of American reality as "a kind of embarrassment to one's own meager imagination?" (224). Or the suspicion that American culture has been running on two parallel currents—the "two rivers, one visible, the other underground," by which Norman Mailer distinguished the practical "history of politics" from those "untapped, ferocious, lonely and romantic desires" that comprised "the dream life of the nation" in 1960 ("Superman" 38)? Or the ecological recognition that everything is connected, shared by Barry Commoner's *The Closing Circle* (1971) and Pynchon's *Gravity's Rainbow* (1973)? Or the satire on plastic made famous in Mike Nichols's *The Graduate* (1967) reappearing in the bit on Erica Demming's love for her "rubberoid gloves" (519–20) and Lenny Bruce's condom rap (581–82)? Or the suggestion that art is made from cultural waste and detritus (see Duchamp *inter alia*)? All the language of Cold War paranoia, conspiracy, the association of all technology with the bomb and Lenny Bruce's "*We're all gonna die!*" (594), even Eric Demming's parody of the paranoid:

"You can never unterestimate the villingness of the shtate. [. . .] To ahkt out its own massif phantasies" (421)—all this is Cold War shtick. Counterhistory itself develops during the Cold War period, emerging from suspicions of state power and authority of every stripe, following upon the movements for free speech, civil rights, women's liberation, and opposition to the Vietnam War. Narrative itself came under suspicion, as the constructed character of narrative history became newly recognized and theorized (see Hayden White, *Metahistory* [1973]).

These improvisations on Cold War culture frequently take the forms of inverted order, repetition, and parataxis. An especially revealing example of such improvisation develops around the word "pocket." We learn that Nick Shay's brother, Matt, works in an "underground operation" called "the Pocket, where weapons were conceived and designed" (404), a passage which serves to connect the word "pocket" and the military-industrial complex with sexual reproduction. This association comments upon a passage five pages earlier, drawing that scene into a loose system of ideas and associations. Klara Sax recalls a double-date with her girlfriend Rochelle, and remembers thinking she "heard the boy's finger actually enter the fleshy pocket between Rochelle's legs" (399). It anticipates Nick's later detailing of early bomb design as the fitting of a male "element" into a female counterpart (791), which links the womb to both the origins of human history and holocaust, and reprises the Lenny Bruce routine about a girl who can place a cigarette in her vagina and blow perfect "O"s—"Because isn't it possible that all these O's coming out of her womb refer to the Greek letter that means The End?" (630; DeLillo lifts this scene from *Emmanuelle* [1974], a soft-core spin-off of Pauline Réage's *Story of O* [1954]). DeLillo reinforces these echoing associations with the language of "furrow," "tunnels," and "the slot" (402, 728), all variations on the "pocket." As J. Edgar Hoover thinks at the ballpark that day in 1951, "they are sitting in the furrow of destruction" (28).

All of these people are downwinders in the wake of history, and passive in the posture of reception, as it were. One might think of this as Cold War estrus, examples of the sexualized discourse of the Cold War, of the missile as a penis, and bombing as figurative fucking. This is something civilization does to itself, an act of collective masturbation. Matt Shay "loved the way power rises out of self-caressing secrecy to become a roar in the sky" (one of many overt references to *Gravity's Rainbow*); after experiencing a "steroid jolt" from two F-4 Phantoms taking off near them, both he and his girlfriend, Janet, "needed a moment to collect themselves, speechless in the wake of a power and thrust snatched [amusing pun] from nature's own greatness" (468). Strapped inside an aircraft known as a "BUFF" (for "Big Ugly Fat Fuck"), radar-bombardier Louis T. Bakey tells Chuckie Wainwright, "I find myself in a very pussy-minded mood today" prior to takeoff for Vietnam (607), while Wainwright himself, as navigator, responds from "[i]n the hole" (608); by the end of the chapter, their chorus of "First we bomb them"/ "Then we fuck them" has been reprised as "First we fuck them"/"Then we bomb them," the reversal signaling the conflation of the two acts in Cold War discourse (607, 616).

Another implication of these dispersed associations of female pockets and male weaponry during the Cold War period—one recalls Slim Pickens with the missile between his legs in *Dr. Strangelove*, riding the warhead down to its point of impact after the mechanical malfunction of his plane's bomb doors—was the idea that mankind is in love with its own death. Readers of Pynchon have been familiar with this idea for years. In *V.* (1963), the narrator appears to quote an as yet unidentified source: "the act of love and the act of death are one" (410); in *Gravity's Rainbow*, the theme is reproduced in the coinciding maps kept by Pointsman (of V-2 strikes) and Slothrop (of sexual trysts). This quasi-Freudian hyperbole of the 1960s counterculture reinforces the feeling—and it is an affect created by the novel—that much of *Underworld* collects and replays typical Cold War thinking. DeLillo reproduces this particular idea in Sister Edgar's thoughts: "Not that she didn't think a war might be thrilling. She often conjured the flash even now, with the USSR crumbled alphabetically, the massive letters toppled like Cyrillic statuary" (245). If anyone doubts the calculation with which DeLillo reprises the death wish as a period piece, or the fun he's having while so doing, consider his reference above—"the massive letters toppled like Cyrillic statuary"—to Martin Campbell's post–Cold War Bond movie, *GoldenEye* (1995), with its depiction of abandoned Soviet relics in St. Petersburg's Statue Park.

There isn't any systematic payoff in this spray of associations, or others noted above, because DeLillo has always been a mood artist, a creator of atmospheres. That he is more interested in feeling than agency has always distinguished DeLillo's books from Pynchon's. While DeLillo works to create the affect of sublime mystery, or the feeling of being an unknowing participant in some vast system, Pynchon's books are more inclined to name names and target particular agents, such as DuPont, Sandoz, Shell-Mex, and IG Farben. The Jamf Ölfabriken Werke AG, a.k.a. "Technology," thus defends itself in *Gravity's Rainbow*: "do you think we'd've had the Rocket if someone, some specific somebody with a name and a penis hadn't *wanted* to chuck a ton of Amatol 300 miles and blow up a block full of civilians?" (521). By contrast, one might cite what has become a critical touchstone of DeLillo's novel, the set of references in *Underworld* to the color orange. "One could list dozens of such motifs," Mark Osteen observes. "But in this novel they point to a deeper level of connection that Matt [Shay] senses when he asks: 'how can you tell the difference between orange juice and agent orange if the same massive system connects them at levels outside your comprehension?'" (465; qtd. in *American Magic* 215). The answer is that one cannot tell the difference, but the question is specious if not paranoid because in such thinking all differences are dissolved into effects of "the same massive system." By such random salting of his narrative, DeLillo, as many readers suggest, may be offering a model of the postmodern sublime produced by late capital. The novel's final section, after all, is titled "Das Kapital," but it may be more accurate to shift the emphasis a bit: to say that DeLillo seeks to *produce* in the reader affects of the sort Matt Shay expresses. If the chief affect the novel represented through the character of Nick Shay is the "longing" that creates history, the chief affect produced within the reader—quite apart from the enormous pleasure provided by DeLillo's evocative prose—is recognition, at once of a time gone by and of words repeated in novelistic space.

Prufrock in Cyberspace

In the third of the novel's temporal movements, *Underworld* abruptly transports the reader forward in time to the post–Cold War of "Das Kapital." This abrupt shift serves to underline the difference between the disorderly vitality of Nick Shay's youth and the sterile culture of cyberspace consumption. The sharp division enforced by the narrative structure suggests an incommensurability of the 1951 era with that of the early 1990s, for coming after the inverted narrative has reached its earliest point, the world of post–Cold War capital appears not as a continuity with, much less an evolution of, the past (though it surely was). In Nick Shay's mind, there is a difference between the "cold war ideologies of massive uniformity" and the "furtive sameness," the "planing away of particulars," in the current dispensation (786).

Although the depiction of cyberspace that concludes the novel might be thought to be a model of the novel itself, DeLillo sets the power of memory to recall history against the power of cyberspace to create the future. Memory and cyberspace connectivity are contending forces in the book, both doing the work of making connections, but the connections forged by memory—the memories "worked" from objects and events signifying the past—Shay's, Lundy's, DeLillo's—are lived connections, invested with experience and attachment however somber or mysterious. Such connections lack the arbitrariness and isolation of the person at the computer, linking one thing to another at the click of a mouse. In fact, precisely because cyberspace does away with time and space, it is, in the novel's imagination, the perfect capitalist medium, a system far more vast than the conspiracies generated by the Cold War. "Is cyberspace a thing within the world," the narrator of "*Keystroke 2*" wants to know, "or is it the other way around?" (826). Is the narrator—are the novel's readers—inside cyberspace, like Sister Edgar in the "grip of systems" (825)? Here at the end we arrive at perhaps the most ominous of Cold War analogies, the one between the social systems of human beings and the closed system doomed to entropy, only in this closed system, in which everything is connected, the cybernetic network only grows and thrives, "difference itself, all argument, all conflict programmed out" (826).

In the face of such power, the self is left to sit at the monitor, clicking away, "willing to be shaped, to be overwhelmed," like Eliot's Prufrock, "docile," willing to dwell in "easy retreats, half beliefs" (826), DeLillo's version of "muttering retreats" and "restless nights in one-night cheap hotels" ("Love Song" ll. 5–6). In the last movement of "*Keystroke 2*"—one of American literature's most evocative and eerie conclusions—the word "Peace" surfaces on the monitor, a passive apparition that emerges from no mouse click or intended hyperlink, though once the word appears "you" can execute the last of the novel's many etymologies. This imagined "you" compares the word's meanings that emerge from cyberspace to the "thick lived tenor of things" taking place outside the window of the house, and tries to "imagine the word on the screen becoming a thing in the world," but cannot (827). That "lived tenor" is precisely what the novel has sought to evoke, and which its major character laments the loss of.

One tendency among DeLillo's readers is to see in this ending a tentative stance about the possibilities for peace in the world, but the eerie narrator seems pretty clear that the word is "only a sequence of pulses on a dullish screen" (827). Besides, from the novel's viewpoint the threat of nuclear conflict has passed, and "peace" seems like an odd thing to wish for when only seventeen pages earlier Nick has told the reader that he longs for "the breach of peace, the days of disarray when I walked real streets and did things slap-bang and felt angry and ready all the time, a danger to others and a distant mystery to myself" (810). On the other hand, DeLillo may intend his novel as "a peace offering," like the Thomson baseball that Chuckie Wainwright's father gave to his son, a "spiritual hand-me-down" (611). Primarily, "peace" is a word, not a thing in the world, and, like the novel itself, an occasion for one last improvisation on the Cold War era evoked in language, the novel's last affect: all it can do is make you pensive.

CHAPTER 6

Underworld and the Architecture
of Urban Space

David L. Pike

It would have been fitting if DeLillo's 1997 novel had been composed on an Underwood, the typewriter of choice of Faulkner and Fitzgerald, and a perfect fit for the dense and tightly woven imagery that opens outward from its title, *Underworld*. But it is perhaps even more delightful that, according to DeLillo (Echlin 147), he typed it up on an Olympia: without the world above, the underworld cannot exist. The background heights that underpin the novel's structure are famously visible on Hungarian émigré André Kertész's 1972 photograph on its cover, in which the twin towers, their top halves lost in the clouds, loom behind the low, dark steeple of a venerable church in the foreground. While most criticism of the novel has focused on the lower depths to which the church's black cross seems to lead and to which the title beckons, DeLillo's portrait of New York City and of the world that seems to radiate out from that city depends just as much on the Olympian perspective obscured in the clouds of the twin towers and named by the typewriter's moniker. The relationship between high and low mapped out by the book is not so simple as either a traditional verticality or an inverted one, however; DeLillo in many ways aims to complicate a vertical order at the same time as he avails himself of its powerful metaphorics to ground the meanings of his novel.

There is, in fact, little that is new about the underground metaphorics of *Underworld*. Encyclopedic compendia of every underground in the city and around the world were something of a specialty of the nineteenth century. Nor is DeLillo's novel unique even in its turn-of-the-century moment. The mid-to-late 1990s, in fact, spawned a number of ambitious summas of the second half of the twentieth century carried out under the aegis of an underworld. David Palmer has noted the "'underworld' of alternative and seemingly irrational popular belief systems" that challenge the "status quo" of crumbling empire in both DeLillo's work and Haruki Murakami's epic history of Japan since the late 1930s, *The Wind-Up Bird Chronicle* (1994–1995), mediated through the powerfully chthonic site of a dry well in a suburban Tokyo backyard (7–8). Controversial Serbian filmmaker Emir Kusturica retold the history of postwar Yugoslavia through the concentrated allegory of a decades-long resistance in a vast cellar/commune/munitions factory in *Underground* (1995). British artists Jake and Dinos Chapman rehearsed the bloody history of the twentieth century in the hallucinatory sculpture *Hell* (2000), remade and expanded as *Fucking Hell* (2008) after a fire destroyed the original, in which a series of gruesome tableaux were acted out by distorted, perverse, and bloodied plastic figures on adolescent hobby tables gone wild.

What distinguishes DeLillo's vision from these and other contemporaneous underworlds is the vertiginous scale of its metaphorical sweep. Murakami, Kusturica, and the Chapmans use infernal and subterranean imagery to condense historical complexity into an intensely implosive allegory—paradoxically containing the sweep of history in the emblematic space of a single well, a single cellar, a single battlefield. In contrast, DeLillo's strategy is paratactic in the extreme: he just keeps accumulating more undergrounds. Tom LeClair has enumerated a fair number of these, suggesting that the "punning title" includes "Dante, the Mafia, hollowed earth, humankind's sediment, ghetto life, underground politics, the subconscious, and linguistic roots" ("Underhistory" 116). But this is only the tip of the iceberg. A more extensive but by no means exhaustive list of the novel's subterranean imagery would also include: physical undergrounds (bank vaults, bunkers, basements and cellars, catacombs, caves, landfills, mines and miners, sewers, subways, all manner of tunnels, underground nuclear test sites, underground waste disposal sites, under highways and bridges, and under the seats at the Polo Grounds); hell, the devil, and Bruegel's painting *The Triumph of Death*; garbage, shit, and waste; the science of *dietrologia*, or "what is behind something" (280); and an almost limitless series of figurative underworlds ("deep time," "deeper forms of truth," "memory tunnel," "seamy underside," "underreal," "undervoice," "underground consciousness," "underground literature," "underground press," "underground rumor," "underground souls," "underworld of images," "underworld of words").

It becomes apparent as one works through the book, however, that DeLillo's ambition is not limited to paratactic accumulation. He certainly strives, sometimes overreachingly, to catalogue the full extent of the ways in which the term "underworld" functions as a dominant image of modernity, postmodernity, and the dialectical relationship between the two. But he is also striving somehow to combine the nineteenth-century propensity to catalogue for the sake of variety and novelty with the postmodernist need to reduce all meaning to an overarching and overwhelming univocality. In this essay, I discuss the relationship of DeLillo's strategies of spatial representation to prior models and examine the result of his decision to place a number of mutually contradictory strategies together within the fraught space of a single novel and single ruling metaphor. For the underground has never been a simple or straightforward space, and DeLillo's laudable refusal to dissolve the components of his syncretism results in an underworld that in its figurative and literary ambitions has perhaps no comparable model since the three canticles of Dante's *Commedia*. I will examine this city under the rubric of three underground topoi that help to define the representation of the modern city: the halting devil, the wall and bunker, and the waste land.

The Halting Devil

> Downtown is where things lay hidden, waiting for people to find them. And one of the hidden things, not only downtown, is the rooftop world—the water towers, gardens, architectural ornaments—and this is the world I tried to explore in Part Four, in the rooftop summer sequences. And of course the fact that Klara Sax is a painter and sculptor helped me see Manhattan in those terms.
> —Don DeLillo to Gerald Howard,
> "The American Strangeness" (1997)

The halting devil Asmodeus was invented in late seventeenth-century Spain as the motor of a literary panorama: using his magical powers, he was able to fly above the city of Madrid, lift off the rooftops, and demonstrate to his young human protégé the myriad secret activities going on beneath their cover. In addition to the frequent presence of Asmodeus as a framing device for the survey of urban activity that was a dominant popular genre during the eighteenth and nineteenth centuries, the "Asmodeus flight" was a common emblem for the problematic power of the omniscient narrator of the realist novel (D. Pike, *Metropolis* 120–23). On the one hand, the term lays claim to supernatural knowledge on the part of the novelist; on the other hand, it intimates the moral taint that could become associated with a fictional overreaching and revelation of things perhaps better left hidden. Moreover, because Asmodeus was merely a minor devil in the satanic hierarchy, this emblem self-consciously ironized diabolical ambition with the implicit recognition of the impossibility of realizing the ambition of conjuring ontological truth out of the fictions of language. DeLillo's novel echoes this trope in two ways: by substituting the more epistemologically, metaphysically, and associatively capacious term "underworld" for the more materially-based "underground" or the specifically Christian "Hell" or "inferno"; and by sustaining a rooftop vantage point throughout the novel that clearly echoes his own authorial position typing away on his Olympus.

This vantage point is clearest in part four, "Cocksucker Blues," which primarily recounts the "rooftop summer" of Klara Sax, providing a panorama of 1974 New York City that includes, among other phenomena, screenings of Robert Frank's *Cocksucker Blues*, a 1972 cinéma vérité documentary of the Rolling Stones distinguished by its "tunnel blue light" (383), and Sergei Eisenstein's apocryphal nuclear holocaust film *Unterwelt* (invented by DeLillo); and references to the nearly finished World Trade Center towers and the art deco Fred F. French building on Fifth Avenue. The only episode not told from Klara's point of view is the voyage underground into the "Pocket," the top-secret desert research facility where Matt Shay is employed in developing nuclear weapons. Its presence declares DeLillo's intent to limit himself neither to the city nor to the artist character, Klara, who in many ways stands in for his narrative viewpoint. But where urban surveys of the halting devil tended simply to string one rooftop vision along after the other, DeLillo, borrowing from the indirect free style of Virginia Woolf's modernist novels (in particular her London panorama *Mrs. Dalloway* [1925]), provides loose associational transitions between narrating subjectivities. For example, we move from Klara to Matt via the Bronx neighborhood association of Klara's memory of her friend Rochelle musing on the "F" in Fred F. French (399) and the related linguistic echo that leads from the "accidental marvel to come upon a memory floating at the level of a glazed mosaic high on a midtown tower—the *old* spoked sun that brings you luck" (400) to "[t]he poets of the *old* nations of the basin [who] told stories about the wind" (401, my italics). We return to New York and Radio City Music Hall via the thematic promise that will be embodied in the Eisenstein film shown there, "the map, where he would try to find a clue to his future" (422), the reference to Matt's existential confusion carrying over to the broader historical vision of the film's underworld.

Ira Nadel has astutely noted the association of Matt and the other researchers in the Pocket with the explicitly urban eighth circle of Dante's *Inferno*, Malebolge (literally "evil pouches"), in which the myriad sins of fraud are punished (184–89). Nadel is primarily concerned with the relationship between the vulgar diction employed by Dante in these cantos and DeLillo's use of the scabrous comic routines of Lenny Bruce to structure part five of the novel; however, the concatenated structure of part four is equally indebted to the form of Dante's canticle as a whole. Like *Underworld*, the *Inferno* (and the three-part *Commedia* as a whole) combines an omnisciently voiced panorama with the unique experience of the narrator himself. This is a paradoxical structure: only the divine perspective can claim full knowledge of the afterlife, while only the human perspective is able to render the experience of that afterlife in the finite terms of space and time. As Teodolinda Barolini has argued, Dante uses many of the tools of the realist novelist in order to lend the weight of truth to his fiction (3–20). The narrative strategies of the *Commedia* were also highly influential on modernist writers, who attempted to ground Dante's assumption of divine omniscience in the immanent flow of subjective perception (D. Pike, *Passage* vii–xiii). DeLillo's *Underworld* falls somewhere between these two approaches: the novel strives relentlessly for the prophetic power of divine knowledge expressed, for instance, in the linking "clue to [the] future" between the Pocket and *Unterwelt*, but it also refuses to reduce its characters to allegories as, for instance, Woolf had done with her most Dantesque creation, Septimus Smith, in *Mrs. Dalloway*.

DeLillo's Asmodeus flights are significant, but they are also subject to constraints. Whereas Klara's view from above defines her character, Nick Shay, the other dominant narrator figure and the only character given the privilege of narrating in the first person, finds himself above the action only once. Early on in the novel (and late in the chronology), he takes his wife, Marian, up in the air for an early morning birthday ride in a hot air balloon (123–26). In perhaps the single happy moment we see the couple share, they float over Klara's ongoing desert art project, *Long Tall Sally*, in which she and her volunteer assistants are repainting hundreds of B-52s left derelict and obsolete by the end of the Cold War. We have already accompanied Nick on a ground-level visit to the site, but only from above, DeLillo implies, can the scale and import of the artifacts and of Klara's project be grasped. "And truly I thought they were great things, painted to remark the end of an age and the beginning of something so different only a vision such as this might suffice to augur it," Nick asserts in diction redolent of biblical prophecy. "And I wondered if the piece was visible from space like the land art of some lost Andean people" (126).

The first manned flight by hot air balloon was performed by the Montgolfier brothers in Paris in 1783, and the balloon perspective soon became an important component of the urban panorama, the mechanical counterpart of the magical Asmodeus flight. As in the aerial view of Klara's piece, the urban panorama suggested that no single narrative on the ground could encompass the scope of the modern city; at the same time, its high vantage point schematized the inhabitants, reducing them to types, occupations, classes, and neighborhoods rather than individuals. Recognizing this duality, DeLillo is careful to modulate the view from above with which he privileges certain of his characters. No matter that he is up in a balloon, Nick in 1992 is still able to spot the "blond girl in the flouncy skirt painted on a forward fuselage" that gives the B-52 project its name (125). Back in 1969, by contrast, Chuckie Wainwright and Louis T. Bakey rehearse a darkly comic version of the opening struggle over Bobby Thomson's home-run ball while deep in the "squat black hole" of a B-52 still in service in Vietnam (607); all outside vision cut off by the windowless lower deck in which they work, they ruminate on the past—Louis on his experience as a test subject for the effect of atomic bomb explosions on pilots, Chuckie on the baseball his father (we eventually discover) had bought from the father of Cotter Martin, the boy who had captured it at the stadium—and argue inconclusively about the race of the original Long Tall Sally. As art, the B-52s provide some form of aesthetic experience; however, as a source of vision, they are as if a dark underground lifted up into the air. Working in Vietnam reviewing aerial reconnaissance photos, Matt, similarly, has no guarantees of recovering any "lost information" from the images he pores over or of identifying even the "minutest unit of data" correctly (462).

Nevertheless, there are moments of genuine insight from above. As in the case of Klara's rooftop summer, the most extended of these visions occur within the space of New York City. There is the radio booth perspective of Russ Hodges deliriously announcing the Giants' unlikely victory in the 1951 baseball game that is the subject of the prologue. There is the window of the Wall that looks down into the wild no-man's-land of the lots to catch sight of Esmeralda, the feral child who will provide a different sort of vision near the end of the book (244). And there is the young Klara looking out of her Bronx window to watch the even younger Nick Shay loitering across the street in part six of the novel (749). Klara's perspective dominates the view from above; elsewhere, other women—Marian in the balloon, Sister Edgar in the Wall—are present in the scene. Recalling Sullivan in *Americana* (1971) and anticipating Lianne Glenn in *Falling Man* (2007), these female characters display a measure of insight often denied DeLillo's men: when they are absent, vision is occluded. The primary exception to this pattern in *Underworld*, Russ Hodges, still exhibits a crucial blind spot: he is unable to witness the key individual actions at the game's periphery, remaining ignorant both of the fight over the baseball below the bleacher seats and of the epiphany experienced by J. Edgar Hoover when faced with a photograph of Bruegel's *Triumph of Death* in *Life* magazine. That we the readers know of all these events should remind us again of the narrator's controlling presence, able not only to peer into every dark and secret underworld of a fifty-year span, but also to reverse the very passage of time, derailing plot in favor of a journey back to origins. As such, the novel's reverse chronology is not a journey back to before original sin, as it is in Dante's trip through hell, up the mountain of Purgatory, and through the heavens to the origin and goal of God's Empyrean realm outside of time. For all his omniscience, DeLillo's narrator resolves nothing. We cannot take Nick and Klara's affair and Nick's shooting of George Manza as an etiology for the world historical events through which the characters will have guided us. But neither can we dismiss their biographical singularity in favor of a paranoid resolution of all meaning into a single sense of "Underworld." The halting devil has enough chthonic power to unroof the secrets of the urban world to us but not enough either to gloss them or to make them cohere. That is the job of divinity, and, despite the resurrection of Sister Edgar in cyberspace at the end of the book, the inexplicable apparition of the murdered Esmeralda in a Minute Maid billboard resonates more as a strange refraction of the Gypsy dancer of Victor Hugo's *Notre-Dame de Paris* (1831) and the pair of Roman children who have a "vision" of the virgin in Federico Fellini's film *La Dolce Vita* (1960) than any genuine introduction of the miraculous into the mundane cityscape of a Harlem River bridge.

Wall and Bunker

> In the book there's a wasted section of the South Bronx called the Wall. It's an area outside the reach of basic services such as water and electricity. And these passages are set around the time of the fall of the Berlin Wall. There is certainly no explicit connection. There is a kind of shadow, a whisper. And there are themes of weapons and waste. The beautiful, expensive, nobly named weapons systems. And then the waste, many types of waste, and the Wall is a particular part of the waste—the part that includes human lives.
>
> —Don DeLillo to Gerald Howard,
> "The American Strangeness" (1997)

Although the historical existence of the Berlin Wall (1961–1989) is easily encompassed by the time span of the novel and although DeLillo clearly regarded it as part of the book's Cold War thematics, it is named only a single time in the course of the book. Significantly, this single mention serves only to negate its presence, as a word Matt Shay cannot pronounce in conversation with a female protester outside the confines of the Pocket: "He didn't use words such as American and Soviet. They seemed provocative somehow. Or NATO and Europe and the East Bloc and the Berlin Wall. Too soon to be so intimate" (419). The literal presence of its "whisper" within the novel, the South Bronx Wall, is also slight—a single fifteen-page chapter in part two (237–51) and another fifteen pages in the epilogue (810–24)—but its tendrils stretch out in a number of directions. Sister Edgar, a nun who distributes food to the Wall's needy, was Matt's grade-school teacher in the 1950s; Ismael Muñoz, the artist responsible for the spray-painted wall memorial, was Moonman 157 back in the 1970s; and Esmeralda, the girl who lives in the wild lots and is the last victim of violence we see commemorated as an angel in graffiti on that exposed wall, provides, in the 1990s, the novel's penultimate image. The association between the bunker, in which weapons systems are conceived and designed in New Mexico, and the Wall, in which lives laid waste are memorialized in the devastated slums of the South Bronx, is surely not accidental, implicit as it is in DeLillo's words to Gerald Howard cited above. It is as if two underground systems overlap. There is the urban underworld of "lost streets, a squander of burnt-out buildings and unclaimed souls" (238), and there is the new city, all bunkered and protected, "a concrete space about the size of a basketball court, somewhere under the gypsum hills of southern New Mexico" (401). There is the organic city of the past, of the lower depths, of devolution and waste, and there is an inorganic city of the future. Both are buried and both somehow emerge from the same Bronx neighborhood in the 1950s.

The main connection is provided by Matt and Sister Edgar, for it is in her class, in late 1951 and early 1952, that he learns the comforts of duck and cover which remain with both of them throughout their lives: "The overbrained boy of the thirty-two [chess] pieces and the million trillion combinations liked to nestle in his designated slot, listening to Sister's voice repeat all the cautions and commands like a siren lifting and dipping in the dopplered haze of another nondescript day" (728). The feeling of security from which both characters are cut loose later in life is the security of Cold War ideology at its most mendacious, but this fantasy of security is no less powerful for being mendacious: "The Pocket was one of those nice tight societies that replaces the world. It was the world made personal and consistently interesting because it was what you did, and others like you, and it was self-enclosed and self-referring and you did it all together in a place and a language that were inaccessible to others" (412). It is tempting to treat this description ironically, as we do the glimpse of Matt's colleague Eric during his youth, masturbating into a condom while his mother, Erica, churns out Jell-O creations in the nearby kitchen. But that is the difference between suburbia and the Fordham neighborhood of the Bronx where Matt, Nick, and DeLillo grew up in the postwar years. And as a characterization of those years in that place, it is much harder to take such descriptions of Cold War security ironically. When Nick longs for "the days of disarray, when I didn't give a damn or a fuck or a farthing" (806), it is the urban place he longs for from the distance of postmodern Phoenix as much as the time of adolescence. DeLillo famously writes near the beginning of the novel that "[l]onging on a large scale is what makes history" (11), and he concludes the book with longing as well, the longing for peace, for "the word on a [computer] screen becoming a thing in the world, [. . .] a word extending itself ever outward" (827). Both times, the longing emerges from the same couple of miles either side of the Harlem River.

That the city is the means to peace as well as the cause of disruption is a commonplace of modernity. And there is no question that DeLillo, like most urban writers, privileges the longings of the damned souls over the desires of the powers-that-be, of Cotter Martin over J. Edgar Hoover, of waste over weapons. In this regard, the tunnel has always been the spatial and thematic counterpart of the wall (D. Pike, "Wall" 74–76). To the visible challenge of a blocked path, desire responds by creating hidden ways around, under, and through. Walled-in prisoners dig tunnels to escape; the underground exceeds and overflows the bounds set for it in the world above. The bunker of the Pocket extends the principle of the wall into the very territory of the tunnel itself, commodifying and regimenting the underground as it earlier has brought order and security into the space of the child's classroom and fantasy life. The conflicting and diverging paths of Matt and Nick plot this divide: Matt progresses from duck and cover to Vietnam image analyst to the Pocket to a think tank; Nick kills a heroin addict in a secret basement room and makes his way through prison to an isolated Jesuit school before becoming a waste specialist. But while DeLillo charts the emergence of this problematic out of the Bronx in the 1950s, there is nothing conclusive about his findings. Klara Sax, for example, takes an oblique path in relation to waste and weapons, refusing either to wall herself in or to dig herself out. Her former husband, science teacher Albert Bronzini, by contrast, never leaves, holding on to the traces of his old neighborhood the way Father Paulus of the Jesuit collegium clings to the meanings of words. It therefore is no accident that the final permutation of underworld to appear in the novel undermines cyberspace with history to introduce the ancient word with which the book will end: "You can examine the word with a click, tracing its origins, development, earliest known use, its passage between languages, and you can summon the word in Sanskrit, Greek, Latin and Arabic, in a thousand languages and dialects living and dead, and locate literary citations, and follow the word through the tunneled underworld of its ancestral roots" (826).

DeLillo structures the Wall episode like a descent into hell; indeed, it is the only moment in the novel when he uses the word "hell" in its religico-topographical sense. There is the "motif of souls-in-hell graffiti on the cab, deck and mud flaps" of the flatbed truck used by Ismael and his crew (241). And there is the portentous line, "People in the Wall liked to say, When hell fills up, the dead will walk the streets" (245). Urban hell has been a commonplace of lower depths writing since cities first were industrialized, making conditions materially much closer to the imagined world of the inferno. Yet long before industrialization, the purported immorality of urban centers had made them the target of moral condemnation as Babylons, dens of iniquity, and infernos. True to form, DeLillo trots out the atrocity exhibition here, prefaced with a highly Dantean and highly self-conscious anaphora. For over a page, he begins each paragraph (thirteen in all, for the numerologically inclined) with the pronoun "They" followed by a predicate, most frequently the visionary form, "They saw":

> They saw a man with epilepsy.
> They saw children with oxygen tanks next to their beds.
> They saw a woman in a wheelchair who wore a Fuck New York T-shirt. [...]
> They saw a man who'd cut his eyeball out of its socket because it contained a satanic symbol, a five-pointed star. (246–47)

Similarly, Sister Edgar is reminded by the subway tunnels of the Capuchin crypt of Santa Maria della Concezione in Rome, where the monks had arranged the bones of the dead in pleasing geometric patterns (249). The conclusion at which she arrives, "death, yes, triumphant" (249), invokes Bruegel's *Triumph of Death*, pictured in the prologue as "the entrance of some helltrap, an oddly modern construction that could be a subway tunnel or office corridor" (41), which, in turn, causes one to wonder about "Pafko at the Wall" (1992), the title under which the prologue was originally published in short story form. The baseball passes beyond the Wall, setting off a chain of searches and coincidences that exceeds a certain kind of boundary and confounds the set meaning of the waste-and-weapons pairing.

But if the Wall as hell looks back to the shot heard 'round the world as collective longing become history (except for Dodgers fans), it also looks forward to the novel's second atrocity exhibition, the epilogue's

Museum of Misshapens (799–803), the Kazakhstan medical record cum cabinet of curiosities documenting the mutations resulting from the effects of years of atomic testing on the local populace (and echoing the rumors recounted by Eric in the Pocket of the "Downwinders"). The Tchaika scheme in Kazakhstan is a brilliant way to wrap up the book, using weapons to vaporize waste, one canceling out the other. Nevertheless, the epilogue's title, "Das Kapital," underlines DeLillo's suspicion of this tail-eating zero-sum game, using the underworld somehow to eliminate the underworld. So perhaps it is not surprising that he returns instead to the Wall to remind us of another zero-sum game: the accumulating mural of angels redeeming each victim of violence, the Christian promise of redemption for suffering, the Dantean proposition that going through hell willingly will finally get you into heaven.

There is no question that DeLillo is suspicious of the power embodied in walls, but it is also evident from the novel that he refuses the alternative consolation proposed by the underworld, the easy answer of undermining, or subverting, the world above. His inferno is just physical enough to preclude the metaphysical—there is nothing allegorical about the atrocities he describes, they simply are what they are—but just surreal enough to preclude the false materialism of the sensation scene, effect for effect's sake. Like the mythical/not mythical barge laden with toxic waste tracked by Nick's colleague Sims and perhaps glimpsed by baseball hunter Marvin Lundy in San Francisco, the urban legend of the Downwinders casts a self-conscious credibility pall over the ghetto episodes and the Central Asian sensationalism. What do we do with the "human waste," the excess excreted by the system, the ones excluded from the bunkers and fallout shelters of the new city?

The Waste Land

A fortress of indestructible leftovers surrounds Leonia, dominating it on every side, like a chain of mountains. [...] Leonia's rubbish little by little would invade the world, if, from beyond the final crest of its boundless rubbish heap, the street cleaners of other cities were not pressing, also pushing mountains of refuse in front of themselves. Perhaps the whole world, beyond Leonia's boundaries, is covered by craters of rubbish, each surrounding a metropolis in constant eruption. The boundaries between the alien, hostile cities are infected ramparts where the detritus of both support each other, overlap, mingle.

—Italo Calvino, *Invisible Cities* (1972)

In his comparison of Pynchon and DeLillo, Timothy L. Parrish argues that while the former "asks his readers to experience the loss of nature as a moral outrage," the latter conceives of nature "only as a wasteland of death and destruction" (86). Organic nature, in other words, is present only as garbage, as the detritus of capital. We see it in the overgrown vacant lots of the South Bronx that refract the no-man's-land space between the east and west sections of the Berlin Wall. Like New York City's High Line, a disused elevated freight railway overgrown from decades of neglect, or the similarly overgrown cutting that contains the *petite ceinture*, the long abandoned railway that circled the city of Paris near the line of its outer boulevards, the neglected landscapes of vacant lots are simultaneously traces of the wastefulness of urban capitalism and the resurgence of organic nature within the spaces created by that wastefulness. They are powerful, magical spaces within the contemporary cityscape because they exceed the control and supervision of urban planners; by the same token, they are spaces of danger.

DeLillo signals this ambivalence with his association of the lots in the Wall with the child Esmeralda, "moving among the poplars and ailanthus trees in the most overgrown part of the rubbled lots. [. . .] a lanky kid who had a sort of feral intelligence, a sureness of gesture and step [. . .]. There was something about her that mesmerized the nun, a charmed quality, a sense of something favored and sustaining" (244). She is a *genius loci*, a spirit of the place in a topos inherited especially from the depiction of the undeveloped site of Rome in book eight of Virgil's *Aeneid*, which Burton Pike has identified as a persistent presence in modern urban literature (71–99). It is a resolutely unromanticized spirit and an unromanticized nature—Sister Edgar's assistant Gracie later comes across a colony of bats in the "thickest part of the lots," feeding on the toxic waste that is regularly dumped there (249)—but it is wild nature nonetheless. DeLillo makes the association with the child's perspective all the stronger when he depicts the teenage Nick and his younger brother, Matt, visiting the same spaces several decades earlier. Nick spends half his time "down the yards," visiting George the Waiter in his storage room crib cum shooting gallery in the "network of alleyways that ran between five or six buildings clustered here. [. . .] Close-set buildings, laundry lines, slant lights, patches of weeds, a few would-be gardens and bare ailanthus trees and the fire escapes that fixed fretwork patterns of light and shade on the walls and paved surfaces" (721). It is the ailanthus tree, or tree of heaven, that makes the connection for us, a deciduous flowering tree that grows quickly and densely where few other trees are able to survive—that and the garbage that accumulates here as it does in the lots. Matt opts for the lots themselves, "rambling waste[s] with a higher and lower level, boulders, weeds and ruined walls, signs of old exploded garbage here and there" (which thematically if not literally occupy the same space as Esmeralda's haunt in the Wall), where the rough kids hang out and where he gets his hand "busted up in a card game called shots on knucks" (743). This is waste on an intimately human level, which also makes it waste that is not simply a technical problem but something that can be productive of meaning and experience, the way Klara Sax uses waste as the material at the core of her art.

DeLillo counterpoints this experiential encounter with waste on the level of lived space with its existence as a commodity (usually an undesirable one) within the circulation of capital. It is not clear how Nick's path has taken him from "down the yards" into waste management— and, indeed, the reverse chronology of the novel suggests that clarity on this question is not achievable in any simple sense. But he becomes the novelist's vehicle for exploring this issue, just as Matt allows DeLillo to explore the related issue of weapons. In one of the denser of Nick's waste narratives, he recounts a trip to Holland:

> I went to VAM, a waste treatment plant that handles a million tons of garbage a year. I sat in a white Fiat and went past windrows of refuse heaped many stories high. Down one towering row and around to another, waves of steam rising from the tapered heaps, and there was a stink in the air that filled my mouth, that felt deep enough to singe my clothes. Why did I think I was born with this experience in my brain? Why was it personal? I thought, Why do bad smells seem to tell us something about ourselves? The company manager drove me up and down the steaming rows and I thought, Every bad smell is about us. We make our way through the world and come upon a scene that is medieval-modern, a city of high-rise garbage, the hell reek of every perishable object ever thrown together, and it seems like something we've been carrying all our lives. (104)

Disposal of waste is not a new problem. It has troubled urban culture since cities have existed. What was new in the modern city was the industrial component of the problem and the stark contradiction it posed to the ideology of urban progress that was fundamental to nineteenth-century conceptions of modernity. Urban filth in the nineteenth century was invariably described in terms of its archaic quality as *not*-modern. As an 1841 article on London's "Underground" put it with an allusion to a notorious contemporary slum, "London generally must have been then [the late 1600s] almost as bad as St. Giles's is now!" (Platt and Saunders 230). Like DeLillo's "medieval-modern" scene above, filth was recognized as part of the problem of the modern city but generally regarded as composed of anti-modern traces to be eliminated rather than made integral to the process of modernization itself. The great public works of the nineteenth century were primarily concerned with circulation: people were to be moved efficiently around cities via buses, trams, and subways; waste was to be flushed away through vastly ambitious and monumentally conceived (or re-conceived) sewage systems; bodies were to be buried or incinerated away from the homes of the living. Both spatially and conceptually, the underworld was rationalized.

As a concept, "waste" meant something that should not exist. And while plenty of nineteenth-century writers decried the horror of its existence, as when Edward Walford wrote in the 1870s of a central London charnel house that "[i]t is indeed strange to think that such foul abuses were not swept away until the reign of Victoria" (32), the great majority of them shared with urban planners the belief that it need not exist. The practical or theoretical valuation of filth, dirt, or other terms by which the various organic phenomena associated with the nineteenth-century underground might be qualified was almost unheard-of before the twentieth-century modernists. Indeed, the only writers who touched on the topic—Baudelaire, Freud, and Nietzsche, to name the most prominent—can be characterized by their status as modernist writers. Nomenclature, as William A. Cohen argues, is essential to the definition of the subject: "Anything designated *filthy* cannot be reused, at least until it is renamed or reconceived as waste or trash, which can be recycled" (x). DeLillo uses the term very sparingly in his novel, once as Cotter Martin ironically terms himself a "[w]alking talking filthman from the planet Dirt" (139) in exaggerated response to his mother's criticism of his cleanliness, and a couple of times when Marvin Lundy refers to a Czech ironworker's pride in "the smoke and filth that hung over the landscape, this was progress" (310), right around the same time that he notices that "[t]he deeper into communist country, the more foul his [own] BMs" (311). Nevertheless, as Cohen also notes, filth can be productive, primarily in a figurative way, for "purposes of self-formation and group identification" (xi), like the ironworker's revolutionary solidarity above, or as a theoretical category, as which it was fundamental to modernism and, later, to poststructuralism.

Echoing David Trotter's critique of the new historicists' inability to approach filth phenomenologically (39–45), David H. Evans notes the tendency of DeLillo scholars to locate "the significance of garbage in *Underworld* in its capacity to represent *something else*" (110), an "unwillingness to let garbage be garbage" that is at odds with DeLillo's plunge "into the material immediacy, the concrete and sensuous, oleaginous and viscid substance of garbage itself" (111, 116–17). Evans makes a strong distinction between what he terms "recycling," the practice of making useful what has been discarded by a system, and work such as Klara's that "is created by interrupting the cycle of consumption-reprocessing-and-reconsumption" (122), what Walter Benjamin termed the work of the collector, who "redeems" obsolete objects by removing them from circulation and granting them new meaning within a collection (282–85). As I have been suggesting in various ways throughout this essay, DeLillo's novel is motivated by a desire to restore the thingness to things, a leitmotif of recent work in the study of waste (see, for starters, the collections edited by Cohen and Johnson and Campkin and Cox). As such, a primary function of the long Bronx episode that climaxes the book with its revelations about Nick's past is to prevent us from allegorizing the discrete moments of *Underworld* into a cohesive, if not paranoid, whole—to prevent us from, to use Evans's term, recycling them or, to use the language of waste and underworld, excavating them out of the world below.

At the same time, DeLillo populates his novel with so many smart characters unable to do what he apparently wants us to be able to do—restore the thingness to things, and quotidian experience to the alienation of everyday life—that it is no wonder many reviewers and scholars have seen in *Underworld* a paranoid vision, a summa of post-modernism, the vision of a city that four years later would somehow seem to undergo exactly the disaster he had appeared to prophesy. The edge of paranoia around the novel rests on its affiliation not just with what Luc Sante terms the "bomb novel" (4) but with the apocalyptic wing of the science-fiction genre, where writers such as J. G. Ballard and Philip K. Dick extrapolated a partial situation in the present day into an absolute condition in the future. In Ballard's "The Concentration City" (first published as "Build-Up" [1957]), for example, overpopulation has resulted in a city stacked in a vast three-dimensional grid with trains circulating in endless loops all the way around the globe, except nobody manages to see beyond the limited horizon of his or her local cubicle. There is nothing left to waste. DeLillo's scenarios, especially the ones related to waste management, are plausible enough to be credible to a paranoid reader but implausible enough to be received as science fiction. Rather than such Cold War era "secure paranoia," to use Peter Knight's term, *Underworld* offers, in Knight's account, a "history of para-noia" that contextualizes and redefines the term, "not the simple story of the replacement of bomb-induced fears by newer anxieties resulting from the fragmentation of those former geopolitical certainties. It is instead an underground current of increasing awareness and conster-nation that slowly everything is becoming connected" (825). For all its isolation as waste land, the Wall is also, according to Sister Edgar, a tourist destination (248–49). In contrast, Fordham in the 1950s was *not* connected in this way, but in the old, Cold War paranoid way.

It is an obsessively patterned novel, and if the warp of the pattern is the end of the Cold War, its weft has to be the title, *Underworld*. DeLillo's Olympian perspective suggests that the book has been perfectly woven to reveal truth, and his characters provide that truth over and over again, as occurs when "garbage archaeologist," UCLA professor, and former "garbage guerrilla" Jesse Detwiler comes up with a cultural theory of garbage as the origin of cities that any self-respecting cultural theorist would kill to have formulated (281, 286): "Detwiler said that cities rose on garbage, inch by inch, gaining elevation through the decades as buried debris increased. Garbage always got layered over or pushed to the edges, in a room or in a landscape. But it had its own momentum. It pushed back. It pushed into every space available, dictating construction patterns and altering systems of ritual. And it produced rats and paranoia" (287). This is hilarious, but it is also a perfectly plausible ventriloquism of anthropologist Mary Douglas's influential pronouncement that dirt is "matter out of place" (36). The only difference—and it's a significant one—is that Detwiler's garbage is not symbolic; it's material.

DeLillo's Olympus is a typewriter and his Bronx emerges from "a sense of intimate knowledge" (Howard 126). It is not so much that the city is the only source of authentic, irreducible, quotidian experience and language, although an implicit argument of the prologue is that only in the uniquely diverse and vast crowd at a 1950s ball game could the variety of "happy garbage" depicted by DeLillo in that game be found (45). It is that the model of social and spatial organization developed and perfected in the city has spread throughout the rest of the world without the natural defenses, resistances, and contradictions to that organization having similarly spread. Or have they? Perhaps that is why we have Nick in waste disposal, Matt in the Pocket, Klara with B-52s in the desert, and Marvin Lundy chasing a baseball all the way to San Francisco. Here, too, *Underworld* resembles Dante's *Commedia*, for both are almost bafflingly syncretic in their method of accumulating narrative data and both refuse to allow the disparate and conflicting sources they accumulate either fully to cohere or fully to cancel each other out. The tangibly real fight over a baseball between Bill Waterson and Cotter Martin coexists with the portentously allegorical raining of *The Triumph of Death* onto the head of J. Edgar Hoover. And even though documentary evidence attests to the painting in that week's *Life* and to Hoover's attendance at the 1951 game, the battle under the seats exists only in DeLillo's god-like Olympian imagination.

CHAPTER 7

Underworld, Ethnicity, and Found Object Art: Reason and Revelation

Josephine Gattuso Hendin

Underworld (1997) is Don DeLillo's tribute to the power of ethnicity as a pathway into postwar experience. While the novel holds other ethnicities in its reach, it is animated by Italian American lives and culture. With the exception of two early short stories, "Take the 'A' Train" (1962) and "Spaghetti and Meatballs" (1965), DeLillo has not lingered in the Bronx Little Italy that formed him. But in *Underworld* its streets are the crucible of meaning and crossroads where the ethnic story and the American story intersect. DeLillo uses the passage of Nick (Costanza) Shay from a Bronx Little Italy in the 1950s, through the upscale suburbs of the Southwest, toward the global prospects at the end of the twentieth century, to describe the arc of American postwar experience and to measure the gains and losses along the way. Reversing the mainstream's dictation of the American story, DeLillo uses an Italian American journey to convey the dance of mainstream ideologies and ethnic ideals.

Even as the jacket art of *Underworld* visually positions our now lost cathedrals of capitalism, the twin towers of the World Trade Center, above the small church whose crucifix transects and visually "links" the towers in its reach, the spiritual is never far from the material. DeLillo introduces a constant interplay between systems of materialism and spirituality, of profane and sacred seeking, of achievements of order and meaning and the agonies of impotence and waste that can attend both. Antonio Gramsci lamented that the *cultura negata*, the folk culture of the dispossessed—its faith in family, its everyday beliefs as well as its art and hopes—was inculcated in the underclass by those in power to maintain their own control. Jürgen Habermas and Max Weber lamented the eclipse of the life-world by intellectual elites whose political and scientific expertise was removed from common life. All saw a world shaped and afflicted by opposition and duality.

What courses through *Underworld* is a more complex search for shared affinities. In it both the life-world and the hegemonic culture are portrayed as encountering an age of limitation, an attrition of difference caused by their shared subjection to a larger process in which old certainties are undermined by challenges in public and private life, all of which force alterations in how we define our experience. We have surpassed the world of either/or, joined the realm of both/and, as in Jacques Derrida's theory of the *supplément*, only to look for more extreme forms of "desedimentation" in once settled beliefs and language. The former enables new syntheses and exchanges in the status of "high" and "low"; the latter permits an unsettling of language that detours from English to embrace the use of Italian to define moments of mystery or deep meaning. Both involve forms of reconciliation that acknowledge the mainstream, triumphal narrative of American culture, but also enable a larger and more encompassing story. This appears in *Underworld*'s complex search for a reconciliation of opposites, a privileging of analogies that break the wall between insider and outsider and redefine what constitutes high and low, secular and spiritual. That process not only carries forward the mainstream's narrative of American wealth and power, but also accounts for the undermining forces that challenge it, and unites both along a quirky ethnic journey that colors, shapes, and redefines all the terms of success and failure.

Emerging through the novel are visions of power in eclipse, industrial prosperity spawning toxic wastes and garbage, and counter-processes of reclamation through fusions of spirituality, science, and art. In this climate, the art of the life-world, the found object art that Italians call *arte povera*, reflects renewal and revival in its awareness of the use value of discarded objects and once abandoned ideals. It creates what Gordon Graham has called "enchanted spaces" that are "the secular world's naturalistic counterpart to worship" (129). Found object art flourishes in *Underworld* in those pockets of invention where the act of making and building affirms human effort in nature and culture, celebrating the human hand in the given world.

Such art reflects an Italian emphasis on living and succeeding through making and working—as in the immigrant phrase "making America"—rooted in the classical celebration of man as maker, that *homo faber* whose fabrications create the social world apart from nature. Pellegrino D'Acierno has pointed out that Italians see order in daily life as something one creates: it can be the development of "*sistemare*," or "worldly tactics," but also "*l'arte dell'arrangiarsi*," the art of "making shift," both expressions of the "Italian art of making the most out of the least"

(753). In *Underworld* what was once called "outsider" art is, in fact, more in tune with the processes of change and the ferment of everyday, common life than mainstream art. Its reclamation of lost, discarded objects creates new structures of reason and worship. Far from being "outside" society, it is its soul, its animating core.

DeLillo's Bronx Little Italy of the 1950s dramatizes an ethnic world of intense experience. It has a seething street-corner culture whose pillars are the pool hall, the Catholic school, and the delicatessen that is a "cathedral of pork" (214). Looming over it on Rose Hill is its monument to Catholic doctrine and disputation: Fordham University. DeLillo himself graduated from that Jesuit domain whose scholar-priests can claim that Aquinas's *Summa Theologica* can explain it all. But what flourishes on neighborhood streets is a vernacular theology. Italians and Italian Americans have their own dogma—the *l'ordine della famiglia*, the strict rules and values governing family life. These enshrine the father as head of the family and the mother as its heart, establishing the certainties of family stability. These enable the everyday to become the all important and the simple pleasures of men playing the card game *briscola* to be a form of communion with each other. These are practiced by people who, in summer heat, "sat on the stoop with paper fans and orangeades. They made their world. They said, Who's better than me? [. . .] They knew how to sit there and say that and be happy" (207). The family's solidarity, the father's protection of it, the mother's competence in implementing its rules, all constitute the order of their lives.

Nick is not one of them. He is partly DeLillo's portrait of postmodern uncertainty as a product of an *infamia,* the violation of the rules of the family by the disappearance of his father: "He did the unthinkable Italian crime. He walked out on his family. They don't even have a name for this" (204). The blow to the authority of the father and family cohesion, and Nick's disbelief that his father voluntarily abandoned his family, shape his agonistic journey through postwar experience, searching for patterns of cause and effect and the meaning of order itself.

Like the architecture of a medieval cathedral which encompasses the milestones of sacred history as the passage from the creation to the annunciation through the crucifixion to the resurrection and Judgment Day, *Underworld* is a multifaceted compendium of an Italian American vision of the postwar world in its public and personal dimensions. Even the challenge to American military and global supremacy is writ small in the progressive questioning of faith in patriarchal institutions, in unraveling family ties, in authority itself—all these only fuel a search for a reconciliation between stability and chance, spirituality and secularism. *Underworld* reflects DeLillo's reenchantment with purpose.

Frameworks of Reconciliation: The Art of the High and the Low

In its extended quest for reconciliation between all that makes up the hidden underworld and mainstream life, DeLillo's novel affirms both as having a common transcendent source. John Dewey, in *Art as Experience* (1934), developed a theory of art as celebrating American ideals by defining human nature dynamically, as an interaction between active and passive forces, which he described as "doing" and "undergoing" (45–47). *Underworld* is driven by comparable energies that intertwine American and Italian approaches to defining self through action, performance, and experience. Emphasizing ordinary experience as a crucible for the formation of larger meaning, the novel recuperates Dewey's "doing" as the building and crafting that yield, for example, visual art. "Undergoing" emerges as those transformative revelations of meaning that come from culling insight from experience in its fullness.

Dewey meets Aquinas in DeLillo's South Bronx. *Underworld* depicts it as an environment of catastrophe and destruction with its swaths of rubble in the 1980s and 1990s, but also recuperates that rubble as a form of *arte povera*, South Bronx Surreal, the ironic destination of tour buses that is also a place where graffiti art memorials to the dead bring dignity to life's discards. Here the definition and reach of what is human can emerge through both active and contemplative processes defined in symbolic or artistic form. As Umberto Eco points out, Aquinas believed that all is created by God and all art is consequently "an accidental" product of human beings, created out of things God made (175). In that sense, *all* art simply *is* found art, and all artists are always "outsiders" working with materials God made that they rearrange for new purposes.

Even as DeLillo's favored creators are those who build art out of garbage, so he himself creates in Nick a protagonist of the streets who has "wasted" another man and his own ability, but eventually become a waste management expert obsessed with recycling all forms of "waste" and loss into self-understanding and enlightenment. Embracing paradoxical relationships between nihilism and purpose, DeLillo roots the energies of the novel in the inversions, paradoxes, and confrontations of a Bronx Little Italy, mysteries of the Roman church, and Fordham's Jesuits, permitting the 1950s Italian American street to open to a mythic past of ancient Mediterranean religious traditions that insist on the interpenetration of common or low things with the divine. In this he follows established mystical traditions.

As Rosalie L. Colie has pointed out, Dionysius the Areopagite held that "Divine things should be honoured by the true negations, and by comparisons with the lowest things, which are diverse from their proper resemblance" (qtd. in Colie 25). Writing in *Paradoxica Epidemica*, Colie traces that impulse in literary traditions, observing that these "rhypological" images of low and sordid things "become by Dionysius' argument appropriate to attempt comprehension of the divine essence. Against this background, several things become clear, among them, the curious habit of devotional poets' using 'low things' in immediate juxta-position to the highest, such as Herbert's likeness of Christ to a bag [in "The Bag"], or of God to a coconut [the "Indian nut" in "Providence"], and Donne's of the flea's triple life to the Trinity [in "The Flea"]" (25).

This tradition thrives in DeLillo's Little Italy. He celebrates the larger meanings contained in ordinary lives and common things, and endows Nick with a similar appreciation learned from the Jesuits: "There's a word in Italian. *Dietrologia*. It means the science of what is behind something. A suspicious event. [. . .] The science of dark forces," the "imaginary" sciences as opposed to the "hard sciences" (280). *Under-world* offers litanies of the street, intensities of sex, mysteries of violence, labor, abandonment, and the earthy sanctity of Italian American fami-lies for whom spicy sausage and sauces stirred and cooked for hours offer a richness of scent and taste that reaffirm being *a tavola* as a form of communion. DeLillo creates a world and its meanings with intellec-tual roots in Aquinas, an agonistic vision of spirituality rooted in the textures of the Italian American Bronx, its multiple forms of Catholi-cism, and DeLillo's synthesis of its moral and aesthetic drives. DeLillo incorporates the spiritual force of low and high—the revelations felt in the street and the luminous logic of Aquinas. The interplay between currents in mainstream America and Italian American visions emerges through DeLillo's exploitation of those crossroads where "insider" and "outsider," public reality and private truths, meet.

Emerson Meets Aquinas in the Polo Grounds: Baseball and the Sport of Analogy

The sophisticated use of analogy in *Underworld* serves as a means of mediation in terms of bringing about an attrition of differences, whether between opposing teams in a pennant game or between the architects of mainstream and ethnic ideologies. Analogy can be used rhetorically to suggest an equilibrium between American radical, mystical Protestant-ism and Catholicism's embrace of reason as a road to faith. DeLillo secularizes a use of analogy comparable to the elaborate theory of anal-ogy developed by Aquinas. It is based on both a recognition of human incapacity as compared with God's intellect and an affirmation of human reason as a pathway to that felt experience of truth some call faith. Analogy for Aquinas involved not only recognizing differences between reason and revelation, or "systematic or speculative" truth, but also placing them in a hierarchy in which reason could lead to faith. It suggested that both originated in a common divine source. The way to discover that unity was through the *quaestio*, a process that required communal reasoning and argument to uncover the structures and patterns inhering in experience. As theologian Frederick G. Lawrence puts it, the *quaestio* is how "meanings and values" go from "the world of community (common sense), which unfolds in the dramatic, artistic, symbolic, and mystical patterns of experience, to the purely intellectual pattern of experience" (442).

The climactic game in the 1951 subway series between the Giants and Dodgers in DeLillo's prologue introduces the communal experience of the fans on both sides. The game serves several functions. It dramatizes class, racial, and ethnic differences approaching the age of the melting pot and celebrates postwar American democracy and diversity. The game takes place in the Polo Grounds, named after a polo stadium long since demolished even as the aristocratic sport of polo has given way to baseball. The new stadium, a concrete and steel structure with an ornate, Italian marble façade, was built on what had been Brotherhood Park on W. 155th Street and Eighth Avenue, off Harlem River Drive, and serves a diverse population. The teams and the audience are multiethnic and racially mixed, a "brotherhood" in action. The novel opens with the stunning success of a poor, fourteen-year-old African American fan, Cotter Martin, who gets past the guards and ticket sellers, skillfully jumps the turnstile, and gets to see the game "for free." Willie Mays plays for the Giants. Dodger mainstay Ralph Branca, who has an Italian father and Hungarian mother, pitches. Branca will fatefully confront the Giant hitter Bobby Thomson, himself an immigrant from Scotland who came to the United States at the age of two.

DeLillo uses this microcosm of America to subject winning and losing to a scrutiny of their long-term effects, letting *dietrologia* determine ultimate success or failure. In the process, he opens up entrenched ideologies of triumph and optimism at America's height as a munificent superpower. DeLillo populates the stands with icons of American power and celebrity in the 1950s—J. Edgar Hoover, the idolized Frank Sinatra, and the celebrated Jackie Gleason, whose *The Honeymooners* will set the comedic standard for television's love of everyman. The Dodgers seem assured of victory as Branca pitches to Thomson. But when Thomson hits the ball out of the park into the stands, winning the game for the Giants, the outcome turns into a meditation on the nature of power, triumph, and security, those American games forever based on the will to beat the odds, but encountering, as the prologue's title suggests, "The Triumph of Death."

Emerson and Aquinas equally mediate DeLillo's treatment of winning and losing. That American national character and ideology constitute a large theme is underscored by the fact that the game is heard by Nick Shay on his Emerson radio (133) and Thomson's hit is referred to by the press as "The Shot Heard Round the World" (669). DeLillo exploits this designation, actually used by reporters in the sports news of the day, to evoke the "Concord Hymn," Emerson's 1837 tribute to the memorial built to commemorate the battle of Lexington and Concord, and underscore his own vision of the fate of triumph.

Emerson celebrates the farmers who began the struggle that would, after many years, see the American army beat the odds to defeat one of the most powerful, well-trained armies of the day.

> By the rude bridge that arched the flood,
> Their flag to April's breeze unfurled,
> Here once the embattled farmers stood
> And fired the shot heard round the world. (ll. 1–4)

Yet the poem's next stanzas treat these farmers as forgettable men and usher in Emerson's take on the inevitable mitigation of triumph by time, and the hope that the "votive stone" of the memorial will "their deed redeem" from nothingness (ll. 10, 11). The impermanence of all human achievement as a rebuke to vanity is a familiar poetic convention, but Emerson is particularly graphic about the similar fate of the British soldiers, the farmers, and even the bridge:

> The foe long since in silence slept;
> Alike the conqueror silent sleeps;
> And Time the ruined bridge has swept
> Down the dark stream which seaward creeps. (ll. 5–8)

Emerson's emphasis on the erosion of difference between enemies is paralleled by DeLillo's fatalistic vision of all victory as only part of a cycle, a moment that begets its opposite. As the novel accurately reports, the media also used "The Shot Heard Round the World" to describe the Soviets' explosion of an atomic bomb (668–69). This detonation not only undermines America's triumph as the sole superpower, but also evokes the Cold War that would dominate the following decades. In the pennant game, the moment when Thomson's bat hits Branca's pitched ball, and victory and defeat meet, is also not a momentary union, but one that shadows lifetimes.

Sparking meditations on the bond created between winners and losers, that moment opens up the difficulty of determining the long-term effects of either victory or loss: "Branca and Thomson appear at sports dinners all the time. They sing songs and tell jokes. They're the longest-running act in show business" (98). Their bond is even acknowledged at the beginning of the 1990s by "official" culture: they are photographed "standing on the White House lawn with President Bush between them, holding an aluminum bat" (100). Yet the actual hit that makes them famous is eclipsed in value, for it too proved a temporary triumph—the Giants' pennant victory was soon neutralized in the World Series when, in another subway series, the Giants were defeated by the Yankees. In DeLillo's hands, the 1951 pennant game is about the "mystery of loss," the tie that Nick believes binds him to the event and prompts him to buy the home-run baseball years later: "It's about the mystery of bad luck [. . .]. To have that moment in my hand when Branca turned and watched the ball go into the stands—from him to me" (97).

DeLillo takes sports into multiple theologies of order as Nick claims Branca's luck as his own, invoking a mysticism of numbers with a focus on the unlucky number thirteen ("Branca wears number thirteen. Branca won thirteen games this year" [678]) to provide a clue to nature's design, "organizing principles," in the words of the neighborhood science teacher, Albert Bronzini, that "make us less muddled" (735). Thus Nick continues: "Take the name Branca and assign a number to each letter based on its position in the alphabet. [. . .] You end up with thirty-nine. What is thirty-nine? It is the number which, when you divide it by the day of the month of the game, gives you thirteen. Thomson wears number twenty-three. Subtract the month of the year, you know what you get" (679). The bond between Nick and Branca is not an accident, but a revelation of Nick's quest for an explanatory structure and purpose, inspired by a personal "mystery of loss" that predates Branca's ("My father's name was James Costanza, Jimmy Costanza—add the letters and you get thirteen" [102]), and joins together public and private, spiritual and secular, through knowing the meaning of losing out, shame, and failure.

Aquinas again meets Emerson in DeLillo's larger implication of a universal, cosmic purpose that supersedes human intention. There is an operative analogy at work between a Thomistic universe governed by Natural Law and Emersonian Nature operating by the Law of Compensation. DeLillo encodes his idiosyncratic use of Catholicism in the radical Protestantism of Emerson by focusing on Emersonianism as key to Nick's hearing the ball game with a mind attuned to concepts of Natural Law. Aquinas saw Natural Law as "the rational creature's participation [in] the eternal law" ("*Summa Theologica*" 12; Q91. A2), defined as the wisdom to accept that all life originates in a common source and is directed toward a divine purpose that no one can fully comprehend.

Emerson saw Nature as a force for moral poise and for social justice, an extra-human force for balancing good with evil, darkness and light. Declaring in his 1841 essay, "Compensation," that "[p]olarity, or action and reaction, we meet in every part of nature; in darkness and light; in heat and cold," including "the nature and condition of man" (172–73), he nevertheless concluded: "Every excess causes a defect; every defect an excess. [. . .] every evil its good. [. . .] the varieties of condition tend to equalize themselves," for Nature "keeps her balance true. [. . .] Every thing is made of one hidden stuff; as the naturalist sees one type under every metamorphosis" (173–74). In his letter on the relocation of the Cherokee, Emerson would simply declare that his Law of Compensation is also a law of social justice.

Emerson's belief that nature finds in "every evil its good" is paralleled by Aquinas's affirmation of the light in darkness. As Aquinas writes on Origen in *Catena Aurea* (1. 5), his commentary on the Gospel according to St. John, "darkness is not always used in a bad sense, but sometimes in a good, as in Psalm xvii: *He made darkness His secret place:* the things of God being unknown and incomprehensible. This darkness then I will call praiseworthy, since it tends toward light, and lays hold on it: for, though it were darkness before, while it was not known, yet it is turned to light and knowledge in him who has learned" (23). In the ruins of DeLillo's Little Italy during the 1980s and 1990s, Sister Alma Edgar, now an aged Catholic school enforcer of memorizing the Catechism, may not understand darkness as part of Natural Law, but she understands the power of a "faith of suspicion and unreality," the "faith that replaces God with radioactivity, the power of alpha particles and the all-knowing systems that shape them, the endless fitted links" (251). Darkness and light are flip sides of a universal purpose and order.

The Rules of the Family

For most Italian Americans, Natural Law and the Law of Compensation are less persuasive than *l'ordine della famiglia,* the rules of the family. The master narrative of Italian American family life is the story of the authority of the father and the cohesion of the family. Nick tells that story through its unexpected disruption: his father not only walked out on the family, the crime so infamous there is no name for it in Italian, but his mother, in retaliation, performed the equally radical act of erasing his father's Italian name from his sons and insisting they use her own Irish maiden name, Shay. Lack of a name for a father's crime of family abandonment is matched by the lack of the father's name as an *infamia.*

Nick's father was a numbers runner who went out for a pack of Lucky Strikes and never came back. The modernist search for a father is turned into a complex meditation on the meanings contained in words—lucky (chance), strike (hit or miss)—and the loss of patriarchal systems of order. Denied both the Italian mother and the involved father or even his name, Nick recognizes himself as "a country of one," not unlike his father, whom he describes as "a loner" (275, 203). He cultivates a mock "mob voice" for jokes. He questions: was his father murdered by the mob, an irate winner he couldn't pay off, or did he just want to abandon his family? Was his disappearance a willed act or an accident? Intention matters.

In George the Waiter, who is "the loneliest man" he's ever met, Nick seems to find a father surrogate who proves that one can live without a family (724). Nick and George seem to get along. Nick performs the services of a first-generation son to an immigrant father who cannot read or write: he fills out forms for George without embarrassing him; he spots George shooting heroin but never reveals what he has seen. George, in turn, encourages Nick not to steal cars, not to work at a job loading perishables into a freezer that will literally keep him on ice, and helps him to get a delivery job. Yet when George, with a strange smile, hands Nick a gun he claims is not loaded, Nick discovers that the man whom he has cast in the role of father has cast him in the role of executioner. The stereotype of Italian American male violence dictates that, given a gun, Nick will shoot. As Nick playfully points the gun at George, squeezes the trigger, and the bullet he fires kills George, Nick has "the thumbmark of George's face furrowed in his mind" (780).

The community on the street closes around Nick like a Greek chorus in a tragedy, but only *dietrologia*, that science of hidden forces, reveals the accidental murder as an Oedipal drama. It discloses a suicidal complicity against the certitude, trust, and confidence once associated with patriarchy and opens up ambiguities of intention and commission, questioning their long-term effects. Because the killing eventuates in Nick's being sent after "correction" to the collegium of Father Paulus, a Fordham Jesuit who has founded a special school in Minnesota to convey systems of thought that mediate between the life-world and systematic Catholic logic, it turns out to be Nick's "lucky strike," the "shot" that catapults him from a life without purpose in the Bronx to a life in which the culture of the street can be connected to those rational norms that lead to meaningful action. In such a process, as Bernard Lonergan points out, theology is a "mediat[ion] between a cultural matrix and the significance and role of a religion in that matrix," whose effectiveness depends "on the clarity and accuracy of its grasp of [. . .] external cultural factors" (qtd. in Lawrence 438).

Reversing the outward role of priestly "father" to penitent "son," Father Paulus places himself squarely in the life-world on the street of shortcomings, confessing to Nick that he has "[t]oo much irony, too much vanity," and too little intensity (538). Celebrating the energies of the street, he asks: "how serious can a man be if he doesn't experience a full measure of the appetites and passions of his race, even if only to contain them or direct them, somehow, usefully?" (539). For him, violence in the life-world signals "elements of productive tension in a soul" that "can serve the fullness of one's identity": "One way a man untrivializes himself is to punch another man in the mouth. [. . .] And I think a man's ability to act in opposition to his tendencies in this direction can be a source of virtue, a statement of his character and forbearance" (538–39).

Father Paulus insists that intensity and depth of thought and feeling are ideally attached to will and essential to becoming "a serious man" (538). In so doing, he moves Nick out of an aimless street-corner culture toward a theological structure that systematizes the difference between vigorous intentional action and weak will as a theological fact. He explains the concept of "velleity" to Nick in Thomistic terms that encompass his own lack but that suggest prospects for fulfillment. He first defines velleity as "[v]olition at its lowest ebb" (539). Yet he sees Nick as capable of intensity: "Aquinas said only intense actions will strengthen a habit. Not mere repetition. Intensity makes for moral accomplishment. An intense and persevering will. This is an element of seriousness. Constancy. This is an element. A sense of purpose. A self-chosen goal" (539). This kind of will is generally defined as *velleitas ratio*, a reasoned purpose that carries with it a mandate to action. It is intention implemented in action and a valorization of *homo faber*.

Father Paulus quickly gives an example of its extraordinary value in the making of ordinary things. In what amounts to that Thomistic definition of art in which beauty is defined as a system of order and purpose revealed in the quotidian, he demands that Nick describe his own shoe in complete detail. As Paulus explains, "Everyday things represent the most overlooked knowledge. [. . .] Quotidian things," the adjective a "gorgeous Latinate word" that "suggests the depth and reach of the commonplace" (542). "Latinate" words are crucial for expressing not only explicit meaning, but also the sacralized importance of the everyday in a logic that defines common experience as the grounding of knowledge. DeLillo associates this with the Italian world and its instantiation in the Bronx. Understanding depends on knowing the names of things, a charged issue for Nick who has lost his father's name. Father Paulus tells Nick that "everyday things lie hidden" because "we don't know what they're called" (541); in Nick's particular case, "You didn't see the thing because you don't know how to look. And you don't know how to look because you don't know the names" (540).

Understanding the larger importance of the shoe exercise as a metaphor for the way he can define and order his own life, Nick wants to look up "velleity" and "quotidian" and "say the words for all they're worth" (543). Knowing the full importance contained in them, he believes, is "the only way [. . .] you can escape the things that made you" (543). At the same time, what "made you" and what you make underscore a Thomistic conception of all art as accidental, determined by a serious will to build, create, and make something of value out of materials that God made. Naming parts of the shoe thus serves as an intellectual exercise in Thomistic aesthetic invention that requires an understanding of both the use value and purpose of man-made designs and the overarching importance of design as symbolic of universal order. In the fitness of each part of the shoe for use in the whole inheres a key to the larger importance of function and aesthetic understanding. As Umberto Eco notes, citing Aquinas's aesthetic theory, "The drive toward perfection in things is an aspiration, whether conscious or confused, toward God" (183); "Values are not autonomous. [. . .] They are defined with reference to their consequences" (184). Aquinas sees the end of art-making (and, presumably, shoemaking) as the "good." As he wrote: "Everything tending to its own perfection tends toward the divine likeness" (*Summa Contra Gentiles* 3. 21. 6, qtd. in Eco 183). This is an aesthetics that links the everyday and divine.

Made Men, Makers of Art, and the Art of *Lontananza*

The man who wishes to create must appraise both himself and the objects available for use. Nick has the distance needed to engage in his own self-reclamation and self-construction. Acknowledging "a certain distance in my makeup, a measured separation like my old man's," he invokes the Italian word "*lontananza*" as explanation, a word he interprets with respect to "the perfected distance of the gangster, the syndicate mobster—the made man": "Once you're a made man, you don't need the constant living influence of sources outside yourself. You're all there. You're made. You're handmade. You're a sturdy Roman wall" (275).

A symbol for the construction of self that Nick variously attributes to the mob's made man, the strong architecture of doctrine of the Roman church, and the process of self-construction he has undertaken, the "Roman wall" resonates in multiple ways. Nick recalls walking as a child with his father and being surprised when, seeing two men on a neighborhood street who were messing up a job building gateposts, his father took off his coat and showed them how to lay brick correctly and how to do a "skillful brickwork bond" (277). The passage invokes the saintly Geremio, the master bricklayer in Pietro di Donato's *Christ in Concrete* (1939) who offers up his life on the altar of family love and responsibility and is buried alive on an unsafe job he kept to support his wife and children. A secretly skilled bricklayer who knows how to build a "sturdy Roman wall" but not how to be one, Nick's father, by contrast, has turned from the iconic work of bricklaying and family-building to numbers-running, embracing chance and instability. If a man fails so completely in the Italian American ideal of masculine value as a husband and father, can anything else he does count?

DeLillo's references to Sabato Rodia provide an answer. Of all the examples of *arte povera* or found object art in *Underworld*, Rodia's Watts Towers in Los Angeles are the most powerful. A ninety-nine-foot tower flanked by lower towers and surrounding installations built out of cement, wire, broken Milk of Magnesia bottles, broken dishes, sea shells, colored tiles, and other fragments, the complex installation of gates and other structures surrounding the towers looms before Nick, upon his visit, like a "jazz cathedral" (277).

Folklorist Joseph Sciorra adopts a similar terminology when comparing the towers to the *gigli*, the towers carried by men in religious processions in honor of St. Paulinus of Nola. Sciorra relates the construction as a whole to a "Catholic-inspired aesthetic" of "layering and accretion," commenting that the "predisposition to repetition and redundancy in the Catholic art tradition of sacramentality informs Rodia's six towers, as well as the various decorative elements found among the inlaid objects and pressed patterning" (13), and seeing in its concerns for form and proportion an "expression of Italian everyday aesthetics" (14). It is also an expression of *homo faber* as a redemptive agent.

As Sciorra notes, Rodia spoke of himself as "one of the bad men in the United States. [. . .] all the time a drinkin'. That's why I built the tower for, I quit the drinkin'" (19). A Neapolitan immigrant who brutalized his wife and children until he left them to live alone in Watts, laboring at construction jobs by day and working, after hours, for thirty-four years on the Towers, Rodia found the making of art out of junk a redemptive act in which the failed husband and father who could not make his family cohere became *homo faber*, the creator of an alternative environment. In comparing the Watts Towers to the *gigli*, Sciorra sees the towers resembling the "ambulatory bell towers that festivalize the Italian notion of *campanilismo*," the "attachment to place" (22). *Campanilismo* refers to the attachment to the central square, anchored by the bell tower in Italian towns. It is in that square that everyone gathers. Rodia, Sciorra reports, "christened his towers 'NUESTRO PUEBLO,' Spanish for 'OUR TOWN' and/or 'OUR PEOPLE'" (22). That public space created by Rodia displaces his failure in the private space of the family home. Reminded of his father the more he looks at it, Nick marvels at "the whole complex of structures and gates and panels that were built, hand-built, by one man, alone" (276), a singularity of purpose reflected in its "structural unity," its "sense of repeated themes and deft engineering," and the "initials here and there, SR, Sabato Rodia, [. . .] SR carved in archways like the gang graffiti in the streets outside" (277). Built by a man who "went away, he said, to die" after the work's completion, the Towers evoke in Nick memories of another man who departed: "the power of the thing, the deep disturbance, was that my own ghost father was living in the walls" (277).

In the Bronx neighborhood of the 1980s and 1990s, swaths of which look like a bombed-out war zone, the redemptive power of *arte povera* is continued by other ethnic artists who affirm the meaning of the life-world. Ismael Muñoz, a graffiti artist, has AIDS and lives amid the ruins in an area called "the Wall, partly for the graffiti facade and partly the general sense of exclusion—it was a tuck of land adrift from the social order" (239). On a Wall that still stands amid the rubble, Ismael's graffiti art memorializes the dead in pink and blue angels, giving their names and causes of death: "TB, AIDS, beatings, drive-by shootings, measles, asthma, abandonment at birth—left in a dumpster, forgot in a car, left in Glad Bag stormy night" (239). The dying memorialize the lost in Ismael's graffiti art that reclaims them from oblivion.

In the Southwest of 1992, found object art rises to embrace and over-come large systems dedicated to death. Nick's former lover Klara Sax, an artist once known as the "Bag Lady" for her work with castoffs, is repainting B-52 long-range bombers with Day-Glo colors and using a desert that is "all distance" for their installation (70, 64). Here *lontan-anza* is imprinted in geography. Her art encompasses the quotidian as well as the life-world. She is devoted to "the ordinary thing, the ordinary life behind the thing," but driven in her work with the abandoned air-planes "to find an element of felt life," a "sort of survival instinct here, a graffiti instinct" (77). Klara is the artist of the life-world not in eternal battle with abstract systems of violence, those "great weapons systems" that "came out of the factories and assembly halls," but one who sees those systems as capable of yielding up their souls (77). She believes the ultimate meaning of the bombers is less in the payload they once carried than in the nose art painted by the men who flew and serviced them. Her focus is on pinups like "Long Tall Sally," who, in being "not amazonian or angelic or terrifically idealized" (78), is a reflection of everyday hopes and fantasies that outlive the vicissitudes of war.

A Plea for Help: "*Aiuto*" and the Road to "Peace"

The end of reasoning is recognition of its limits. By the novel's epilogue, all structured systems seem part of a "marathon of danced-out plots" (802). Sex initiates Nick's movement toward a series of acceptances of the peace beyond understanding. As he talks with a pickup, Donna, at a conference hotel, she undresses and places his hand between her legs. She makes him feel young and reckless. But Nick's foreplay includes an account of his discovery of the limits of reason after reading a book given to him by a priest: *The Cloud of Unknowing*, written by an anonymous medieval mystic, an English monk. The book made Nick take stock of himself, realize his own limitations, and begin to "think of God as a secret, a long unlighted tunnel," to try to "understand our blankness in the face of God's enormity" and to "approach God through his secret, his unknowability" (295). Donna believes this is an attack on her public sexuality as a member of swinging couples' club. Nick, however, is concerned about knowing God: "Maybe we can know God through love or prayer or through visions or through LSD but we can't know him through the intellect. [...] How can we attempt to know such a being?" (295).

According to Nick's reading, *The Cloud* suggests the mystical solution of trying "to develop a naked intent that fixes us to the idea of God" and "recommends that we develop this intent around a single word. Even better, a single word of a single syllable" (295). Nick's word is "Help." But realizing that the word is inadequate, even "a little pitiful," he decides he "need[s] to change languages, find a word that is pure word" (296). Only an Italian word will do, the word of his father and grandfather: "A word to penetrate the darkness. *Aiuto*" (296). *Aiuto* is his plea for God's grace, for an event that is not the product of human making. It comes to *Underworld* in a series of revelations of incorporation, cultural interpenetration, and experiences of wholeness and peace.

In those episodes of reconciliation and fusion that end *Underworld*, cultural interpenetration enables a sense of modernity as the experience of multiversity: a polyglot urban linguistics in an American English that incorporates Italian words; a close interaction between a premodern culture of heritage and the present; a fusion with the mother in spiritual fullness; and an extension of the search for revelation on the Internet, in a website with a Latin name, *http://blk.www.dd.com/miraculum* (810). Ancient hopes have incorporated modern technology; cyberspace has soul.

Nick's journey through the novel enables him to discover the ghost of his father in Rodia's "jazz cathedral," but with his mother's death Nick becomes one with the spirit of the Irish Madonna whose memories and reality define his understanding of the spirit of the life-world: "When my mother died I felt expanded, slowly, durably, over time. I felt suffused with her truth, spread through, as with water, color or light. I thought she'd entered the deepest place I could provide, the animating entity, the thing, if anything, that will survive my own last breath, and she makes me larger, she amplifies my sense of what it is to be human. She is part of me now, total and consoling" (804).

The Bronx, as the life-world in all its intensity, is the site of miracles of community that fuse present and past, material and spiritual experience. It is where immigrant waves—poor Italians and then poor Hispanics, to name only two—have settled. All who come there bring their mythologies of redemption and self-transcendence. In the book's penultimate scene (818–23), a crowd waits expectantly for a miraculous vision to break through an ordinary advertisement on a billboard that shows a woman's beautifully manicured hand pouring Minute Maid orange juice from a pitcher. But that billboard ad reveals the hidden hand of God when the light cast by a careening elevated train illuminates a miraculous vision to the crowd. Marginality and solitude are defied in this community of rapture as the face of Esmeralda, a dead Hispanic child who had lived in the Bronx rubble, emerges in the light as a divine apparition. The crowd's shared epiphany casts its own light, linking categories of meaning, connecting the resurrection of hope and innocence to commercial, secular culture, and reconciling differences. Nick's son finds a website for miracles and on it gleams the Bronx in its revelation: the mystical apparition of Esmeralda looming like a visitation of the Blessed Virgin.

The ferment of *Underworld*—its quests, journeys, games, and traumas—culminates in its closing word, "Peace." Peace is more than a wish or a word of farewell. It is the climax of the interplay between the doctrines, systems, and life-world that fuels the novel and drives its movement toward reconciliation. Umberto Eco, following Aquinas, calls peace "a balance of energies," the "total delight of a contemplative perception which, freed from desire and effort, experiences love of the harmony which the intellectual judgment has shown to it" (200). Aquinas says, "Peace implies the removal of disturbances and obstacles to the obtaining of good" (*De Veritate* 22. 1 ad 12, qtd. in Eco 200). In *Underworld*, it is what you hope to find after recognizing the limits of reason.

In its scrambled times sequences, interplay of secular and spiritual concerns, and focus on the art of the life-world, *Underworld* is a complex formal structure wrought from tools of mediation that break the wall between theology and experience, systems and soul. *Underworld* offers a vernacular theology, a celebration of the ethnic life-world in its violence and grace, its afflictions and hopes, joined in the abundance and mystery of experience. In that immense diversity one finds patterns of interaction and possibilities for order. Nick's voyage through the novel may not end in the fullness of faith, or even in happiness, but it produces a validation of the effort of reason that ends in moral poise, in the cessation of turmoil, and, most of all, in a celebration of experience itself as the source of wisdom. And it may lead to the peace of the mystic who advised: "I urge you: go after experience rather than knowledge. [...] Knowledge is full of labor, but love, full of rest" (*Cloud* 176).

PART III

Falling Man (2007)

The visionary quality of Don DeLillo's writing, the way his portraits of the contemporary *Zeitgeist* are informed by an ability to prefigure the events that will make up that *Zeitgeist*, is by now a matter of critical consensus. Nothing more wrenchingly attests to that prescience than the images of the World Trade Center that punctuate his fiction prior to 2001. Dwarfed by the sheer size of the buildings, characters in these earlier works typically remain at a loss to express what the twin towers signify. Pammy Wynant keeps going into the wrong tower on her way to work in *Players* (1977), surrounded as she is by elevators conceived as "places" and lobbies as "spaces"; aware that only "abstract terms" are commensurate with "such tyrannic grandeur" that is the Center (24), she nonetheless cannot figure out which terms are most appropriate: "Was it a condition, an occurrence, a physical event, an existing circumstance, a presence, a state, a set of invariables?" (48). Brita Nilsson is appalled by the "deadly" size of the complex in *Mao II* (1991), and suspects that her feeling has something to do with homeless people and people with multiple residences occupying the same urban grid; but it is not until she later sees a reproduced painting of the twin towers in an art journal that she understands the provocative "comment" inherent in "two black latex slabs that consumed the available space" that formerly has escaped her (40, 165).

Those endowed with broader historical and, more to the point, geological sensibility are attributed greater understanding by DeLillo, however. The "counter-archaeolog[ists]" of the future envisioned in *Great Jones Street* (1973) do not dig into the earth but climb "vast dunes of industrial rubble and mutilated steel, seeking to reach the tops of our buildings," and cite, as a primary reason for cultural demise, "the fact that we stored our beauty in the air, for birds of prey to see, while placing at eye level nothing more edifying than hardware, machinery and the implements of torture" (209). Those who journey to the Mani to seek "[w]here Europe ends" in *The Names* (1982) and find a "pair of towered cities set at the end of the continent" also see a "modern skyline" in ruins, proof of the inevitable fate that awaits all modern skylines regardless of epoch (180, 185). When *Underworld* (1997), then, delineates the Fresh Kills landfill—where the remains of those who worked in the twin towers would, four years later, be taken—as a "poetic balance" to the World Trade Center (184), it advances in words what already can be ascertained by looking at the elegiac images of the towers that grace the novel's cover.

It is DeLillo's refusal to offer any kind of significant compensation—a Watts Towers to offset the twin towers as in *Underworld* (276–77, 491–92), an "Oral New York" of "fibrous beauty" to balance the "woven arrangements of decay" as in *Players* (206–07)—that, upon first reading, most distinguishes his portrayal of the devastation of 9/11 in *Falling Man* (2007). The choice of an irredeemable free fall as his governing image—borrowed from Richard Drew's photograph (later censored) of a man plunging to his death from the towers—clearly refutes the triumphant nationalist discourse that almost immediately followed on 12 September, as Kristiaan Versluys argues (23). It also refutes the two traits that, as Versluys has meticulously documented (14), typically characterize novels that deal with 9/11: the tendency to express the actuality of 9/11 by way of allegory and indirection (e.g., the 6 December 1917 Halifax harbor explosion in Anita Shreve's *A Wedding in December* [2005], the 1945 firebombing of Dresden and atomic bombing of Hiroshima in Jonathan Safran Foer's *Extremely Loud and Incredibly Close* [2005]), and the tendency of the imagination to blunt the impact of 9/11 with recuperative measures (e.g., the invocation of poetry as source of transcendent meaning in Ian McEwan's *Saturday* [2005], the reconciliation of marriage in Joseph O'Neill's *Neverland* [2008]). DeLillo's re-creation of the attacks on the World Trade Center at the end of *Falling Man*, by contrast, leaves Keith Neudecker where he is at the book's beginning: witnessing a white shirt falling from the sky. And the mid-paragraph juxtaposition of Keith's perspective and one of the jihadists' as American Airlines 11 blasts a hole into Tower 1 portrays to chilling effect the collision of two forces—capitalism and terrorism—that continue to produce, in the words of *Cosmopolis* (2003), "[h]ysteria at high speeds" (85).

The three chapters that follow all, at different points, employ the falling man of DeLillo's title to comment on the extended ramifications that falling and the fall have within DeLillo's text. John Carlos Rowe's consideration of the novel with respect to global politics portrays the

U. S. fall from grace that occurs when the nation's abuse of moral authority is set against the values on which it claims to be based. Linda S.
Kauffman's focus on corporeal bodies in free fall exposes the provisional
nature of all existence as a fact confirmed, rather than caused, by 9/11.
And John N. Duvall's discussion of falling bodies represented in
various media—silhouette, sculpture, and photography as well as
fiction—queries the degree to which any artwork can effect the kind of
healing that a trauma experienced collectively requires. As a result,
while each of these chapters situates DeLillo's novel with respect to a
very specific historical context—mention is made in their pages of
the 1993 bombing of the World Trade Center, the 2008 attack on
Mumbai's Taj Mahal Palace and Tower Hotel, the 2009 shootings at Fort
Hood, and the ongoing wars in Afghanistan and Iraq—each chapter
also extends its discussion of the novel's topicality to consider the issues
raised by the novel with respect to a broader historical context.

Significantly, part of that broader context is literary. The genealogy
of terrorism that John Carlos Rowe traces back to the political radicalism of the 1960s is complemented by his tracing the terrorism in
Falling Man back to the figure of Lee Harvey Oswald in *Libra* (1988).
The precariousness of life after 9/11 that Linda S. Kauffman traces back
to the existentialist tenets of a century earlier is matched by her juxta-
position of the movement toward death in DeLillo's book against the
portraits of that inevitable passage found in the works of James Joyce,
Samuel Beckett, and William Faulkner. The falls staged by David Janiak
that John N. Duvall examines with respect to performance artists who
do not appear in DeLillo's novel are also traced back to the work of
those outsider artists that do increasingly play a role in his more recent
fiction.

Fittingly, these final chapters return to the question of aesthetics and
the limits of representation that has been an undercurrent of this entire
volume. Is DeLillo's increasing reliance on what John N. Duvall terms
the "gestural poetics" of the performance artist a comment on the
limitations of the novel in representing the events of 9/11? Or, as
John Carlos Rowe argues, are the limitations to be found in DeLillo's
continued reliance on isolationist national paradigms that prevent a
critical awareness of America's failures in global affairs from developing
into an appreciation of alternatives to Western thinking? Is it now only
the outsider artist—not the novelist—who can successfully compete
with the terrorist in, to recall the phrasing of *Mao II*, "alter[ing] the
inner life of the culture" (41)? Or is it a question of the Keatsian
Negative Capability that, as Linda S. Kauffman shows, enables some
of the women in DeLillo's later fiction to enter imaginatively into the
subjectivity of others remaining a quality out of reach of the novelist
himself?

CHAPTER 8

Global Horizons in *Falling Man*

John Carlos Rowe

> *We have met the enemy, and he is us!*
> Walt Kelly, The Pogo Papers *(1953)*

The consequences of globalization are central to Don DeLillo's fiction and since *Libra* (1988) have informed his meditation on the future of literary authority. We like to think that after the assassination of John F. Kennedy, America changed forever, but in *Libra* DeLillo makes clear that it was Lee Harvey Oswald's life, not John F. Kennedy's death, that changed America or was at least symptomatic of how impossible it has been after that November day in 1963 to *be American*. Oswald is unimaginable apart from his transnational circulation as U.S. serviceman in Japan, Communist fellow-traveler in the USSR, CIA spy in Mexico, pro-Castro supporter in Miami, and anti-Castro advocate in New Orleans. A world-traveler with contradictory credentials, Oswald is a baffling postmodern cosmopolitan who warns us of the dangers of the persistent liberal myth of the enlightened cosmopolitan, recently revived in Kwame Anthony Appiah's *Cosmopolitanism: Ethics in a World of Strangers* (2006). Trembling on the brink of DeLillo's later terrorists, Oswald charts a path beyond national identification that DeLillo insists we follow, if only because we have no choice. Propping up our unstable, increasingly fantastic Americanness is not an option, even though many of his characters insist upon maintaining such a facade.

DeLillo has developed an imaginative genealogy from Oswald in *Libra* to the Lebanese terrorists in *Mao II* (1991) to the 9/11 terrorists in *Falling Man* (2007). As assassins, they change the world through destruction, and for that very reason they are compared often and agonizingly to the novelist, either DeLillo or his surrogate, like Bill Gray in *Mao II*.

Their destructive acts are, of course, quite specific and diverse: the assassination of a U.S. president, the murder of a Swiss-French hostage (and the collateral death of an American author on the ferry ride to Lebanon), and the deaths and traumas experienced by those immediately affected by the attacks on the World Trade Center. Taken together, their violence is a grand symbolic act directed against the prominence of U.S. state power or more generally Western Civilization. DeLillo admires and detests their destructive powers, just as he is enchanted and disgusted by their perverse cosmopolitanism. In each work, terrorism and imaginative violence, guerilla war and aesthetic critique, are compared, often favorably, if tentatively. Although concerned with the decline of the novelist's powers of social criticism, DeLillo still seems impressed that an assassin, like Oswald, finally does act alone and that a small group of terrorists with few resources can achieve their ends, however immoral we may judge them. At the same time, DeLillo is trained in the great traditions of Western modernism, in which imaginative action is the best sublimation of murderous rage, however justified. In "How 'Bigger' Was Born" (1940), Richard Wright famously compares himself with his character, Bigger Thomas, only then to distance himself as an artist from his character's violence.

What, then, is the equivalent in our postmodern, terror-centered era for the aesthetic sublimation that allowed Wright to substitute artistic rage for Bigger's fearful murder? DeLillo asks this question not simply for his own sake as an artist, but also because he believes we all live in and through our symbolic constructions of everyday reality. What happens to this ontology when the comfortable symbolic framework of the nation-state loses credibility? Faced only with the transnational anomie of Oswald or Abu Rashid, leader of the Beirut terrorists, DeLillo's protagonists also drift. In *Mao II*, Bill Gray wanders from his aesthetic seclusion in upstate New York to New York City, London, Athens, Cyprus, and then dies in his bunk on the ferry to Junieh. In *Falling Man*, Keith Neudecker stumbles blindly out of his office in the World Trade Center back into his dysfunctional family life, an aimless affair with another 9/11 survivor, and then into the bathos of international poker competitions. Initially sympathetic characters, versions of a waning humanism, Gray and Neudecker degenerate into specters of their terrorist antagonists: aimless, stateless, socially determined beings following others' orders.

Terrorism and the Nation-State

Both Gray and Neudecker are far more existentialist than their terrorist *Doppelgänger*; each meditates on the randomness that terrorism both exposes and exploits. However goal-oriented Abu Rashid and Mohamed Atta may be in the cause of radical Islam, DeLillo makes clear that both serve the much higher purpose of metaphysical contingency. Atta is clearly identified by DeLillo in *Falling Man* by his given name "Amir"— "Amir spoke in his face. His full name was Mohamed Mohamed el-Amir el-Sayed Atta" (80)—but DeLillo represents al-Qaeda in the novel through the character Hammad. An Iraqi veteran of the Iran-Iraq War (1980–1988), "a baker, here in Hamburg maybe ten years," who "prayed in the same mosque" as Hammad, tells him his war stories, especially about the boys the Iranians sent in waves of assault on the contested borderland between Iraq and Iran (77). The nameless baker concludes that "Most countries are run by madmen," and as Hammad listens distractedly he "was grateful to the man" (78). Hammad's attention is not on macropolitical issues but women and sex—"he kept thinking that another woman would come by on a bike, someone to look at, hair wet, legs pumping" (78)—even though he knows he must suppress such desires, especially for German women. When he does satisfy his sexual desires, he does so with a Syrian immigrant to Germany, but even that relationship seems foreign to him. Hammad's gratitude to the baker seems less for the specific lessons to be learned from the futile Iran-Iraq War and more from the bare human contact such conversation provides.

DeLillo's analysis of al-Qaeda's motives and the personal and social psychologies of the terrorists is brief, scattered through the novel in two chapters ("On Marienstrasse," 77–83; "In Nokomis," 171–78) and a portion of the concluding chapter, "In the Hudson Corridor" (237–43), in which the actual impact of Hammad's flight on the World Trade Center is represented. DeLillo is careful, however, to make sure each of the three parts of the novel—1. Bill Lawton, 2. Ernst Hechinger, 3. David Janiak—includes some part of the terrorists' story. Even so, only twenty-two pages of a 246-page novel deal with al-Qaeda, most of them focusing on Hammad's distraction and confusion, torn between basic human desires for social and sexual contact and the false society of al-Qaeda. DeLillo seems to stress Hammad's ordinariness, his lack of intellectual sophistication, both as part of his common humanity and his willingness to be recruited. When Hammad asks Amir Atta about "the others, those who will die," he is told: "[T]here are no others. The others exist only to the degree that they fill the role we have designed for them. This is their function as others. Those who will die have no claim to their lives outside the useful fact of their dying." DeLillo can only conclude: "Hammad was impressed by this. It sounded like philosophy" (176).

DeLillo trivializes the terrorists by minimizing the attention he pays to them in the novel, reinforcing his arguments in *Underworld* (1997) and *Cosmopolis* (2003) that first world, hypercapitalist nations, especially the United States, have created their own antagonists in al-Qaeda and any other "terror" (domestic or foreign) we might experience in our postmodern condition. The currency trader in *Cosmopolis* smugly watches on television the Seattle demonstrators opposing the global economic policies of the World Trade Organization and International Monetary Fund as they chant, "*A specter is haunting the world*" (89). For the currency speculator, the symbolic action of the demonstrators is pure theater, mere entertainment, not a symptom of the impending collapse of global credit markets, admittedly historically ahead of any of these novels and yet systemically predictable, given the conditions of vastly growing disparities in wealth and poverty dividing individuals, institutions, and nations. Unintentionally recalling Jacques Derrida's *Specters of Marx* (1993), DeLillo approximates its argument: we need a new intellectual-activist paradigm and a new international to overcome the failures of Marxism *and* the impending collapse of global capitalism. There is no difference between the home-grown American assassin, Lee Harvey Oswald, and the imported terrorists of al-Qaeda: terror is the inevitable by-product of a system built upon unstable master-servant relations that inevitably prompt the servant's rebellion. Keith Neudecker's son, Justin, hearing the endlessly repeated news stories about Osama bin Laden begins looking for "Bill Lawton," the homophonic resemblances between the Arabic and Anglo-American name at first lost on his family.

"There is no purpose, this is the purpose" are Amir Atta's words (177), and they echo in Hammad's head throughout his brief appearances in the novel, but they also function as a sort of horrible *leitfmotif* in the same way "The future belongs to crowds" organizes *Mao II* (16). Once the veneer of social organization and the symbolic structures of affiliation—family, neighborhood, religion, nation, et al.—collapse, each of us is exposed to what Giorgio Agamben, in *Homo Sacer* (1995), has termed "bare life," a condition that can be simulated by totalitarian regimes but is also the fundamental condition to which we respond in our efforts to "be human." Of course, the application of Agamben's term "bare life" to the characters in DeLillo's novel seems at first immoral, insofar as Agamben uses the phrase to represent how the Nazis reduced their victims to the most minimal existences to justify their extermination. Atta's contention that the "others" exist only for al-Qaeda's purposes recalls Nazi rationalizations of their genocide.

Agamben develops the concept of "bare life" in part out of Hannah Arendt's notion in *The Origins of Totalitarianism* (1951) of the "naked life" experienced by refugees of all sorts displaced by World War II. Even before we witness Keith Neudecker escape the World Trade Center after the 9/11 attacks, we know him to be a "refugee," deeply traumatized and displaced, incapable of dealing with his family life and work, driven relentlessly by forces he does not understand finally to the triviality of competitive poker. Drifting from pre-9/11 poker games with friends as a mere social pastime to the gambling parlors of Atlantic City and Northeastern Indian casinos after 9/11, finally pursuing competitive poker as his vocation in Las Vegas, "Neudecker" does indeed get a "new deck" or "new cover" that actually exposes to the reader the randomness of everyday life. The existentialist as fundamentally alienated can thus connect with other "refugees," such as the African American woman Keith meets when he identifies her name inside a briefcase he has carried out of the North Tower.

The brief affair between Florence Givens and Keith Neudecker is possible only because of their shared bond of post-traumatic stress: "She talked about the tower, going over it again, claustrophobically, the smoke, the fold of bodies, and he understood that they could talk about these things only with each other, in minute and dullest detail, but it would never be dull or too detailed because it was inside them now and because he needed to hear what he'd lost in the tracings of memory" (90–91). Florence is described as a "light-skinned black woman," whose "odd embodying of doubtful language and unwavering race" suggests a community outside Neudecker's society (92), even though she lives just across Central Park (admittedly a proximity that also suggests class distinctions of the East and West sides of New York). DeLillo just barely eroticizes her ethnic identity, albeit strictly through Neudecker's perspective: "[W]hen she laughed there was a flare in nature, an unfolding of something half hidden and dazzling" (92). And she is predictably in tune with the Brazilian music she plays on her CD player for him, "clapping her hands to the music" and finally dancing, "arms up and away from her body, nearly trancelike, [. . .] facing him now, mouth open, eyes coming open," until Neudecker "began to crawl out of his clothes" (92–93).

"I've never been to Brazil," Florence admits (93), but it is her racial identity in the novel that permits her to respond, however awkwardly, to music that finally moves Neudecker out of his middle-class propriety. The music (and thus this possible contact between the two characters) was what was inside the briefcase Neudecker returns to Florence: "This is the disc that was in the player that you carried out of there," she tells him (93). Three pages from the end of the novel, as Neudecker makes his way down the stairways of the North Tower, an "old man, smallish, sitting, [. . .] resting," hands him the briefcase, explaining, "I don't know what I'm supposed to do with this. She fell and left it" (244). Parodying some classic detective plot, DeLillo gives us the "treasure" inside that briefcase as the Brazilian rhythms of Samba or some hybrid musical form, intended to liberate us from the confines of capitalism, print-knowledge, Western Civilization: "He heard the music change to something that had a buzz and drive, voices in Portuguese rapping, singing, whistling, with guitars and drums behind them, manic saxophones" (92). Neudecker, the real estate investment banker— "[s]mall outfit called Royer Properties. [. . .] We were Royer and Stans. Then Stans got indicted" (53)—can only respond professionally: "I'm talking to somebody. Very early in the talks. About a job involving Brazilian investors. I may need some Portuguese" (93).

Like the white man drumming his fingers methodically on the juke joint's table in Zora Neale Hurston's "How It Feels to Be Colored Me" (1928), Neudecker never really makes contact with Florence, even if they do have a brief sexual relationship. "Music. The great blobs of purple and red emotion have not touched him," Hurston writes. "He has only heard what I felt. [. . .] He is so pale with his whiteness then and I am *so* colored" (154). But DeLillo does not draw this conclusion, even if he gestures in the direction of Keith's and Florence's cultural, ethnic, and class differences, overlooked briefly as a consequence of a shared, but passing post-traumatic stress. Their undeveloped interlude is strange indeed in the novel, because it is one of the very few times characters in the novel actually cross the boundaries of their small worlds, apart from the framing act of al-Qaeda's attack, in itself a fundamental transgression of realms. The other instances of transgression in the novel, by contrast, are either fantastic, trivial, or merely reinstate the boundaries they threaten. Hammad longs for the German women cycling in the street, but then sleeps with a Syrian woman. Lianne angrily tells her neighbor, Elena, to turn down the Arabic-sounding music— "women in soft chorus, singing in Arabic" (119)—shortly after 9/11, complaining, "The whole city is ultrasensitive right now. Where have you been hiding?" (120). At some level, DeLillo suggests that these personal failures—whether Keith's inability to hear the Brazilian rhythms Florence so clearly feels or Lianne's reduction of the music Elena plays to "noise" (68–69)—are symptomatic of our national problem and explain in part our susceptibility to terror.

The Genealogy of 1960s Political Radicalism

Linda S. Kauffman has argued convincingly that *Falling Man* draws on DeLillo's nonfictional prose, both before and after 9/11, to comment on the relationship between 1960s radical protest movements in Europe and the United States to contemporary global terrorist movements ("Wake of Terror" 353–77). Lianne's mother, Nina, has a twenty-year-long relationship with a mysterious German art dealer, Martin Ridnour, aka Ernst Hechinger, who is rumored to have been associated with Kommune 1. Like Antonio Negri, convicted *in absentia* for his role in the Italian Red Brigades' kidnapping and murder of Christian Democratic Prime Minister Aldo Moro, Ridnour/Hechinger represents the intersection of radical politics and culture.

DeLillo explicitly identifies Ridnour/Hechinger with "Kommune 1," not Baader-Meinhof, although Nina also suggests "he was in Italy for a while, in the turmoil, when the Red Brigades were active. But I don't know" (146). Kommune 1, or "K1," was a short-lived political commune founded in Berlin in 1967 by a group of radicals led by Dieter Kunzelmann, Rudi Dutschke, Bernd Rabehl, and including Hans Magnus Enzensberger's ex-wife, Dagrun, and his brother, Ulrich. By 1969, this anti-government student activist group had fallen apart, but in its heyday was known for planning and occasionally carrying out Dadaist-style "performance" acts of social satire. Such acts included the planned "Pudding Assassination" of Vice President Hubert Humphrey during his visit to Berlin in April 1967—so called because one plan called for attacking him with pudding, yogurt, and flour—and the famous K1 photograph of communards' buttocks posed against a wall with the headline: "*Das Private ist politisch!*" ("The personal is political!"). The symbolic actions of Kommune 1 were usually linked to specific political acts, such as their demonstration against the Shah of Iran's visit to Berlin on 2 June 1967, but they were often criticized by German left-activists as more interested in publicity than in political change.

Kommune 1 nevertheless comes close to DeLillo's earlier versions of the radical artist, and its leaders were headlined as "Eleven Little Oswalds" in *Die Zeit*'s coverage of the abortive "Pudding Assassination" plot. Thanks to their members' connections with well-known German writers, Kommune 1 members lived for a time in Hans Magnus Enzensberger's Berlin apartment and later in Uwe Johnson's studio apartment until Johnson, abroad in the United States, grew alarmed at the negative publicity Kommune 1 had attracted and asked his neighbor, Günter Grass, to have them evicted. Whereas the Red Brigades in Italy and Baader-Meinhof in Germany really did commit urban terrorist acts with lasting consequences, Kommune 1 worked primarily through symbolic actions. However different these political activist groups are, they still have in common their origins in 1960s European left politics and their associations with the 1960s Left in the United States.

DeLillo includes very few political debates in the novel and all of them take place among the scholars and artists surrounding Lianne's mother, Nina, the distinguished Professor of Art History, and her lover, Martin/Ernst, the cosmopolitan art dealer and former radical. At the lunch following the memorial service for Nina, Martin announces the "thought" of "American irrelevance," of "the day [that] is coming when nobody has to think about America except for the danger it brings," that "America is losing the center" (191). Martin's different thoughts are in fact the same for DeLillo: irrelevance equals marginal; marginal equals dangerous. These equivalences suggest the ultimate one: America = terrorism. This conclusion, of course, comes predictably from the suspected 1960s radical, Ernst Hechinger (aka Martin Ridnour), pontificating on a subject we are led to believe he knows too well.

But what, then, should we conclude about the brief, undeveloped relationship between Florence Givens and Keith Neudecker, whose German surname adds to his vague family relationship to Ernst Hechinger through Keith's mother-in-law, Nina? Michael Hardt and Antonio Negri conclude *Empire* (2000) with a final section, "The Multitude against Empire," in which they predict an emerging coalition of oppressed peoples rising against the Euroamerican Empire that has caused so much human misery in the names of modernization, progress, freedom, and selfhood in the previous five hundred years (393–413). If it does arrive, Hardt and Negri argue, it will not come from within the system of Euroamerican hegemony and privilege. "What comes after America?" Martin asks Nina's mourning friends and her daughter (192), but he has no more idea what to do with this knowledge than did the historical members of Kommune 1. Lianne understands the problem: "Maybe he was a terrorist but he was one of ours, she thought, and the thought chilled her, shamed her—one of ours, which meant godless, Western, white" (195).

Why, then, does DeLillo so marginalize his other characters, his characters of *otherness*, ranging from the ordinary but nonetheless ethnically specific Florence to the terrorists Hammad and Amir Atta? Florence Givens's surname suggests the various gifts with which she is associated, ranging from the suitcase (with its CD player and its Brazilian music) to the human contact she gives Keith, perhaps hinting at a new "gift economy" of human relations, rather than social relations based on property and commodities. Yet DeLillo, like Keith, seems merely to entertain her as an impossible alternative, a means to non-Western knowledge she merely implies in her yearning, albeit clumsy, dance to those Brazilian rhythms. Keith Neudecker's response is finally trivial, personal: he will confess his affair to his estranged wife, Lianne, and she will "get a steak knife and kill him" (162). Trivializing any revolution from within the first-world system, DeLillo refuses to explore the possibility of any transvaluation from *outside*, apart from the dogmatism of the terrorists, represented as the nearly perfect opposite, the inevitable product, of Western ambiguity and doubt.

In his representation of a specific terrorist, DeLillo gives some human definition to Hammad only to Westernize him, a strategy reinforced by the fact that Hammad is fictional, whereas the historical Amir Atta is dogmatic and totalitarian. Hammad stumbles along in Hamburg, Afghanistan, Nokomis (Florida), even on board the jetliner hurtling down the Hudson Corridor toward the North Tower of the World Trade Center. He has his doubts about the use of children in the Iran-Iraq War, the promise of salvation to all martyrs in the *jihad* against the West, the prohibition against sex for the terrorists, even the demand that Muslim men grow beards. Critical of most of these lessons, he nonetheless accepts the basic premises: that the West is making war on Islam and that a blow against Western dominance shows "how a great power can be vulnerable. A power that interferes, that occupies" (46). And yet those final words are spoken by Martin/Ernst, the descendant of the 1960s Euroamerican Left, not by Islamic fundamentalists or such groups as Hezbollah and Hamas, who repeatedly condemn Euroamerican support of what they consider Israeli imperialism in the Middle East.

The Existentialist Aura

DeLillo understands fully how the existentialist aura of modernity, in which he and I were both educated, does not adequately motivate the social bond. To argue as philosophical existentialism did that the fundamental absurdity of our existence as humans, our insurmountable alienation from the external world, is what calls us together and thus should motivate us passionately to create human habitation and social institutions is too abstract and paradoxical to motivate the ordinary person. DeLillo cannot transcend his earlier education, and he still believes in the fundamental abyss, the randomness of existence that the mind transforms into patterns, plots, characters, destinies, and empires. Behind the dogma of Amir Atta lies the skepticism of Hammad, so that even the jihadists will be tricked into nothingness in the end. But DeLillo no longer believes that this universal truth of human contingency can motivate anything beyond the ceaseless history of a will-to-power that thrives on warfare and the production of subalterns who deserve our domination (whoever "we" may be in the particular historical moment).

Lianne "loved Kierkegaard in his antiqueness, in the glaring drama of the translation she owned, an old anthology of brittle pages with ruled underlinings in red ink [...]. He made her feel that her thrust into the world was not the slender melodrama she sometimes thought it was" (118). But Lianne's life *is* a "slender melodrama," only expanded into significance by the suffering of untold others, victims of foreign policies, wars, economic cheats, whereby Lianne lives in relative comfort and Hammad remembers nothing but crowding, narrow rooms filled with other lodgers, and ceaseless displacement. Yemen, Saudi Arabia, Afghanistan, Hamburg, Florida, New York, the Hudson Corridor—Hammad is always in some foreign place, experiencing to be sure the fundamental estrangement of DeLillo's and modernity's existentialist thesis. Are we *all strangers*? Yes and no; Hammad more than Lianne. Does Lianne recognize this impasse when she turns oddly, unpredictably, casually to religion in chapter 14, just a few pages before Hammad and Amir Atta begin their fateful flight toward the North Tower? "She wanted to disbelieve," perhaps because her father, Jack, a suicide, believed so passionately and contradictorily "that God infused time and space with pure being, made stars give light," as if this gave purpose to his own career as "an architect, an artist," someone in the business of producing order (232).

But it is not the "will to disbelieve" that motivates her; instead, Lianne turns to Catholicism, as if in direct reply to the passionate will to believe DeLillo attributes to Amir Atta: "Others were reading the Koran, she was going to church. [. . .] She followed others when they stood and knelt and she watched the priest celebrate the mass, bread and wine, body and blood. She didn't believe this, the transubstantiation, but believed something, half fearing it would take her over" (233). Lianne's religious conversion is still some version of Christian existentialism, a lingering trace of the antiquated Kierkegaard she loved in college and before 9/11, but it is nonetheless Catholicism, especially when it says: "God is the voice that says, 'I am not here'" (236). Although Lianne waffles between several versions of Christianity in a few pages, her conversion does enable her "to be alone, in reliable calm, she and the kid," apart from Keith, who has chosen the radical contingency of hypercapitalism (236).

Displaced from the North Tower to Florence's apartment "across the park" to the Sport and Gambling clubs of Atlantic City (89), then finally to Las Vegas, where he "works" fitfully as a competitive, compulsive poker player, Keith Neudecker acts out hypercapitalism's response to the existentialist predicament. If it is all a lie, merely a passing game, then we can only expose the fiction by ceaselessly demonstrating it, always living on the edge, facing every day the sheer contingency thinly veiled in the "risks" of the stock, credit, and currency markets of the Wall Street world where Keith once felt secure. Almost forty years ago, Robert Venturi, Denise Scott Brown, and Steven Izenour's *Learning from Las Vegas* (1972) appeared as a postmodern manifesto, even if its title underscores the irony that serious architecture and urban planning should follow the lead of Las Vegas's *kitsch*. DeLillo's conclusion in *Falling Man* is that Las Vegas has only led us to the bathos of capitalism, the absolute point of contradiction when the system can no longer hold, and he turns Las Vegas into the capital of America's "own shit" (191), recalling the main argument of *Underworld*.

The dilemma staged in DeLillo's *Falling Man* is exemplified in the eponymous act of David Janiak, whose repeated enactment of "falling" reminds New Yorkers of the pathos of the American "fall." Of course, what he stages is literally a "memento mori," that old poetic trope, of the several victims of 9/11 who chose to throw themselves from the top of the towers, rather than be incinerated or asphyxiated within. Much has been written about these "falling" people, whose peculiar positions were primarily the consequence of the basic physics involved, rather than any final gesture in response to the horrifying events of 9/11. Lianne witnesses one of Janiak's performances when she picks up her son, Justin, at school and chances on Janiak "falling" from an elevated subway platform visible from the schoolyard. Years later, she comes across his obituary, then searches his history on the web. A trained actor with "a heart ailment and high blood pressure" (220), he is found dead at thirty-nine years old in Saginaw County, Michigan, "more than five hundred miles from the site of the World Trade Center" (223), perhaps preparing to perform his "last jump" without a harness.

The performance art DeLillo stages in the novel invokes the rich history of street performance in New York City and recalls the specific act of the French aerialist, Philippe Petit, who on 7 August 1974 defied security at the World Trade Center, still under construction, to stretch a cable between the towers and tightrope-walk between them. Celebrated and criticized in James Marsh's recent documentary, *Man on Wire* (2008), in which no reference to 9/11 is made, Petit anticipates DeLillo's Janiak, just as Marsh's documentary offers an unwitting commentary on DeLillo's mysterious figure. Both call attention to the human being in the overwhelming scale of late-modern urban space; both depend upon the World Trade Center as symbol of modernist dehumanization, pitting either Petit's daring or Janiak's victimized human form against such a cityscape.

Yet even as news photographs of Petit's daring act circled the globe and Janiak leaves New York City, presumably to spread his own news to the Midwest and across America, both figures occlude the events of 9/11. Americans did not attack themselves on September 11, even if DeLillo argues convincingly that Americans contributed to the global conditions that have prompted the rise of numerous anti-imperialist, non-state affiliated, politically radical groups at war with first-world nations and global financial powers since the end of the Cold War in 1989 (Rowe, "*Mao II*" 38–39). Understanding "our fall" as a powerful nation, which has abused its moral and political authority in that same historical period, is certainly an important task. *Falling Man* contributes to this ongoing analysis by left intellectuals around the globe by detailing the instability of the values on which the United States has based that moral authority: religious tolerance, the nuclear family, intellectual and cultural criticism of the state, equal opportunity, anti-imperialism, and universal human rights. Janiak "falls" in the novel to demonstrate our failings in each of these areas. Islamic terrorism drives Lianne to Catholicism. Lianne and Keith's shaky marriage only briefly recovers after his escape from the North Tower; as he struggles with post-traumatic stress, the marriage totters and falls again. Nina and Martin/Ernst's artistic circle typifies the "radical chic" that no longer has any traction in global politics. Neither Kommune 1 pranks nor serious art can change the system from within. The white walls of the art dealer Martin Ridnour's apartment suggest not only his impermanence but also the erasure of aesthetic and intellectual critique. Postmodern intellectuals and artists have been contained by a pervasive U.S. anti-intellectualism, as well as by their own complicity in the global class/caste system. Like those elegant Giorgio Morandi paintings that hang in Nina's apartment in which slender bottles and spare boxes barely appear against white backgrounds, contemporary art criticizes late capitalism merely by stressing our impoverishment and commodification. In Morandi's paintings, *we* are those bottles and boxes, still-lives without natural referents, distilled into useless, expensive objects in a shop window.

But none of this explains Mohamed Atta and al-Qaeda. Hammad's Westernized desires and confused soul do not adequately represent the rage or the violence directed against the United States by groups and individuals who are willing to die for the barest chance to "speak out" against first-world arrogance. The ten rural peasant youths who carried out the attack on Mumbai between 26 and 29 November 2008 paused in the lobby of the Taj Mahal Palace and Tower Hotel to wonder at the television screens, personal computers, and vast array of technological devices available to the hotel guests. Those young revolutionaries were witnessing a disparity of global wealth also evident in the social and economic inequities of rapidly modernizing Mumbai. Of course, the motives of their Pakistani-based militant organization, Lashkar-e-Taiba, are in part driven by religious differences between Muslims and Hindus in South Asia, but the attack also indicated how these local religious politics are now inflected with a deep anti-Semitism that seems to bind together globally Islamic terrorist groups. The religious, political, economic, social, and personal cathexes of global terrorism cannot be represented adequately, much less successfully analyzed and criticized, entirely within the framework of Euroamerican ideologies. British imperialism in the Subcontinent, U.S. neoimperialism around the world, and global capitalism of the first-world nations are all to blame for the production of terrorism, but terrorism is neither a unified global movement nor entirely the *effect* of these causes.

Written before 9/11 and published in the same year, Salman Rushdie's *Fury* (2001) does attempt to understand the psychology of the minoritized non-European faced with first-world economic, political, and personal hegemony. Rushdie's protagonist, Malik Solanka, is not a poor peasant from an undeveloped country but a Cambridge-educated Bombay millionaire, whose invention of the doll, "Little Brain," has brought him fortune and fame. Perhaps for all of these reasons, Solanka feels an overpowering "fury," which he fears he will wreak violently on his own family, so he exiles himself from London to New York. Yet in New York City, he reads compulsively newspaper stories about a serial killer Solanka fears may be himself, acting out his uncontrollable rage in some repressed or somatic state.

Malik Solanka turns out not to be that psychopathic killer, but Rushdie makes clear that his character's anger against the West is so real, so palpable even to him, that it may erupt at any moment. When on 5 November 2009, Nidal Malik Hasan, a U.S. Army major serving as a psychiatrist at Fort Hood, Texas, entered the Soldier Readiness Center, shouted "*Allahu Akbar!*" and opened fire, wounding forty-three and killing thirteen people, his fury adds to that of the 9/11 terrorists and others, whether al-Qaeda inspired or not, bombing trains in Madrid and London, nightclubs in Bali, foreign naval ships in Yemen, resorts in Egypt and Israel, as well as the countless foiled attempts to bomb public transport and spaces throughout the imperialist first world. Was Major Hasan a "terrorist"? Did his cell phone and e-mail contacts with Anwar al-Awlaki in Yemen *prove* that Hasan was part of this "global war," or was he just another psychopath, a "madman" ironically trained to treat others' post-traumatic stress disorder?

Rushdie's pre-9/11 attempt at a literary interpretation of the "consciousness" of third-world fury by no means "covers" the issue, which today is at the center of our global anarchy. John Updike's *Terrorist* (2006) brilliantly captures the inner fury of Ahmad Ashmawy Mulloy, the eighteen-year-old Northern New Jersey convert to Islam who was raised by an Irish-American mother abandoned by her Egyptian husband when Ahmad was three. Sentimental in its conclusion when Ahmad changes his mind while driving a truckload of explosives into the Lincoln Tunnel, *Terrorist* nevertheless is a valiant effort by a thoroughly bourgeois writer to employ the techniques of the novel to help American readers comprehend this other-worldly fury. It is not, then, the "failure" of the novel as a genre that makes it so difficult for us to "represent" terrorism and terrorists. Whatever its limitations, the novel can still help us think through an "other," however fraught with problems of language, style, cultural and religious differences, and reader competency this process may be.

The fatal impasse in DeLillo's *Falling Man* is not the fault of the literary genre, but DeLillo's excessive reliance on the U.S. national form. Throughout his career, DeLillo has been one of our greatest critics of the limitations of thinking only from inside the United States. I began this chapter by arguing that DeLillo's Lee Harvey Oswald cannot be understood in exclusively national terms. America "changed" the day Oswald assassinated John F. Kennedy, because from that moment on we could never again understand "America" apart from Mexico, Cuba, Japan, the Soviet Union. Should we *ever* have thought of "America" in a culturally isolationist way? In recent years, American Studies has turned significantly toward transnational and international work to demonstrate that "national" knowledge—the old "American Exceptionalism"— has blinded us to the historical and geopolitical scope of U.S. imperialism, its global deployment of domestic racial and ethnic and sexual stereotypes, class and related economic inequities, and its extension of slavery "by other means."

Rushdie's Malik Solanka in *Fury* is never tricked into believing that New York City is some cosmopolitan or multicultural utopia. Worse even than that old imperial metropole, London, New York City poses as egalitarian, inclusive, diverse, and functional, when in fact Solanka clearly sees it as a microcosm of the inequities, political barriers, and occupied territories that continue to enrage so many outside the "first world." DeLillo's *Harper's* essay, "In the Ruins of the Future: Reflections on Terror and Loss in the Shadow of September," was published in December 2001, only three months after 9/11, and it predicts accurately what he would write in *Falling Man*: a searching criticism of our national failings without a complementary understanding of the global forces we have helped to produce and yet have exceeded our cultural, political, and military control. In this respect, both his nonfictional and fictional responses to 9/11 contribute to, rather than challenge, what I have elsewhere termed the "hypernationalism" whereby the U.S. state has attempted to incorporate and thereby domesticate global problems ("Culture" 38–39). That one of our most powerful social critics and insightful writers could be so captured and captivated by the national form is another reason why we so desperately need ways of thinking beyond the nation to theorize anew the political, economic, and human relations of a genuinely global order of things.

CHAPTER 9

Bodies in Rest and Motion in *Falling Man*

Linda S. Kauffman

It is difficult to write about relationships between men and women in *Falling Man* without sounding like the sociologist John Ray, Jr. in Nabokov's *Lolita* (1955)—pompous, self-righteous, and wrong. Critics who reduce literature to sociology will find numerous traps in Don DeLillo's 2007 novel. For starters, while the title is singular, the novel portrays many falling men—and women. First is the man in a white chef's coat and black shoes, plunging head first from the World Trade Center, immortalized in Richard Drew's photograph—the shot seen round the world. The second falling man is Keith Neudecker, who survives the twin towers' collapse, but is haunted by his colleagues' deaths. Thirdly, Keith sees a white shirt float to earth. The novel begins and ends with this—literally disembodied—image of pity and terror. The fourth is a performance artist billed as "Falling Man," who stages impromptu parachute jumps around New York City. It is as if the parachutist wants to put a body back in that white shirt. The women are falling too: some are "fallen women"; others are falling in and out of love. Some are spiraling downward psychically; others are slowly dying. This is a novel obsessed with the corporeal body—in motion, in bed, in suspense. Few characters rest, even when they are nearly dead.

Portrait of a Marriage

The stress (in both senses of the word) on bodies extends to the marital relations between Keith Neudecker and his wife, Lianne Glenn. Although they had been separated for over a year, Keith wanders home on September 11. They resume a semblance of family life, though the conflicts that drove them to part remain unresolved. The conflicts seem to involve drinking, gambling, and (possibly) philandering on Keith's part, and recriminations on Lianne's. DeLillo alternates between Lianne's consciousness and Keith's. While Keith disassociates from his body, Lianne is preoccupied with hers and her mother's (whose health is failing).

The second chapter opens with her reverie about sex. Lianne remembers their courtship and the early days of their marriage, before things soured. Every interaction was electrified by a sexual current— reading; watching television; walking down the street; entering a rented beach house, while the pounding surf "marked an earthly pulse in the blood" (7). They recapture some of that passion after September 11, but it is now overshadowed by their new-found awareness of how vulnerable they are to injury, loss, and death. For Lianne, their lovemaking is the only interval that does not seem "forced or distorted [. . .] by the press of events" (69). After they reunite, they make out in taxis and make love at home. They both want contact. At one point, Lianne presses her naked body to the full-length mirror, steamy from her husband's shower. Elsewhere, she recalls a fling she had during her separation from Keith. Her lover traces the ridges of her body with his finger, comparing each one to a geologic era. She opens herself and laughs.

The word "opening" reverberates throughout *Falling Man*. Sometimes it connotes desire. Sometimes it is a sign of willingness to explore the unknown, a leaning into something that does not have a name. It entails surrender—a letting go of preconceptions, abstractions. In this sense, "opening" resembles Keats's Negative Capability—the ability to enter imaginatively into the subjectivity of another person or thing. As Keats describes it, his own personality disappears in the process of imagining the Grecian urn or the nightingale. Lianne possesses this quality: ever since she was a little girl, she has imaginatively absorbed the sensations around her, as if her body were a permeable membrane. In this regard, she resembles Karen Janney in *Mao II* (1991), who absorbs the suffering of the homeless and the dispossessed, her heart an open wound. Similarly, Lianne tries to enter imaginatively into the experience of those who were in the towers, including her own husband. Not only does she have empathy, but she almost seems psychic: she is "a sensitive" who registers the emotions around her, as if her body were a tuning fork. Negative Capability, moreover, is sensual, as when DeLillo writes that making love is "a laying open of bodies but also of time" (69). It is one of the few experiences that slows time down to discrete, still moments.

Keith embodies this stillness, even though his relation to his body differs dramatically from Lianne's. After 9/11, he "was not quite returned to his body yet" (59), which makes him sound a bit like a package, waiting to be mailed C.O.D. Keith feels as if he is hovering above or beyond his body, watching himself from a distance. Since his office was destroyed when the twin towers fell, he is out of work, stripped of the normal routines that used to preoccupy him. As a result, he sees things differently, as if he had been sleepwalking through life before, but is now awake:

> He began to think into the day, into the minute. It was being here, alone in time, that made this happen, being away from routine stimulus, all the streaming forms of office discourse. Things seemed still, they seemed clearer to the eye, oddly, in ways he didn't understand. He began to see what he was doing. He noticed things, all the small lost strokes of a day or a minute [. . .]. (65)

Rather than being aware of the present moment, most of us live in a constant state of distraction—until something singular happens to snap us to attention. Keith's new-found awareness is corporeal—playing catch with his son, Justin; tasting bread crumbs; hearing music; smelling the acrid metallic air of lower Manhattan; seeing himself, as if for the first time: "Nothing seemed familiar, being here, in a family again, and he felt strange to himself, or always had, but it was different now because he was watching" (65). His acute self-consciousness implies heightened alertness, but no one knows better than Keith that alertness does not keep terror—or terrorist attacks—from happening.

Keith is tense, in suspended animation. The fact that remains unstated throughout the novel is that Keith is suffering from the after-effects of trauma, particularly that of seeing his buddy Rumsey die in the office they shared. These details appear as flashes of memory, brief but recurring. The burden Keith carries centers on bodies—burned, shrieking, falling. When he has surgery for his own injury, the anesthesia is supposed to be a memory suppressant, but the last thing he remembers before going under is "Rumsey in his chair [. . .], which meant the memory was not suppressed [. . .], a dream, a waking image, whatever it was, Rumsey in the smoke, things coming down" (22). The unconscious erupts, despite Keith's strenuous efforts to repress it. Instead of trying to work through trauma the way Lianne does, Keith acts out (see my "World Trauma Center" 647–59). He refuses to discuss what happened—until he meets Florence Givens, a black woman whose briefcase he inadvertently picks up while evacuating.

Precarious Lives

Keith is drawn to Florence because she gives voice to the very emotions he has been repressing. They share the same compulsion to go over and over that ghastly day. Even when he walks in the park with Justin "[h]e was still back there, with Florence, double in himself, [...] the deep shared self" (157). It is Florence who recounts some of the most horrific details of what it was like in the towers: the firemen racing upstairs and not coming down; water bottles passed up the line; the joking bravado of the equity traders; people with asthma, gasping for air; employees trying to use their cell phones; and above all, the darkness and the interminable stairs, floor by floor, spiraling down. "I feel like I'm still on the stairs," she says. "If I live to be a hundred I'll still be on the stairs" (57). Florence and Keith are both stuck, fixated on a moment neither of them can transcend. They are like "dreamers bleeding" (58), a description Florence applies to the wounded office workers who were all around her that morning.

Florence is frankly sensual. She and Keith become lovers. With her, he shares things that he has never confessed to his wife. He once aspired to be an actor, an appropriate career for a man who feels that he's acting the role of husband and father, imitating his own father's role (88). Keith is eager to skate on the surface of things, but the terrorist attacks defamiliarized the habits of everyday life, making ordinary occurrences seem surreal. For example, when Keith meets Florence in the mattress section of Macy's department store, forty or fifty people, mostly women, are wantonly bouncing on the mattresses. Each consumer is trying to *feel* something—a sensation of desired firmness, soundness, support, as if sheer consumption will fulfill her, or make her feel safe. The scene strikes Keith as "remarkable" (132); all the consumers "falling down" (133), publicly engaging in a ritual that is normally intimate. Just as *Mao II*'s mantra is that "[t]he future belongs to crowds" (16), *Falling Man*'s is that "all life had become public" after September 11 (182). The terrorist attack makes Keith feel that life is "meant to be lived seriously and responsibly, not snatched in clumsy fistfuls" (137). Nevertheless, he snatches the odd hours with Florence. He is aware of the contradiction, and its unfairness to her: she is "not someone to be snatched at" (137). While Florence tests one of the mattresses, a male bystander makes what Keith presumes is a lewd comment about her. Keith punches the man, "ready to kill him" (133). Perhaps the bystander's remark has racial overtones; DeLillo doesn't say. Nevertheless, one wonders if Keith's supercharged reaction arises because he secretly knows that his own behavior is not honorable.

Florence calms him, but she soon discovers that she wants more from Keith than he has to give. Although her firm is moving across the river to regroup, she does not want to move, because it would put too much distance between the lovers. She believes Keith saved her life by appearing at her door, because she has no one else to turn to. All those who might help her after 9/11 are missing or dead. But Keith terminates the affair, and the rejection Florence feels reconfirms old, unnamed wounds she has already suffered, presumably at the hands of men: "This was the old undoing that was always near, now come inevitably into her life again, an injury no less painful for being fated" (158). Florence was a fallen woman long before she is taken in adultery, but she isn't "fallen" in the Victorian sense. Her condition isn't sexual, but existential. It resembles Sartre's *Nausea* (1938) more than Hardy's *Tess of the d'Urbervilles* (1891). No rake has "ruined" her; instead, she is living in what DeLillo, in an essay published in *Harper's*, calls "the ruins of the future" (33–40). Existence has suddenly become provisional. Or perhaps terrorism simply stripped the veil of familiarity from her eyes, laying bare her vulnerabilities. Her first name evokes Florence Nightingale, the kindly nurse who ministered to wounded men. Her last name suggests that while she gives and gives, men do not reciprocate. Instead, it is a "given" that Keith will leave her. Moreover, "Given!" is the penultimate one-word sentence in *Finnegans Wake* (1939; 628), a work that reverberates throughout DeLillo's novel, as I will show presently.

Ironically, when Lianne first met Keith, her mother, Nina Bartos, warned her that Keith was made for affairs, not marriage. Nina astutely observes that Keith's style is "to get a woman to do something she'll be sorry for" (12). By novel's end, Florence becomes that woman. *Falling Man* is filled with such disappointments and misperceptions. For example, at the very instant when Lianne lies in bed thinking how nice it is that Keith is finally growing into his role as husband, he is already involved with Florence. The reader is thus aware of an infidelity Lianne never discovers. However, she has her suspicions, sparked by a single word: *actually*. "When she asked him about the stranger's briefcase in the closet, why it was there one day and gone the next, he said he'd actually returned it to the owner" (105). From long experience, Lianne knows Keith uses that word when he is lying. But she never voices her suspicions, and Keith continues to come and go as he pleases.

Both before and after 9/11, Keith is full of contradictions, one more case of that conflicted masculinity that Ruth Helyer has explored in DeLillo's work (125–36). On the one hand, he wants to live on the edge; on the other, he needs contact with his family. He nevertheless finds domesticity stifling. Perhaps, like John Marcher in Henry James's "The Beast in the Jungle" (1903), he fancies that he is destined for greater things: he "used to want more of the world than there was time and means to acquire" (128). Perhaps he drank to anaesthetize himself from these contradictions. But before I start to sound like John Ray, Jr., it's important to highlight the Sophoclean irony of Keith's fate, which is simply to have survived the terrorist attack, just as the Sophoclean irony of John Marcher's destiny is to be the man of his time to whom *nothing* happens.

Falling Man contains many moments of mordant black comedy. It is comedy Italian-style, which combines insult, bravado, and menace. It is often cruel, and frequently scatological. For instance, Lianne recalls how Keith used to come home drunk and defiant, with a look on his face that was "boyish and horrible" (103). His look illuminated "something so surely and recklessly cruel that it scared her, [...] a twisted guilt in his smile, ready to break up a table and burn it so he could take out his dick and piss on the flames" (104). DeLillo's humor echoes Martin Scorsese's *Mean Streets* (1973) and *GoodFellas* (1990) and Francis Ford Coppola's *The Godfather* trilogy (1972, 1974, 1990). Above all, Lianne's recollections remind us of dialogue spoken by Robert De Niro in a film directed by another Italian-American—Brian De Palma. In *The Untouchables* (1987), Robert De Niro (in the role of Al Capone) says with savage glee: "I want you to get this fuck where he breathes! I want you to find this nancy-boy Eliot Ness, I want him DEAD! I want his family DEAD! I want his house burned to the GROUND! I wanna go there in the middle of the night and I wanna PISS ON HIS ASHES!" Nobody holds a grudge like an Italian, and the hallmarks of DeLillo's comedy frequently involve vindictiveness, vendettas, and revenge. If the earth gets scorched while settling scores, so be it.

But beyond comedy lies the larger tragedy of 9/11. After all, the earth around the World Trade Center has literally been scorched. Therefore, the Bush Administration decided that the only way to settle scores against al-Qaeda was to wage war on two fronts, in Afghanistan and Iraq. Throughout DeLillo's novel, violence, delusion, and duplicity are intricately interwoven in passages filled with gaps and silences. Keith and Lianne avoid discussing any issue that might upset the delicate balance of their current arrangement. They deflect the topic of trauma, despite the fact that they are both exhibiting multiple signs of trauma—isolation, fear, irritability, impatience, anger. As the catastrophe's toll mounts, the number of motifs related to falling, the Fall, and the fallen reverberate with heightened intensity. "Falling" is variously described as an opening, a process, something unfolding, terminating, or in motion. All the characters are portrayed as living in suspense: Keith, Lianne, Justin, Florence Givens, the elderly and infirm, the victims and perpetrators of 9/11. Lianne frequently finds herself thinking: "*The whole of existence frightens me*" (118), a sentence from Kierkegaard.

Therefore, while it is tempting to label the men in the novel as destructive (Keith), thrill-seeking (the parachutist), or death-seeking (the jihadists), the men are considerably more complicated. Nor are the women uniformly constructive or nurturing. After all, Keith is not the only one who is filled with rage after the terrorist attack. Lianne is angry too. Her nerves are raw. Just as Keith punches a man in a brawl in Macy's, Lianne slaps a neighbor woman, Elena, because she is playing loud "Islamic" music (67). Although the music may be Greek, North African, or Sufi chanting, Lianne views it as a provocation, a personal affront. To her, Elena symbolizes everything she despises about Muslims who pray using the same rote phrases, rituals, and movements "following the arc of sun and moon" (68). But when DeLillo proceeds to describe Lianne as falling asleep under the arc of the same sun and moon, the implication is that what unites us is that we are all bodies in rest or motion, in space, on a small planet.

The Mania for Evidence

Lianne's attitude toward Elena is all the more paradoxical because Lianne is one of the most analytical characters in the novel. She earns her living as an academic editor, work that is a significant part of her life. She edits one book on Renaissance art, another on polar exploration. Words are like runes to Lianne, mysterious and unyielding. She is trained in ambiguity. She ruminates over language's origin, etymology, and evolution. She edits a book on ancient alphabets which traces all the forms writing took, all the materials that were once used—pictograms, hieroglyphics, cuneiform (149). Although DeLillo does not belabor the point, all these forms took root throughout the Middle East—ancient Egyptian, Sumerian, Assyrian, Mesopotamian cultures—the very region the U.S. begins bombing by *Falling Man*'s conclusion. The author of the book Lianne is editing is a Bulgarian who illuminates the earliest origins of language, for he has translated scores of "inscriptions on baked clay, tree bark, stone, bone, sedge" (23). Meaning, however, remains provisional, for the Bulgarian's "meticulous decipherments" are typed "in a deeply soulful and unreadable script" (23). He is a Bulgarian writing in English—as if to highlight the inevitable gaps between word and thing, where much is lost in translation.

Lianne wants to understand what has befallen her. She feels as estranged from language as she does from her marriage. She learns of a book written by a retired aeronautical engineer who has "been working obsessively for fifteen or sixteen years" (139). It has become legendary among agents and editors who—before 9/11—rejected it as the work of a crackpot. But now, in the wake of September 11, it looks visionary. It details a set of interlocking global forces that converge in time and space on a "late-summer morning early in the twenty-first century." It "might be said to represent the locus of Boston, New York and Washington" (139). Her boss, Carol Shoup, dissuades Lianne from editing it, warning her that it is boring, filled with "[s]tatistical tables, corporate reports, architectural blueprints, terrorist flow charts," and "a long sort of treatise on plane hijacking" (138, 139). The book resembles the manifesto Ted Kaczynski, the Unabomber, wrote (1995), indicting scientists for the sins of technology. Carol highlights the parallel by nicknaming the aeronautical engineer the "Unaflyer" (139). Carol eventually gives Lianne the assignment after another editor quits because the "text [is] so webbed in obsessive detail that it was impossible to proceed further" (155). The sentence reminds one of the fable of the Chinese knotmaker who made such dazzling knots that eventually his own intricate designs caused him to go blind. In *Falling Man*, the Blind Sheik, mastermind of the first attack on the World Trade Center in 1993, complements the Unaflyer's role as a harbinger of doom.

Lianne is searching for some key, some figure in the carpet that will not only unlock the causes of 9/11, but the impenetrable mystery of good and evil, and she fancies that the Unaflyer's treatise might be the ticket. In this respect, she resembles Nicholas Branch, whose task in *Libra* (1988) is to untangle all the interwoven threads of rumor, myth, speculation, and evidence about the assassination of President John Fitzgerald Kennedy. Like *Libra*, *Falling Man* is obsessed with evidence. There is the evidence of the hijackers' movements from Hamburg to the Hudson Corridor, involving the transmission of money, data, information. There is the criminal prosecution of the Blind Sheik for the 1993 bombing. There is the forensic evidence of the dead in the detritus that floats out of the offices in the World Trade Center on 9/11, along with DNA evidence collected to identify bodies and body parts. There are the cell phone, video, camera, media, e-mail, and answering machine recordings of the event unfolding in real time, as well as the surveillance cameras at airports and banking machines (which also contribute to the idea that after 9/11, all life is public). Just as horrific memories of those hours in the North Tower become embedded in Keith's memory, the viscera of the dead literally become embedded in the skin of the living, including Keith's. There are the notes, posters, and photos on makeshift memorials throughout the city begging for evidence of the missing and dead.

The Neudeckers' seven-year-old son, Justin, is equally obsessed with evidence. Justin is a solitary child, quirky and precocious. He seems as enigmatic to his parents as they are to each other. Justin takes things literally, refusing to speak, except in monosyllables. His singsong sentences have a slightly totalitarian ring to Lianne's ears, which she finds unnerving. Lianne does not know if Justin is purposely trying to bait her by obstinately refusing to forsake the practice, or if the problem is more serious than childish willfulness. Is it a sign of trauma? A form of a more serious linguistic and psychological disorder, like Asperger's syndrome? She tries to imagine what Justin is feeling, speculating that it must be confusing to see his father sleeping in the same bed with her again, after having walked out on his wife. Justin, Lianne speculates, must wonder if Keith can be trusted; is he a constant or a variable in the boy's life? "If your child thinks you're guilty of something, right or wrong, then you're guilty. And it happens he was right," Lianne thinks (102). (Her thoughts foreshadow her final confrontation with Keith, which I shall discuss presently.) Although Lianne's anxiety is acute, DeLillo leavens it with comedy. When Justin confuses bin Laden with "Bill Lawton," DeLillo pays homage to J. D. Salinger's little boy in "Down at the Dinghy" (1949), who confuses "kike" with "kite," and is upset that his father has been compared to "one of those things that go up in the *air* [. . .]. With *string* you hold" (129). When Justin refuses to speak at the dinner table, his parents mockingly speculate that he has entered "the next stage" of his "spiritual development," which consists of "[u]tter and unbreakable silence" (100–01), like a monk living in a cave in the mountains. Sometimes it is difficult to distinguish silence from cunning, especially in this kid.

Disappearance and God

The counterpoint to Justin's comedy is the tragedy of the Alzheimer's patients. Lianne runs a volunteer writing workshop to help them document their rapidly fading memories of their lives. After September 11, some of the women in the novel search for God; others want revenge. Some long for revenge *and* God. Lianne is one of the latter. As she listens to the Alzheimer's patients' reactions to the attack, Lianne prods them to talk directly about the terrorists. She privately applauds those who view the terrorists as criminals who should rot in hell. Lianne is secretly gratified by this unvarnished desire for revenge. Nevertheless, Lianne eventually finds herself going to Mass. She takes solace in the community and the ritual. Paradoxically, her discussions with the Alzheimer's patients help her articulate the difference between organized religion (which so frequently relies on power and violence) and a transcendent spirituality. By novel's end, she embraces the latter approach. The Alzheimer's patients are crucial to Lianne's spiritual transformation, particularly regarding her unresolved grief about her father, who shot himself after being diagnosed with Alzheimer's. In the workshop, Lianne realizes that "[t]hese people were the living breath of the thing that killed her father" (62). Lianne watches for symptoms of the hereditary disease in herself—another sign of the obsession with evidence throughout the text. She needs reassurance that she has "normal morphology"

(206). Certainty, assurance, and security have all fallen out of Lianne's world, but the Alzheimer's patients give her some sense of proportion and perspective about the magnitude of her loss, which hardly compares to theirs.

They reveal the preciousness not just of life, but of language. The patients marvel at the sounds of words; some marvel at "the revelation of writing itself" (31). Here too, writing is portrayed as an embodied act, by which I mean an act of the body that engages all five senses: while writing, they eat pastry, hear music, laugh, and cry. One member calls the classroom "their prayer room" (30). In the workshop, Lianne urges each patient to read his or her work aloud, which reveals:

> the first signs of halting response, the losses and failings, the grim prefigurings that issued now and then from a mind beginning to slide away from the adhesive friction that makes an individual possible. It was in the language, the inverted letters, the lost word at the end of a struggling sentence. It was in the handwriting that might melt into runoff. (30)

Dyslexia, aphasia, impotence: the patients are aware of what is happening to them, but they are incapable of preventing it. Lianne speculates that *she* needs the workshop even more than the patients do, because "[t]here was something precious here, something that seeps and bleeds" (61–62). Lianne is moved by their valiant struggle to document the evidence of their existences. She thinks about the beauty of it, "the way they sing their lives, but also the unwariness they bring to what they know, the strange brave innocence of it, and her own grasping after her father" (155). Sometimes the patients' writing resembles a Greek chorus, implicitly or explicitly commenting on the novel's action. For instance, although the storyline sessions are intended "strictly for morale" (29), there is one topic nearly all of the patients seize upon: "They wanted to write about the planes" (31)—about where they were when the terrorist attack happened; about people they knew who were affected; and about God. Is there a God? If so, how could He let this happen? What is the nature of good and evil?

One of Lianne's favorite Alzheimer's patients is named Rosellen, who is another one of the novel's falling women, felled by a particularly cruel disease. Lianne is haunted by Rosellen's final sentences. Rosellen's last scribblings expose her psychic disintegration: "*Do we say goodbye, yes, going, am going, will be going, the last time go, will go*" (156). The sentence evokes Molly Bloom's final soliloquy in *Ulysses* (1922), but whereas Molly's is an affirmation of the life instinct, Rosellen's is a valediction. Even more pointedly, Rosellen echoes the final sentence in *Finnegans Wake*, "A way a lone a last a loved a long the" (Joyce 628). *Finnegans Wake* displays the same syntactical condensation, as when Joyce writes, "My leaves have drifted from me. All. But one clings still. I'll bear it on me. [. . .] Far calls. Coming, far!" (628). The chiasmos stresses the process of moving toward death, just as DeLillo portrays dying as a dynamic process. Joyce's allusion to "my leaves" invokes the autumn of life. Despite Joyce's punctuation (the finality of the period as a full stop), aurally the sentence also means: "All but one clings still." The struggle between surrender versus the desire to cling to life links the two passages with eloquent economy. Just as DeLillo refers to "the last bare state" (156), Joyce puns on "bare" versus "bear": dying is a burden one must bear, as well as something that bears one away, the way one might be borne on the tides. Like Joyce, DeLillo stresses leaving, leave-taking, being left, and being bereft. Indeed, Lianne could be speaking of *Finnegans Wake* when she describes Rosellen's sentences: Rosellen "developed extended versions of a single word, all the inflections and connectives, a kind of protection perhaps, a gathering against the last bare state, where even the deepest moan may not be grief but only moan" (156). Joyce uses the word "moananoaning," which conflates "moan," "owning," and "moaning"—an incessant lament, in and out like the tides of the River Liffey. (It may also be an onomatopoeic allusion to onanism, carrying us back to "penisolate" in Joyce's opening paragraphs [3].) Faulkner's *The Wild Palms* (1939) also comes to mind: "*between grief and nothing I will take grief*" (324).

Rosellen has entered an elemental realm where the body still has a voice, but is no longer in motion, and certainly not at rest. She is inscribing her own epitaph, narrating her own imminent demise. She makes one think of the disappearing acts of Beckett's garrulous, solipsistic figures too. Nevertheless, she still concludes in the future tense, clinging still. Like Keats's "still unravished bride," the idea of "still life" is very nearly an oxymoron in *Falling Man*, which refers repeatedly to the oddness of the phrase "*Natura morta*" (12). Rosellen lives in a state of suspension, neither dead nor fully alive. She has no nostalgia or regret, since both sentiments require a sense of the past which Alzheimer's patients by definition no longer possess. The portmanteau word Joyce uses to combine *memory, memento mori, remember me*, and *commemoration* is "mememormee!" (628). It is a demand, a command, and a lament against oblivion. As I have discussed elsewhere ("Wake of Terror" 368), *Falling Man* portrays Alzheimer's as a metaphor for the post–September 11 condition: all the characters are living in a state of abeyance, with a sense of impending doom that they are powerless to prevent.

Mother and Daughter

In addition to watching the Alzheimer's patients deteriorate, Lianne witnesses her own mother's slow decline. Nina Bartos had "a mane of white hair at the end, the body slowly broken, haunted by strokes, blood in the eyes. She was drifting into spirit life. She was a spirit woman now" (234). Their relationship is frequently testy; each knows how to push the other's buttons. Nina is formidable, opinionated, and brainy. To illustrate, after meeting Jack Glenn on a Greek island—an architect whom she later marries—she writes an article about his design for an artists' retreat on the site, which she describes as "Euclidean rigor in quantum space" (130). In other words, Jack combined the classical with the modern; the practical with the theoretical; geometry with the theory of quantum fields on curved spacetimes—a topic that has long interested physicists (and DeLillo). Nina's description highlights DeLillo's spatial imagination throughout the novel. The compression of time and the telescoping of space—seen literally in the fall of the twin towers—are recurrent motifs that influence the novel's very structure. Its chronology is compressed between the seconds when Keith walks out of the World Trade Center, at the novel's beginning, and the seconds after the planes' impact, at the novel's end. (Its *in medias res* structure is obviously indebted to *Finnegans Wake*.) Nina calls the cluster of architectural structures "a piece of pure geometry gone slightly askew" (130), where angles are joined in unpredictable ways. (DeLillo may have modeled Jack Glenn on the audacious architect Frank Gehry, who is known for fluid, curvilinear designs and structures that seem to defy gravity.)

Nina's description of Jack's architectural design illuminates why the Bolognese painter Giorgio Morandi appeals to her, for Morandi also takes classical elements (specifically, the still life), then deconstructs them. He combines elements which seem purely figurative, then adds lines, shapes, and shadows that bleed into other objects in ways that defy realism. Nina's life work has been devoted to research, writing, and giving lectures on Morandi all over the world (see my "Wake of Terror," 365, 370, 374, for more detailed discussion of Morandi). She is used to being distinguished, and her voice is authoritative. It is the voice of Western Civilization, which Nina adamantly equates with the white, European, Judeo-Christian tradition: "I want to sit in my armchair and read my Europeans" (34). She wants to remain aloof from mass culture and, possibly, the masses. She certainly has no patience with jihadists, whom she defines as the epitome of barbarism.

Lianne thus finds her mother rather intimidating. Far from being nurturing, motherhood seems to have been something of an afterthought for Nina. Nina clearly taught Lianne how to look at art, and as a little child Lianne would pretend to lecture the way her mother did. But as an adult Lianne approaches art in a different way. She finds it a relief "simply" to look, rather than subjecting each work to her mother's method of exhaustive analysis. Lianne prefers to absorb the work, rather than intellectualize it. As Lianne gazes as the two Morandi paintings her mother owns, she finds "a mystery she could not name [. . .]. Let the latent meanings turn and bend in the wind, free from authoritative comment" (12)—meaning her mother's trained eye and expert analysis.

Nina Bartos is equally expert in her analysis of Lianne's attraction to Keith. In Nina's opinion, Keith makes Lianne feel "dangerously alive" (11). She thinks Lianne chose Keith because he reminded her of her glamorous father. But in Nina's view, Lianne has romanticized Jack Glenn: far from being reckless, Jack was, Nina insists, "at heart a careful man" (11). Not only does she shatter Lianne's illusions about her father, but Nina is particularly judgmental about Keith's character flaws. Even more irritating is that Nina is probably right, particularly when she says that "[t]here's a certain man, an archetype," who is "sheer hell on women. Living breathing hell" (59). Nevertheless, their dialogue is frequently funny, as when Nina mockingly observes that Keith "gives the impression there's something deeper than hiking and skiing, or playing cards. But what?" (9–10). Lianne's reply: "Rock climbing" (10). In this exchange, one hears traces of Isabel Archer's disaffected assessment of Gilbert Osmond, whom she describes as having a "genius for upholstery" (James 363). In *The Portrait of a Lady* (1881), Gilbert Osmond is a connoisseur who simulates a self in order to ensnare Isabel. Henry James and Don DeLillo crystallize the spirit of their respective ages—and social classes. In the 1880s, the acquisitive social climber Osmond collects Japanese china, miniatures, and bibelots. In 2001, Keith's hobbies are watching television, poker tournaments, and wilderness excursions—the only thing about him that is outward bound.

In fact, Keith's inner migration was well under way long before 9/11; the terrorist attack merely consolidates his previous tendencies toward withdrawal, flight, diversion. Unlike Lianne, Keith seldom expresses the slightest interest in books, language, or any other kind of art. His true avocation seems to be gambling. When Keith suddenly appears at their apartment on 9/11, Lianne has no idea whether his reappearance is temporary or permanent. All arrangements seem provisional. DeLillo's prose moves back and forth from the domestic crisis to the national crisis; a conversation about whether Keith and Lianne will reconcile turns into a conversation about the nation's vulnerability. There are no guarantees. Lianne is forced to confront that harsh fact. Another fact is even harsher: security was an illusion *before* 9/11 too. We just didn't know it, despite the 1993 bombing instigated by the Blind Sheik. When Nina quizzes Lianne about what comes next with Keith, Lianne turns a personal issue into a political one by replying: "Nothing is next. There is no next. This was next. Eight years ago they planted a bomb in one of the towers. Nobody said what's next. This was next. The time to be afraid is when there's no reason to be afraid. Too late now" (10). Her terse reaction is another sign of the temporal disorientation that afflicts all the characters. "Before" has become "after"; now everything is "after" 9/11. Ironically, as if to highlight the return of the repressed, Lianne gets a summons to serve on the jury that will bring the Blind Sheik to trial.

David Janiak

David Janiak is the name of the parachutist who calls himself Falling Man, whose acts recall those of Jeb Corliss, the professional parachute jumper who has orchestrated jumps from the Golden Gate Bridge, the Eiffel Tower, and the Petronas Towers in Kuala Lumpur (see my "Wake of Terror" 369–70). Another (less direct) inspiration is Philippe Petit, the famous aerialist and funambulist featured in the documentary *Man on Wire* (2008), who on 7 August 1974 managed to walk on a tightrope he rigged between the twin towers. (My thanks to Lewis Gleich for bringing this to my attention.) Janiak's stunts signal the return of the repressed too, since they remind New Yorkers of the bodies that fell from the towers. When Lianne first encounters him, he is wearing a business suit, dangling from a safety harness near the train station entrance on 42nd Street. His pose mimics that of the doomed man in Richard Drew's photograph: one leg bent up, arms at his sides. Just as DeLillo earlier describes lovemaking as a "laying open" of bodies and time, Janiak places his own body up close and personal. Although Lianne is horrified at first, she finds herself thinking that Janiak "held the gaze of the world [. . .]. There was the awful openness of it, something we'd not seen" (33). Although DeLillo never says so explicitly, that is the function of art: to show us something about events, history, aesthetics, or the human body that we have never seen before. Specifically, Janiak compels Lianne to confront "the puppetry of human desperation, a body's last fleet breath and what it held" (33). In this way, he complements Rosellen, whose seemingly nonsensical scribblings cry out so eloquently.

Falling Man is particularly tantalizing because he purposely avoids the celebrity that most of the culture craves. Each jump is spontaneous, so the media cannot record it. He depends on the element of surprise, and refuses to explain his actions, motives, or intentions. He seems to expect hostility, if not actively court it. No New Yorker wants a reminder of falling bodies. Lianne, however, fully recalls the beauty and horror of the image of the "falling angel" captured by Richard Drew (222). Moreover, she intuitively understands why Janiak discourages media attention. Insight like hers is a rarity, and it brings us back to the redeeming value of Negative Capability. She loses her personality (another word for ego) in her attempt to enter imaginatively into Janiak's performance. If all life after 9/11 is public, the corollary is that no experience is unmediated. Janiak, in contrast, wants to create an unmediated experience. Here is how Lianne interprets his art: "There were no photographs of [his] fall. She was the photograph, the photosensitive surface. That nameless body coming down, this was hers to record and absorb" (223). Record it she does, in the same way she tries to absorb Morandi's art, words, random events, and the emotions of those around her—her husband, her mother, her son, her colleagues, the Alzheimer's patients, and the culture at large.

Is Janiak a freak or an artist? DeLillo won't say, but he offers a pitch-perfect satire of the cultural response to Janiak, who gets invitations to speak from the Guggenheim, the Japan Society, and the New York Public Library. Conversely, a concise tabloid headline reads: "MAYOR SAYS FALL MAN MORONIC" (222) (DeLillo's sly allusion, perhaps, to Mayor Rudolph Giuliani's condemnation of the Sensation Exhibition at the Brooklyn Museum of Art [1999–2000]). But to Janiak's credit, he refuses to be co-opted by the media, the politicians, and the cultural mavens alike. Lianne only learns his name when she reads his obituary. Although he died of natural causes, he had planned one final jump—without a harness—a suicide mission.

If the Unaflyer's path leads to madness and Janiak's leads to suicide, the question then becomes: "How is one to live?" The line between belief and delusion is slim. Is God a delusion too? The character who has the firmest conviction that God exists is Florence Givens. She wonders if the lesson of 9/11 is to "obey the laws of God's universe, which teach us how small we are and where we're all going to end up" (90). But she goes on to note that the terrorists also believed in God, despite being against everything Americans stand for. Instead of addressing this contradiction, she is alarmed when Keith states flatly that he never thinks about God. She tells him: "I've always felt the presence of God. I talk to God sometimes" (90). It is tempting to dismiss the discussion of God as a silly superstition, but DeLillo treats the search for transcendence with respect. As John A. McClure has shown, *Players* (1977), *The Names* (1982), *White Noise* (1985), *Mao II* (1991), and *Underworld* (1997) "climax in dramatic episodes of worshipful communion that recall the religious 'mysteries' of DeLillo's Catholic heritage. [...] sacred practices that channel grace to those who perform them from sources that cannot be fully understood" ("DeLillo and Mystery" 166). Those who search for mastery, knowledge, or control (including in organized religion) are doomed to fail, as McClure points out, but those who seek an opening to grace sometimes find it.

For Lianne, however, the resolution of the uncertainties that have plagued her is couched in ambiguity:

> She thought that the hovering *possible* presence of God was the thing that created loneliness and doubt in the soul and she also thought that God was the thing, the entity existing outside space and time that resolved this doubt in the tonal power of a word, a voice. (236, my italics)

As if the word "possible" were not enough to highlight the provisional nature of her epiphany, the following sentence undermines the affirmation in the passage just quoted: "God is the voice that says, 'I am not here'" (236). That is the central paradox of faith: to believe in an absence, unseen and unverifiable. This helps explain the novel's obsessive emphasis on evidence: some things have to be taken on faith, and most are indeterminate, unsolvable.

Some things are also irreconcilable, including the Neudeckers' conflicting views of their fate as a couple. Keith proposes that he continue to come and go, traveling to poker tournaments and returning home, but Lianne sees poker as a "total psychotic folly, [. . .] a séance in hell" (216). Notably, Keith does not deny this. In fact, the gamblers joke about being like vampires returning to their coffins before dawn. But the joking disguises a deeper truth, which is that Keith has chosen an artificial environment that is anonymous, hermetically sealed, ruled by a strict code. It is a denatured world outside of time (no clocks in casinos). For Keith, that's its appeal. But Lianne frames her objections quite specifically in terms of time: "Tick tock tick tock. What happens after months of this? Or years. Who do you become?" (216). Keith has no answer. Even the idea of contemplating an answer makes his "mind shut down" (216). He has consciously chosen life-in-death. Significantly, when Lianne confronts Keith, she describes their conflict in terms of gender, then quickly re-frames it: "I understand there are some men who are only half here. Let's not say men. Let's say people. People who are more or less obscure at times" (213–14). The deflection does not obscure the fact that she really means *men*.

Although Keith is the poker player, it is Lianne who lays her cards on the table and calls his bluff. They must decide whether to be a family. She and Justin must both be able to trust Keith. He wants to drift; she wants permanence. He wants danger; she wants to feel safe. Nevertheless, her analysis of his predicament is not without compassion. She realizes that what he saw in the twin towers filled him with helpless fury: "You want to kill somebody. [...] I don't know how it works or how it feels. But it's a thing you carry with you" (214). Once again, he replies flippantly, but Lianne refuses to be deterred. She has been gathering her strength, deliberately withdrawing from Keith, the way one might withdraw from a drug. She is preparing to cut him loose. Lianne's story concludes when she is at Mass one morning three years after the attacks. She finds herself thinking, "She was ready to be alone, in reliable calm, she and the kid, the way they were before the planes appeared that day, silver crossing blue" (236). Not exactly a happy ending. No one can ever be the way they were prior to September 11. By the novel's conclusion, Lianne has become an orphan. She carries her past selves with her—girl, daughter, wife, lover—but she is capable of carrying on alone.

Conclusion

Falling Man defies tidy categorizations of every sort, including those related to sexual politics. DeLillo's novel has "no moral in tow," as Nabokov famously said about *Lolita* (286). Furthermore, Nina Bartos would agree with Nabokov that the only immortality is art. She shows how one can live for art, just as David Janiak shows how one might die for it. But living is harder, as Keith illustrates. So much of living entails letting go, as both Lianne and Florence Givens discover. The Alzheimer's patients illuminate the fabric of faith and teach us something about the perverse, wondrous nature of language, the ghostly trace of which remains even as they are falling out of this world. DeLillo portrays the séance in hell that has come to be known as 9/11. We gain some insight into discrete moments and movements on that fateful day. We also learn something about the aftermath, including the commencement of the U.S. wars in Afghanistan and Iraq. War brings an even more somber significance to the idea of falling bodies: the fallen soldiers join the ranks of all the men, women, and children who have fallen at home and abroad.

CHAPTER 10

Witnessing Trauma: *Falling Man* and Performance Art

John N. Duvall

Cultural criticism finds itself faced with the final stage of the dialectic of culture and barbarism. To write poetry after Auschwitz is barbaric. And this corrodes even the knowledge of why it has become impossible to write poetry today.
    Theodor W. Adorno, "Cultural Criticism and Society" (1949)

Don DeLillo's *Falling Man* (2007) takes place primarily in New York City, beginning in the immediate aftermath of the collapse of the World Trade Center towers. The story is simple, though the issues of terrorism, trauma, and aesthetics it takes up are not. Keith Neudecker, a lawyer who escapes from the North Tower, wanders injured and confused until an electrician picks him up and offers him a ride. Keith chooses not to go to the emergency room but rather to the apartment of his estranged wife, Lianne. Through this couple's attempted reconciliation, DeLillo stages the effects of trauma.

Focusing on the specific trauma of New Yorkers, DeLillo is aware that the destruction of the towers, broadcast live to the world as it was, psychologically scarred millions of viewers, but he resists the notion of a new American identity based on collective trauma. We hope that Keith and Lianne will successfully make their marriage work, that this reunification will provide the Shakespearian happy ending that will offer a kind of symbolic healing of the wound of 9/11. This hope, however, is frustrated. Lianne may find the strength to go on alone in a return to the forms of her long-forgotten Catholic faith; Keith, in contrast, is left with a belief that the last best hope for free will lies in the turn of the card at professional poker tournaments in Las Vegas. But if DeLillo's novel resists providing an easy narrative resolution to trauma, does *Falling Man* offer any possibility for the working through of a trauma broadly enough experienced that the administration of George W. Bush was able to exploit it in order to wage a preemptive war in Iraq and to suspend the guarantees of the U.S. Constitution?

For a novel that is ostensibly about trauma and terrorism, it may seem perverse that so much attention is devoted to art and artists. Characters, including an art history professor and an art dealer, view and interpret both photographs and the still life paintings of Giorgio Morandi. Moreover, the eponymous character of the book's title is a performance artist whose work points to one of the most iconic (yet simultaneously suppressed) images of one of the people who fell or jumped from the twin towers. The prevalence of art, artists, and art critics in the novel at the very least raises a question about what role art might play in addressing the traumatic events of 9/11. I believe that in *Falling Man* DeLillo illustrates both the inadequacy and the necessity of artistic mediation and meditation to the task of remembering and memorializing 9/11.

A Portrait of the Artist as a Middle-Aged Man

Falling Man's focus on art is hardly anomalous in DeLillo's work. DeLillo has long been interested in the possibilities of the outsider artist to effect change in the world. Early in his career, he fashioned himself as that outsider artist. He had a business card that he would give interviewers that read "I don't want to talk about it" (LeClair, "Underhistory" 113). He also remained aloof, shying away from not only interviews but also from publicly reading his work. For all his postmodern subject matter— the media, advertising, consumption, waste (social elements that often make American culture feel like one giant, Disney-produced simulation), it is DeLillo's investment in the role of the artist that aligns him finally with the high modernist writers of the first half of the twentieth century. In the wasteland of our (post)modernity, the artist, DeLillo believes, still has a vital role to play.

For much of his career, DeLillo felt that the responsibility of the artist was to question those cultural forces that would reduce our human being to so many acts of unreflective consumption. As DeLillo (who before becoming a novelist worked in a Madison Avenue ad agency) early realized, images—especially in a media-driven culture—are inherently charged, and his biggest fear has centered on what can happen when politics are reduced to aesthetics, that is, when politics become nothing more than pretty images. If politics are reduced to images, people don't need to think; they need only believe. For example, when, on 1 May 2003, President Bush landed on an aircraft carrier, emerged in full fighter-pilot regalia, and announced the end of hostilities in Iraq under a banner reading "MISSION ACCOMPLISHED," we had an instance of politics reduced to pure image. What DeLillo hopes to do in much of his fiction of the 1970s through the 1990s is to move us in the opposite direction. If American media tends to reduce politics to aesthetics, DeLillo wants to politicize and historicize the image. He frequently does so by depicting those cultural producers and artists who are marginal to the mainstream. In his novel of the Cold War, *Underworld* (1997), for example, DeLillo celebrates the outsider artist, from graffiti writers to filmmaker Sergei Eisenstein to underground comedian Lenny Bruce. For DeLillo, these are the artists who attempt to reshape the image so that it challenges people's assumptions about the Us-Them politics of the period.

Ironically, even as DeLillo calls on us to think historically, much of his fiction prior to *Falling Man* seems to look into the future—to peer around the corner, so to speak, anticipating and commenting on important cultural trends and tendencies, the full significance of which only emerges after his novels are published. In particular, his earlier depictions of terrorism seem, in the aftermath of 9/11, eerily prescient. In DeLillo's fifth novel, *Players* (1977), a stockbroker becomes implicated in a plot of a foreign terrorist cell to blow up the New York Stock Exchange. In *The Names* (1982), an American expatriate living in Greece, an unwitting agent of the CIA, stumbles onto the existence of an ancient religious death cult; stated more symbolically, the secret agency of U.S. imperialism is forced to acknowledge a violent fundamentalism. In *Mao II* (1991), a reclusive novelist named Bill Gray feels compelled to leave America and travels to civil war–torn Beirut, Lebanon, where a terrorist organization has taken a poet hostage in order to draw attention to its cause.

During this last novel, Bill comes to a moment of doubt about his own art form, saying:

> "There's a curious knot that binds novelists and terrorists. In the West we become famous effigies as our books lose the power to shape and influence.[...] Years ago I used to think it was possible for a novelist to alter the inner life of the culture. Now bomb-makers and gunmen have taken that territory. They make raids on human consciousness. What writers used to do before we were all incorporated." (41)

What the character Bill Gray worries about is something that concerns DeLillo as well. We live in an age of the media spectacle—with unrelenting hype over such corporate-sponsored events as the Super Bowl and the Victoria's Secret lingerie show—that overwhelms the news coverage of the U.S. wars in Afghanistan and Iraq. In such a media environment, terrorists today seem better able than the novelist to cut through the glut of digital images by producing terrible and horrific images of their own. Recall the non-stop media coverage of the events of 9/11, the way that we saw the planes flying into the towers again and again. It was horrifying, of course, that the terrorists used American airliners as weapons, but perhaps the greater technological horror was their using the various forms of our electronic media against us. By doing so, the terrorists effectively said, "You like spectacle? We'll give you spectacle." Part of the problem facing DeLillo in addressing 9/11 is that the terrorist has usurped the role of politicizing the image. If the avant-garde modernist hoped to shock the bourgeoisie, that is precisely the role that the terrorist plays in contemporary society.

Although DeLillo suspects that the novel (as well as, more broadly, narrative) may have outlived its usefulness as a form of cultural critique, he still writes novels. These novels of late, however, have begun to privilege the work of the performance artist as that outsider figure who might still produce a culturally significant aesthetic form that could compete with the terrorist. In *The Body Artist* (2001), a performance artist, Lauren Hartke, must come to terms with a personal trauma, the suicide of her husband, Rey Robles. A film auteur, Rey was sixty-four years old at the time of his death, the same age as DeLillo was when *The Body Artist* appeared. We might speculate about the extent to which Rey is DeLillo's fantasized self-portrait. In the obituary that appears in the novel for Robles, we discover that he had produced several films in the 1970s that used the conventions of the thriller, much as DeLillo's fiction from the 1970s did. Unlike DeLillo, however, Robles's later films "failed commercially" (29), enabling Rey to retain his status as an outsider artist, appreciated critically and by a cult following. What DeLillo almost seems to be acknowledging in his portrait of the artist as a suicide is that he can no longer legitimately claim the status of the outsider artist. After all, a writer who has experienced the commercial and critical success of *White Noise* in 1985, has won numerous literary awards, received a $1,000,000 advance for *Underworld*, and has a secure place in the canon of contemporary American literature is about as inside as one can get. But if he can no longer be the outsider artist, he can still imagine what that artist might look like. DeLillo, the wordsmith, envisions a gestural poetics in Lauren's performance piece called *Body Time*. The voices and fragments of language she includes do not create her meaning. Only by reshaping her body into a variety of male and female characters does she viscerally suggest the bodily tedium of time passing.

Terrorism as Aestheticism

In *Falling Man*, DeLillo again explores the way that art might still vie with terrorism in shaping the American imagination, only this time there is an uncanny sense in which terrorist acts, such as those of 9/11, resonate with performance art. DeLillo builds this correspondence into the very structure of his novel. The three major sections of *Falling Man* are each named for a man, but the names fail to identify correctly or fully: each points to mistaken, secret, or double identity. The first, "Bill Lawton," is simply a misunderstanding, how Keith and Lianne's son and his friends mishear the name "Bin Laden." The middle section, "Ernst Hechinger," is the real name of the art dealer who now goes by Martin Ridnour, an alias that leads to speculation regarding the extent of his involvement in the late 1960s-early 1970s with a left-wing movement that protested against fascist elements in the West German government. The final section, "David Janiak," is the actual name of the performance artist known as Falling Man. In the names of the three main sections, then, we have a terrorist, a political radical turned art dealer, and an artist. But in what sense and to what extent is DeLillo relating terrorism and art? If the terrorist has succeeded in politicizing aesthetics, what might the artist now learn from the terrorist?

Shortly after 9/11, the composer Karlheinz Stockhausen commented in the German press on the terrorist attacks in a fashion that eerily sounds like Bill Gray from *Mao II*. The *New York Times* on 19 September 2001 carried the translation of Stockhausen's remarks in which he called the destruction of the towers "the greatest work of art ever," marveling "[t]hat characters can bring about in one act what we in music cannot dream of, that people practice madly for 10 years, completely, fanatically, for a concert and then die. That is the greatest work of art for the whole cosmos. I could not do that. Against that, we, composers, are nothing" ("Attacks" E3). Stockhausen was roundly criticized for this comment, but DeLillo imagines another German who also sees the 9/11 destruction in terms of the sublime.

Because it is the middle section, "Ernst Hechinger" mediates between the sections named for a terrorist and an artist. Whether or not Martin had ties to the radical Red Army Faction that used terrorism to advance its politics, he is neither a terrorist now nor is he an artist, but he knows how to evaluate (both critically and monetarily) acts of terrorism and works of art. While not equating the act of flying planes into the towers with Marcel Duchamp's adding a moustache and goatee to da Vinci's *Mona Lisa*, Martin is not blind to the aesthetic symbolism of the destruction of the towers. As a European, Martin is an outsider—if not an outsider artist, then an outsider art theorist. What Martin's comments make clear is that the twin towers were not symbolically appropriate targets only because they were buildings in which businesses participated in the global flow of capital; they were equally symbolic as works of art. This is why Martin's view of art is more nuanced than that of his lover, Nina Bartos, the retired art history professor who is also Lianne's mother. Nina sees art only as a closed meaning-making system, while Martin, who makes his living buying and selling art, understands that art is also always embedded in capitalist exchange. The attack on the World Trade Center, in one sense, is an attack on aesthetics inasmuch as architecture is an art form, one more implicated in capitalism than any other because of the enormous amount of labor and material required to realize the architect's design as a material object. The twin towers, each nearly 1,400 feet tall, were designed by Minoru Yamasaki, who surely was making a statement about capitalism's power and aspiration.

In Martin's debate with Nina about the politics of terrorism, his final words comment on the towers as ruins:

> "But that's why you built the towers, isn't it? Weren't the towers built as fantasies of wealth and power that would one day become fantasies of destruction? You build a thing like that so you can see it come down. The provocation is obvious. What other reason would there be to go so high and then to double it, do it twice? It's a fantasy, so why not do it twice? You are saying, Here it is, bring it down." (116)

Martin's comments recall those of another provocateur, the French sociologist Jean Baudrillard, who in comments made on 23 February 2002 asks, "Why *two* towers at the World Trade Center?" (*Spirit* 42). For Baudrillard, the twin-ness signifies "the end of any original reference" (43) that engenders "a secret desire to see [the towers] disappear" (46). The twin towers were the perfect aesthetic realization of postmodern America, their very doubleness underscoring the notion of the simulacrum, for what tourist looking at them in early 2001 could have said which was the original (the North Tower, completed in 1970) and which the repetition (the South Tower, completed in 1971)? Baudrillard continues: "There is, admittedly, in this cloning and perfect symmetry an aesthetic quality, a kind of perfect crime against form, a tautology of form which can give rise, in a violent reaction, to the temptation to break that symmetry, to restore an asymmetry, and hence a singularity" (46).

The relation of terrorism to aesthetics is again underscored through the Morandi still life that Martin gave to Nina. In the aftermath of 9/11, the terrorist act seems to have granted Martin a moment of fresh perception. Looking at the painting, Martin finds he is "seeing the towers in this still life" (49). Lianne joins him and finds in the twinned darker objects a sense of the now-missing towers. In effect, the terrorist act, which destroys the towers, has had an uncannily similar effect to that of the truly new work of art, if we follow T. S. Eliot's argument in "Tradition and the Individual Talent" (1920). In this essay, Eliot articulates a non-linear model of influence. The new work of art does not simply grow out of what came before but fundamentally reshapes the way one sees previously canonical works. At this moment in DeLillo's novel, then, the terrorist act of destroying twinned architectural verticality means that, for Martin and Lianne at least, Morandi's representation of twinned verticality can no longer be viewed as it previously had. For Martin to comment on this painting in terms of 9/11 terrorism is to grant the terrorist a role similar to that of the artist.

Through "Ernst Hechinger" as the middle section and Martin Ridnour as a character, the perspective of the political radical, then, is marked as central to *Falling Man*'s conception of the artist and the problem of representation. One way that DeLillo invites us into what is at stake in representation is through disease. The Alzheimer's patients with whom Lianne works are also, figuratively speaking, falling men and women. As their disease advances, as the towers of their intellect crumble, they too fall into oblivion. Lianne guides these patients in a writing workshop in which they are invited to tell the stories of their lives. She does so even though the doctor who supervises her work tells her that there is no therapeutic value to this writing—it will not stave off the advance of Alzheimer's.

DeLillo's point, as I take it, is related to the act of writing narrative, whether it be journalism, history, or a novel. Can any narrative hope to heal the trauma of 9/11? No. But this is precisely why the attempt to make sense is so crucial. It is less about the product than the process if we are ever to process this trauma. In trying to address 9/11, DeLillo is working with a problem similar to the one that the theorist Theodor Adorno addresses in the aftermath of World War II when the enormity of the Holocaust became clear. For Adorno, "poetry after Auschwitz is barbaric" (34). The question Adorno raises is one about the role of aesthetics and the limitations of representation: How can the imaginary ever hope to address the horror of the historical images of the Holocaust? Without equating the Holocaust and 9/11, this is DeLillo's dilemma as well: How can a novel, or any artistic mediation, hope to engage adequately the horror of 9/11? As DeLillo puts it in "In the Ruins of the Future," "when the towers fell," the moment "was so vast and terrible that it was outside imagining even as it happened. [. . .] The event itself has no purchase on the mercies of analogy or simile" (39).

How can novelistic images ever compete with the digitally archived images of the event, especially when these images implicitly claim to document truthfully the events of 9/11?

Falling Angels

DeLillo's depiction of the performance artist known as Falling Man attempts to address these questions. Shortly after the destruction of the towers, a performance artist begins staging falls throughout Manhattan that recall the people who fell to their deaths from the towers. His unannounced falls are arrested by ropes and harnesses so that he hangs suspended in the attitude of free fall. With the trauma of 9/11 so fresh, Falling Man's art is an outrage. One might say that Falling Man is a terrorist of perception. Moreover, Falling Man's art resonates with other attempts to make these New York deaths the subject of art. The public outrage that attends Falling Man's performances mirrors in a number of ways the responses to two particular artists' attempts to memorialize the jumpers that were presented in New York on the first anniversary of 9/11.

The well-known contemporary artist Eric Fischl, who was born and lives in New York, created a bronze sculpture, titled *Tumbling Woman*, of a nude woman in free fall. Fischl did so explicitly to commemorate those who leapt to their deaths. In September of 2002, the Rockefeller Center contracted to display Fischl's statue for a two-week period, but a public outcry, fueled by a *New York Post* columnist, led to the almost immediate suppression of Fischl's statue: Rockefeller Center officials first covered it in cloth and placed a screen around the statue so that no one could see it and then removed the statue on 18 September (see Gillmore for more details). At the same time, the artist Sharon Paz exhibited a work called *Falling*; it consisted of numerous cutout silhouettes, all in different attitudes of free fall, that were placed in the windows of the Jamaica Center for the Arts. As Paz has noted, she "found the images of people falling the most disturbing and wanted to deal with them" in the hope that her art might "bring out the reality within the memory that this event burns into our mind" (par. 3). The piece was supposed to be on view from 11 September 2002 until 5 October, but, as was the fate of Fischl's statue, negative media attention caused Jamaica Center officials to remove Paz's exhibit two weeks early (Swartz 87–89).

If DeLillo's depiction of another edgy artist who portrays the 9/11 jumpers seems like a meditation on the repression of Fischl's and Paz's work, things take an even stranger turn: DeLillo's fictional performance artist known as Falling Man is anticipated by a real-life falling man. Kerry Skarbakka is a performance artist fascinated by falling, but the falls he stages are at least as much about the photographs he takes of his falls. He has photographed himself falling down stairs, out of a tree, in the shower, and off a railroad trestle. (He positions the camera for composition and has someone else take the photograph.) Skarbakka's interest in falling began after his horror at seeing the images of people falling on 9/11. On 14 June 2005, Skarbakka staged perhaps his most spectacular (and certainly his most controversial) performance, one that deliberately attempted to memorialize 9/11, by doing a series of thirty falls from the roof of the five-story-high Museum of Contemporary Art in Chicago as various photographers captured images of his falls on film. (As with all of Skarbakka's photographs, the wires and pulleys that prevent him from hurting himself were then digitally removed.) The resulting series of images forms a work titled *Life Goes On* (Figure 10.1).

As Skarbakka explained a few days before his Chicago performance, "I wanted to be able to respond intelligently, conceptually, responsibly to what was going on" and that if he could not address 9/11 he would "make an exodus from the world of making art" (Marlan 29). Given his previous work, Skarbakka was surprised by the hostile response from the New York press—a *New York Daily News* headline, for example, screamed "KICK HIM IN THE ARTS" and Mayor Michael Bloomberg

Figure 10.1   Kerry Skarbakka, "Onlookers," from *Life Goes On* © 2005. Courtesy of the Artist.

called Skarbakka's performance "nauseatingly offensive" (Camper A39). It is in fact the negative press that Skarbakka received that makes the link between his work and that of DeLillo's character seem less than coincidental. DeLillo represents a newspaper headline that echoes the negative response to Skarbakka: "MAYOR SAYS FALL MAN MORONIC" (222).

The differences, however, between Skarbakka's falls and those DeLillo imagines for his character, David Janiak, are crucial. In fact, in writing Janiak's obituary, DeLillo seems to highlight the differences between these falling men. Although both Skarbakka and Janiak are denounced for their performances, Skarbakka is not the kind of outsider artist that DeLillo celebrates. In Chicago, Skarbakka willingly talks to the press about the meaning and intentions of his work; Janiak (like DeLillo in the 1970s) will not talk to reporters. Skarbakka publicly apologizes for any offense he may have given; Janiak, once again, has no comment for the press. Skarbakka, whose work is often supported by grants from various foundations, announces his falls from the Museum of Contemporary Art and encourages people to come and watch his performance; Janiak's performances are unannounced, and he turns down an offer from the Guggenheim Museum to stage a jump from its roof when his work's merit finally begins to be recognized.

Ultimately, what the differences between DeLillo's character Janiak and the real-life artist Skarbakka illustrate is that the same act—staging a fall that is modeled on the 9/11 jumpers—may produce art with radically different effects and aesthetics. As is the case of Eric Fischl's and Sharon Paz's art, Skarbakka's remains largely representational. People who find these artists' work objectionable can only understand that its referent is the people who jumped from the World Trade Center. Janiak's art also depends on the 9/11 jumpers as an intertext, but his art is not primarily representational; rather, it carries with it an element of witness precisely because of its effect on his unsuspecting audience: Janiak's art, in other words, allows his viewers themselves to become witnesses of the horror. Rather than simply represent what happened when people jumped from the World Trade Center, Janiak's art extends the moment of 9/11 into the present. By doing so, DeLillo suggests that his imagined performance artist creates an art commensurate with the tragedy. Janiak, as we learn, had planned a final jump without ropes and harnesses, so that this ultimate act—suicide-as-performance—would have further erased the distance between art and the deaths of the 9/11 jumpers.

Lianne twice happens to see Falling Man's performances. The first time she does not actually see him fall but only sees him dangling in his safety harness. Seeing only the result, she finds it simply a "little theater piece" (33). The second time, however, Lianne witnesses all of Falling Man's unannounced performance, one that she does not initially understand to be a performance as Janiak prepares to make his jump. This time, Janiak's art removes for Lianne all distance between reenactment and the actual horrific moment when people chose to jump rather than burn to death. Watching him prepare to jump for an audience that will consist mainly of commuters on a passing train, Lianne has a discomfiting foreknowledge of the horrified responses of those who will not have seen Falling Man attach his safety harness, a foreknowledge that makes witnessing the event almost unbearable, yet her helpless compulsion will not allow her to look away. After Janiak's fall, Lianne panics and runs in terror. For her, then, witnessing Falling Man's full performance is not a representation of the horror of 9/11, it is the horror of 9/11 itself.

Three years later, Lianne happens to read Janiak's obituary and realizes that the way he shaped his body in his falls was "intended to reflect the body posture of a particular man who was photographed falling from the North Tower of the World Trade Center" (221). In this moment, DeLillo makes clear what Janiak has been doing. He has been staging the forbidden image of 9/11 (Figure 10.2), the photograph that

Figure 10.2 A person falls from the North Tower on Tuesday, 11 September 2001, after terrorists crash two hijacked airliners into the World Trade Center. AP Photo/Richard Drew. Used by permission.

ran on 12 September 2001 in the *New York Times* and in newspapers around the country.

Janiak's death causes Lianne to remember her initial response to the image:

> It hit her hard when she first saw it, the day after, in the newspaper. The man headlong, the towers behind him. [. . .] The enormous soaring lines, the vertical column stripes. The man with blood on his shirt, [. . .] or burn marks, and the effect of the columns behind him, the composition, she thought, darker stripes for the nearer tower, the north, the lighter for the other, and the mass, the immensity of it, and the man set almost precisely between the rows of darker and lighter stripes. Headlong, free fall, she thought, and this picture burned a hole in her mind and heart, dear God, he was a falling angel and his beauty was horrific. (221–22)

This photograph was taken by the AP photographer Richard Drew. It caused a hue and cry from newspaper readers on the grounds that this image was immoral, a voyeuristic invasion of the privacy of a man just moments before his death. Tom Junod wrote a fascinating essay, "The Falling Man," on this photo that appeared in *Esquire* on the second anniversary of 9/11. Because of this essay, Drew's image now is commonly known as "Falling Man." The man in the image cannot be positively identified, but Junod's investigation led him to suggest that it is Jonathan Briley, who was an employee at the Windows on the World restaurant, located at the top of the North Tower. Save for Junod's essay, Drew's photo has been strangely absent in the American print media since 12 September 2001, but its presence on the web is maintained by a variety of sources.

The prohibition against viewing Drew's photo is particularly odd in light of Susan Sontag's observations in her final book, *Regarding the Pain of Others*, her meditation on the depiction of death, torture, and war in photography and art. As she notes (and discusses through copious canonical examples from the twentieth century): "To catch a death actually happening and embalm it for all time is something only cameras can do, and pictures taken by photographers out in the field of the moment of (or just before) death are among the most celebrated and often reproduced" (59). Sontag's point is something Drew implicitly has noticed himself. In an article that he wrote at the two-year anniversary of 9/11, he notes: "As a 21-year-old rookie photographer on a supposedly routine assignment, I was standing behind Robert F. Kennedy when he was assassinated. That time, there was no telephoto lens to distance me.

Figure 10.3 The Winecoff Hotel fire in Atlanta, Georgia, 7 December 1946. AP Photo/*Atlanta Journal-Constitution*, Arnold Hardy. Used by permission.

I was so close that his blood spattered onto my jacket. I saw the life bleed out of him, and I heard Ethel's screams. Pictures that, shot through my tears, still distress me after 35 years. But nobody refused to print them, as they did the 9/11 photo. Nobody looked away" (Drew par. 13). Yet how does Drew's "Falling Man" differ, for example, from the Pulitzer Prize–winning photograph by Arnold Hardy of the 1946 fire at the Winecoff Hotel in Atlanta, Georgia (Figure 10.3)—a disaster that killed 119 people, more than any other hotel fire in U.S. history? Most of the dead jumped from the building. Hardy's photo of what we might call "Falling Woman" appeared in newspapers throughout the country. Arnold Hardy wins a Pulitzer, while Richard Drew is reviled as nothing short of a pornographer. Wherein lies the difference?

The answer has something to do with the fact that the Atlanta fire was local and specific. A supposedly fireproof hotel that becomes engulfed in flames is simply a failure of technology, rather like the sinking of the supposedly unsinkable *Titanic,* and, as Hollywood has repeatedly told us with its many film versions, it's perfectly acceptable to be fascinated by *that* disaster. 9/11, however, is different. Far from specific to New York, the collapse of the twin towers directly impacts America's sense of privilege, power, and global supremacy. To be the falling woman is simply to be unlucky—she's just in the wrong place at the wrong time; the falling man of Richard Drew's photograph, by contrast, seems to be, in an almost immediate way, bespeaking the end of the American dream of unassailable global supremacy in the post–Cold War era—or it might if it were not forbidden to view it.

But changes in camera technology between 1946 and 2001 point to another difference between Hardy's and Drew's images that complicates the preceding sense of their difference. There is a danger that Drew's 9/11 image could be reduced to a mere aesthetic object. "Falling Man," as Lianne notes, is strikingly beautiful, and if one did not know the context, one might almost suspect, given its stunning sense of composition, that the image was contrived as part of some high-concept advertisement for a magazine like the *New Yorker*—or that perhaps it was another example of the carefully planned work of photographer/performance artist Skarbakka. The aestheticism of Drew's image is precisely why Junod reproduces not only the iconic "Falling Man" photo in his essay but the eleven other shots that Drew had taken during the approximately fifteen seconds of the man's fall. As Junod powerfully notes:

> Photographs lie. Even great photographs. Especially great photographs. The Falling Man in Richard Drew's picture fell in the manner suggested by the photograph for only a fraction of a second, and then kept falling. The photograph functioned as a study of doomed verticality, a fantasia of straight lines, with a human being slivered at the center, like a spike. In truth, however, the Falling Man fell with neither the precision of an arrow nor the grace of an Olympic diver. He fell like everyone else, like all the other jumpers—trying to hold on to the life he was leaving, which is to say that he fell desperately, inelegantly. In Drew's famous photograph, his humanity is in accord with the lines of the buildings. In the rest of the sequence—the eleven outtakes—his humanity stands apart. He is not augmented by aesthetics; he is merely human, and his humanity, startled and in some cases horizontal, obliterates everything else in the frame. (180–81)

To what extent, however, is Drew's published photo simply a "lie" that is "augmented by aesthetics"? Discussing the dual powers of photography, Sontag seems almost to be commenting critically on Junod's response to Drew's "Falling Man":

> Transforming is what art does, but photography that bears witness to the calamitous and the reprehensible is much criticized if it seems "aesthetic"; that is, too much like art. The dual powers of photography—to generate documents and to create works of visual art—have produced some remarkable exaggerations about what photographers ought or ought not to do. Lately, the most common exaggeration is one that regards these powers as opposites. Photographs that depict suffering shouldn't be beautiful, as captions shouldn't moralize. In this view, a beautiful photograph drains attention from the sobering subject and turns it toward the medium itself, thereby compromising the picture's status as a document. (76–77)

Junod, then, is a prime example of someone who firmly opposes the aesthetic and the documentary elements of Drew's twelve photographs. For Junod, "great photographs" are great because they are art; only bad photos bear documentary truth. If we take seriously Junod's opposition, what exactly constitutes the "greatness" of Drew's "Falling Man"? It is not as though Drew digitally enhanced the published photo to make it more visually pleasing. However, the amateur photographer Arnold Hardy had only one flash bulb left when he took his photo of the falling woman, and even if he had had more, given the limitations of his camera, he could not have sequenced her fall as Drew did that of his falling man. The aesthetic element of "Falling Man" is precisely Drew's ability to select his image from among the dozen in this sequence. And with a trained photographer's eye, Drew selected the image with the most striking sense of composition and symmetry. To this extent, then, Drew's "Falling Man" is already a work of art, an aesthetic, transformative rendering of the experience of the 9/11 jumpers and thus of a piece with the representational work of Eric Fischl and Sharon Paz.

DeLillo's photographer in *Mao II*, Brita Nilsson, is certainly aware of this tension in the photographic image; for her, however, Junod's opposition does not hold. Before deciding to concentrate on portraiture, she used to photograph the urban dispossessed but found that "[n]o matter what [she] shot, how much horror, reality, misery, ruined bodies, bloody faces, it was all so fucking pretty in the end" (24–25). The documentary element of the photograph ("horror, reality, misery") is never absolute because there is never a zero-degree of aesthetics ("pretty") in the photographic image. Yet to the extent that Drew's "Falling Man" is a work of art, does this mean that *Falling Man*'s Lianne has bought into its lie?

Does she recall and (mis)interpret the wrong image? Perhaps, but it does not necessarily follow that Drew's rejected images are the bearers of unmediated truth; each of the other images arrests a fall and depicts an event that no eyewitness would ever have apprehended. By their very immobility, Drew's unpublished images, to invoke Junod's claim, are aesthetic lies as well, even if lesser lies to the extent that they are lesser photographs because they are lesser works of art.

Motion, then, is something that DeLillo's Falling Man restores to the aesthetic meditation on 9/11. Janiak's art combines the chilling sense of falling, a continuity that cannot be perceived as a discrete series of sequenced moments, with the power of Drew's photograph to arrest that same motion. In the disturbing, transgressive art that DeLillo's performance artist Falling Man produces, an art that invokes (and perhaps transcends) Drew's forbidden image of 9/11, the possibility for a degree of healing arises. In imagining Janiak's art, DeLillo is metafictionally commenting on the limitations of, and his desire for, his own narrative art. Janiak's art, like DeLillo's, does not produce a final healing of the wound of 9/11 but probes at hidden recesses of our memories. For Lianne, Falling Man's art, whether definable as truth or lie, ultimately provides a small bit of solace. After experiencing the terror of Janiak's performance, Lianne finds she is able to forgive her father for his decision to commit suicide when he learned that he had Alzheimer's.

What Falling Man's performance and Lianne's reception underscore is the gap between the artistically mediated response to trauma and the individual reception of such a work of art. Even if the work of art (Falling Man's performance) bypasses representation and functions as a form of witness, the individual (such as Lianne) who encounters the work of art is still an individual, not a collectivity. As such, the individual is not solely constituted by some collective trauma but is already the bearer of previous private traumas. This is equally true for the traumatized artist as it is for the traumatized audience and suggests why, in *The Body Artist*, Lauren Hartke has to correct an interviewer's assumption regarding the genesis of *Body Time*: "How simple it would be if I could say this is a piece that comes directly out of what happened to Rey. [...] I want to say that but I can't. It's too small and secluded and complicated and I can't and I can't and I can't" (108–09). Because our multiple traumas interact (overlap, reinforce, or diverge), any particular artist's response to 9/11 or viewer's reaction to such art is radically unpredictable. This is why, even if there is such a thing as collective trauma, there will never be any work of art that can collectively heal this trauma.

In his recent novel, DeLillo adds to the growing list of novelists, which includes Jonathan Safran Foer, Ian McEwan, and John Updike, who have risked exploring the psychological trauma that remains with us more than nine years after the terrorist attacks on New York and Washington. DeLillo's work undoubtedly will not be the last novel to try to make sense of 9/11, but it is one that reminds us that if we are ever to awaken from the nightmare of history, we must lose our political innocence and try to imagine that those who oppose the United States are more than unthinking brutes who irrationally hate democracy. Our innocence, DeLillo suggests, is maintained when we turn away from the disturbing images of 9/11 rather than confront them. What DeLillo asks us to remember is that images—whether identified as documentary or aesthetic—crucially matter, and his performance artist known as Falling Man invites our reflection on the images of 9/11, since they may be all that ever will allow us a partial glimpse into trauma's unknowing.

Works Cited

Adams, Henry. *The Education of Henry Adams.* 1906. Boston, MA: Houghton Mifflin, 1961.

Adorno, Theodor W. "Cultural Criticism and Society." 1949. Rpt. in *Prisms.* Trans. Samuel and Shierry Weber. London: Neville Spearman, 1967. 17–34.

Agamben, Giorgio. *Homo Sacer: Sovereign Power and Bare Life.* Trans. Daniel Heller-Roazen. Stanford, CA: Stanford UP, 1998. Trans. of *Homo sacer: il potere sovrano e la nuda vita.* 1995.

Appiah, Kwame Anthony. *Cosmopolitanism: Ethics in a World of Strangers.* New York: Norton, 2006.

Aquinas, S. Thomas. *Catena Aurea: Commentary on the Four Gospels, Collected out of the Works of the Fathers.* Vol. 4, Pt. 1. Oxford: John Henry Parker, 1841. <http://www.archive.org/details/catenaaureacomme04thom>.

—. *The "Summa Theologica" of St. Thomas Aquinas.* Pt. 2, 1st Pt. Trans. Fathers of the English Dominican Province. 1915. London: Burns Oates and Washbourne, 1927.

Arendt, Hannah. *The Origins of Totalitarianism.* 1951. New York: Harcourt, 1973.

Ash, Timothy Garton. "1989 Was a Very Good Year." *Los Angeles Times* 5 Nov. 2009. <http://www.latimes.com/news/opinion/la-oe-gartonash5-2009nov05,0,5820196.story>.

—. "Attacks Called Great Art." *New York Times* 19 Sept. 2001, late ed.: E3.

Auster, Paul. *Leviathan.* 1992. New York: Penguin, 1993.

Ballard, J. G. "Build-Up." *New Worlds* 19.55 (Jan. 1957). Rpt. as "The Concentration City." *The Complete Stories of J. G. Ballard.* New York: Norton, 2009. 23–38.

Barolini, Teodolinda. *The Undivine Comedy: Detheologizing Dante.* Princeton, NJ: Princeton UP, 1992.

Baudrillard, Jean. *America.* Trans. Chris Turner. 1988. London: Verso, 1989. Trans. of *Amérique.* 1986.

—. "L'Esprit du terrorisme." Trans. Donovan Holn. *Harper's* Feb. 2002: 13–18.

—. *The Spirit of Terrorism and Requiem for the Twin Towers.* Trans. Chris Turner. London: Verso, 2002.

Begley, Adam. "The Art of Fiction CXXXV." *Paris Review* 128 (1993): 274–306.

—. "Don DeLillo: *Americana, Mao II,* and *Underworld.*" *Southwest Review* 82 (1997): 478–505.

Benjamin, Walter. "Edward Fuchs, Collector and Historian." *Selected Writings, Volume 3: 1935–1938.* Ed. Howard Eiland and Michael W. Jennings. Trans. Edmund Jephcott, Howard Eiland, et al. Cambridge, MA: Harvard UP, 2002. 260–302.

Bercovitch, Sacvan. *The American Jeremiad*. Madison, WI: U of Wisconsin P, 1978.

Billen, Andrew. "Up from the Underworld." *London Evening Standard* 28 Jan. 1998: 25–26.

Boxall, Peter. *Don DeLillo: The Possibility of Fiction*. London: Routledge, 2006.

Bush, George H. W. "Address Before a Joint Session of the Congress on the Cessation of the Persian Gulf Conflict." 6 Mar. 1991. <http://bushlibrary. tamu.edu/research/public_papers.php?id=2767&year=1991&month=3>.

—. "Address Before a Joint Session of the Congress on the Persian Gulf Crisis and the Federal Budget Deficit." 11 Sept. 1990. <http://bushlibrary.tamu.edu/ research/public_papers.php?id=2217&year=1990&month=9>.

Calvino, Italo. *Invisible Cities*. Trans. William Weaver. New York: Harvest-Harcourt, 1974. Trans of *Le città invisibili*. 1972.

Camper, Fred. "Life Goes On: Is Art Defaming 9/11 Deaths?" *New York Newsday* 10 July 2005, early ed.: A39.

Campkin, Ben, and Rosie Cox, eds. *Dirt: New Geographies of Cleanliness and Contamination*. London: I. B. Tauris, 2007.

Cohen, William A. "Locating Filth." *Filth: Dirt, Disgust, and Modern Life*. Ed. William A. Cohen and Ryan Johnson. Minneapolis, MN: U of Minnesota P, 2005. vii–xxxvii.

Cohen, William A., and Ryan Johnson, eds. *Filth: Dirt, Disgust, and Modern Life*. Minneapolis, MN: U of Minnesota P, 2005.

Colie, Rosalie L. *Paradoxia Epidemica: The Renaissance Tradition of Paradox*. Princeton, NJ: Princeton UP, 1966.

Coover, Robert. *The Public Burning*. 1977. New York: Bantam, 1978.

Cousins, Norman. "Modern Man Is Obsolete." *Saturday Review of Literature* 18 Aug. 1945: 5–9.

Cowart, David. *Don DeLillo: The Physics of Language*. Athens, GA: U of Georgia P, 2002.

D'Acierno, Pellegrino, comp. "Cultural Lexicon: Italian American Key Terms." *The Italian American Heritage: A Companion to Literature and Arts*. Ed. Pellegrino D'Acierno. New York: Garland, 1999. 703–66.

Danielewski, Mark Z. *House of Leaves*. New York: Pantheon, 2000.

Debord, Guy. *The Society of the Spectacle*. Trans. Donald Nicholson-Smith. 1994. New York: Zone, 1995. Trans. of *La société du spectacle*. 1967.

DeCurtis, Anthony. "'An Outsider in This Society': An Interview with Don DeLillo." *Introducing Don DeLillo*. Ed. Frank Lentricchia. Durham, NC: Duke UP, 1991. 43–66.

DeLillo, Don. *Americana*. Boston, MA: Houghton Mifflin, 1971.

—. "American Blood: A Journey through the Labyrinth of Dallas and JFK." *Rolling Stone* 8 Dec. 1983: 21–22, 24, 27–28, 74.

—. *The Body Artist*. New York: Scribner, 2001.

—. *Cosmopolis*. New York: Scribner, 2003.

—. *End Zone*. Boston, MA: Houghton Mifflin, 1972.

—. *Falling Man*. New York: Scribner, 2007.

—. *Great Jones Street*. Boston, MA: Houghton Mifflin, 1973.

—. "In the Ruins of the Future: Reflections on Terror and Loss in the Shadow of September." *Harper's* Dec. 2001: 33–40.

—. *Libra*. New York: Viking, 1988.

—. *Love-Lies-Bleeding: A Play*. New York: Scribner, 2005.

—. *Mao II*. New York: Viking, 1991.

—. "Midnight in Dostoevsky." *New Yorker* 30 Nov. 2009: 68–77.

—. *The Names*. New York: Knopf, 1982.

—. *Players*. New York: Knopf, 1977.

—. *Point Omega*. New York: Scribner, 2010.

—. "The Power of History." *New York Times Magazine* 7 Sept. 1997: 60–63.

—. *Running Dog*. New York: Knopf, 1978.

—. *Underworld*. New York: Scribner, 1997.

—. *White Noise*. New York: Viking, 1985.

De Palma, Brian, dir. *The Untouchables*. Paramount, 1987.

Derrida, Jacques. *Specters of Marx: The State of Debt, the Work of Mourning, and the New International*. Trans. Peggy Kamuf. New York: Routledge, 1994. Trans. of *Spectres de Marx*. 1993.

Desalm, Brigitte. "Masses, Power and the Elegance of Sentences." Trans. Tilo Zimmerman. *Kölner Stadt-Anzeiger* 27 Oct. 1992. Trans. of "Masse, Macht und die Eleganz der Saetze." 5 Jan. 2010 <http://perival.com/delillo/desalm_interview.html>.

Dewey, John. *Art as Experience*. 1934. New York: Perigee-Penguin, 1980.

Dewey, Joseph. *Beyond Grief and Nothing: A Reading of Don DeLillo*. Columbia, SC: U of South Carolina P, 2006.

—. "DeLillo's Apocalyptic Satires." *The Cambridge Companion to Don DeLillo*. Ed. John N. Duvall. Cambridge: Cambridge UP, 2008. 53–65.

Didion, Joan. *The White Album*. 1979. New York: Farrar, 1990.

Dos Passos, John. *U.S.A.* 3 vols. 1938. New York: Modern Library-Random, n.d.

Dostoevsky, Fyodor. *The Possessed*. 1872. Trans. Andrew R. MacAndrew. New York: Signet, 1962.

Douglas, Mary. *Purity and Danger: An Analysis of the Concepts of Pollution and Taboo*. 1966. London: ARK-Routledge, 1984.

Drew, Richard. "The Horror of 9/11 That's All Too Familiar." *Los Angeles Times* 10 Sept. 2003: B13+. Rpt. Los Angeles Times On-Line. 27 Aug. 2009 <http://articles.latimes.com/2003/sep/10/opinion/oe-drew10>.

Duvall, John N. *Don DeLillo's* Underworld: *A Reader's Guide*. New York: Continuum, 2002.

—. "The Power of History and the Persistence of Mystery." *The Cambridge Companion to Don DeLillo*. Ed. John N. Duvall. Cambridge: Cambridge UP, 2008. 1–10.

Echlin, Kim. "Baseball and the Cold War." *Ottawa Citizen* 28 Dec. 1997: E5. Rpt. in *Conversations with Don DeLillo*. Ed. Thomas DePietro. Jackson, MS: UP of Mississippi, 2005. 145–51.

Eco, Umberto. *The Aesthetics of Thomas Aquinas*. Trans. Hugh Bredin. Cambridge, MA: Harvard UP, 1988. Trans. of *Il problema estetico in Tommaso d'Aquino*. 1970.

Eliot, T[homas] S[tearns]. "The Love Song of J. Alfred Prufrock." 1917. *Modern Poetry*. 2nd ed. Ed. Maynard Mack, Leonard Dean, and William Frost. Englewood Cliffs, NJ: Prentice-Hall, 1961. 130–34.

—. *The Waste Land*. 1922. *Collected Poems 1909–1962*. London: Faber, 1963. 62–86.

Emerson, Ralph Waldo. "Compensation." 1841. *The Complete Essays and Other Writings of Ralph Waldo Emerson*. Ed. Brooks Atkinson. New York: Modern Library-Random, 1950. 170–89.

—. "Concord Hymn." 1837. *The Complete Essays and Other Writings of Ralph Waldo Emerson*. Ed. Brooks Atkinson. New York: Modern Library-Random, 1950. 783.

Evans, David H. "Taking Out the Trash: Don DeLillo's *Underworld*, Liquid Modernity, and the End of Garbage." *Cambridge Quarterly* 35 (2006). 103–32.

Faulkner, William. *The Wild Palms*. New York: Vintage-Random, 1939.

Fiedler, Leslie A. "McCarthy and the Intellectuals." *Encounter* Aug. 1954. Rpt. in *An End to Innocence: Essays on Culture and Politics*. 1955. 2nd ed. New York: Stein and Day, 1972. 46–87.

Fitzgerald, F. Scott. *The Great Gatsby*. New York: Scribner's, 1925.

Foer, Jonathan Safran. *Extremely Loud and Incredibly Close*. Boston, MA: Houghton Mifflin, 2005.

Frank, Robert, dir. *Cocksucker Blues*. Unreleased, 1972.

Franzen, Jonathan. "Perchance to Dream." *Harper's* Apr. 1996: 35–54. Rpt. as "Why Bother?" *How to Be Alone: Essays*. New York: Farrar, 2002. 55–97.

Frost, Robert. "The Constant Symbol." *Atlantic Monthly* Oct. 1946: 50. *Robert Frost: Collected Poems, Prose, and Plays*. Ed. Richard Poirier and Mark Richardson. New York: Library of America, 1995. 786–91.

—. "Conversations on the Craft of Poetry." 1959. *Robert Frost: Collected Poems, Prose, and Plays*. Ed. Richard Poirier and Mark Richardson. New York: Library of America, 1995. 853–59.

—. "Mending Wall." *North of Boston*. 1914. *Robert Frost: Collected Poems, Prose, and Plays*. Ed. Richard Poirier and Mark Richardson. New York: Library of America, 1995. 39–40.

Fukuyama, Francis. "The End of History?" *The National Interest* 16 (Summer 1989): 3–18.

Fussell, Paul. *Class: A Guide through the American Status System*. New York: Simon and Schuster, 1983.

Giddens, Anthony. *Runaway World: How Globalization Is Reshaping Our Lives*. 1999. New York: Routledge, 2000.

Gillmore, Alison. "9/11: How Artists Have Responded: Freefall: The Story of Eric Fischl's *Tumbling Woman*." Canadian Broadcast Corporation 8 Sept. 2006. 24 June 2009 <http://www.cbc.ca/arts/artdesign/tumbling.html>.

Goldberg, Vicki. "Photos That Lie—and Tell the Truth." *New York Times* 16 Mar. 1997, sec. 2: 1, 34.

Goldman, Eric F. *The Crucial Decade—and After: America, 1945–1960*. New York: Vintage-Random, 1960.

Graham, Gordon. *The Re-enchantment of the World: Art versus Religion*. New York: Oxford UP, 2007.

Hardack, Richard. "Two's a Crowd: *Mao II*, Coke II, and the Politics of Terrorism in Don DeLillo." *Studies in the Novel* 36 (2004): 374–92.

Hardt, Michael, and Antonio Negri. *Empire*. Cambridge, MA: Harvard UP, 2000.

Hass, Robert. "Meditation at Lagunitas." *Praise*. New York: Ecco Press, 1979. 4–5.

Hassan, Steven Alan. "Steven Alan Hassan's Freedom of Mind Center." <http://www.freedomofmind.com/>.

Helyer, Ruth. "DeLillo and Masculinity." *The Cambridge Companion to Don DeLillo*. Ed. John N. Duvall. Cambridge: Cambridge UP, 2008. 125–36.

Howard, Gerald. "The American Strangeness: An Interview with Don DeLillo." *The Hungry Mind* 47 (1997): 13–16. Rpt. in *Conversations with Don DeLillo*. Ed. Thomas DePietro. Jackson, MS: UP of Mississippi, 2005. 119–30.

Hungerford, Amy. "Don DeLillo's Latin Mass." *Contemporary Literature* 47 (2006): 343–80.

Hurston, Zora Neale. "How It Feels to Be Colored Me." *The World Tomorrow* 11 (May 1928): 216. *I Love Myself When I Am Laughing . . . And Then Again When I Am Looking Mean and Impressive: A Zora Neale Hurston Reader*. Ed. Alice Walker. Old Westbury, NY: Feminist Press, 1979. 152–55.

Jaeckin, Just, dir. *Emmanuelle*. Parafrance, 1974.

James, Henry. "The Beast in the Jungle." *The Better Sort*. New York: Scribner's, 1903. 189–244.

—. *The Portrait of a Lady*. 1881. New York: Washington Square, 1966.

Jameson, Fredric. *Postmodernism, or, The Cultural Logic of Late Capitalism*. Durham, NC: Duke UP, 1991.

Johnston, William, ed. *The Cloud of Unknowing and the Book of Privy Counseling*. New York: Image-Doubleday, 1996.

Joyce, James. *Finnegans Wake*. 1939. New York: Penguin-Viking, 1976.

—. *Stephen Hero*. Ed. Theodore Spencer. 1944. New York: New Directions, 1955.

—. *Ulysses*. 1922. New York: Vintage-Random, 1961.

Junod, Tom. "The Falling Man." *Esquire* Sept. 2002: 177–81, 198–99.

Kauffman, Linda S. "The Wake of Terror: Don DeLillo's 'In the Ruins of the Future,' 'Baader-Meinhof,' and *Falling Man*." *Modern Fiction Studies* 54 (2008): 353–77.

—. "World Trauma Center." *American Literary History* 21 (2009): 647–59.

Kelly, Walt. *The Pogo Papers*. New York: Simon and Schuster, 1953.

Kierkegaard, Søren. *Philosophical Fragments or A Fragment of Philosophy*. Trans. David F. Swenson. Princeton, NJ: Princeton UP, 1962.

Knight, Peter. "Everything Is Connected: *Underworld*'s Secret History of Paranoia." *Modern Fiction Studies* 45 (1999): 811–36.

Kubrick, Stanley, dir. *Dr. Strangelove or: How I Learned to Stop Worrying and Love the Bomb*. Columbia, 1964.

Lawrence, Frederick G. "Lonergan and Aquinas: The Postmodern Problematic of Theology and Ethics." *The Ethics of Aquinas*. Ed. Stephen J. Pope. Washington, DC: Georgetown UP, 2002. 437–55.

LeClair, T[h]om[as]. "An Interview with Don DeLillo." *Contemporary Literature* 23 (1982): 19–31.

—. "An Underhistory of Mid-Century America." *Atlantic* Oct. 1997: 113–16.

Lukács, Georg. *The Historical Novel.* Trans. Hannah and Stanley Mitchell. 1962. Boston, MA: Beacon, 1963. Trans. of *A történelmi regény.* 1937.

Lyotard, Jean-François. *The Postmodern Condition: A Report on Knowledge.* Trans. Geoff Bennington and Brian Massumi. Minneapolis, MN: U of Minnesota P, 1984. Trans. of *La Condition postmoderne: rapport sur le savoir.* 1979.

Macdonald, Dwight. "A Theory of Mass Culture." *Diogenes* 3 (Summer 1953): 1–17. Rpt. in *Mass Culture: The Popular Arts in America.* Ed. Bernard Rosenberg and David Manning White. 1957. New York: Free-Macmillan, 1964. 59–73.

Mailer, Norman. *The Armies of the Night: History as a Novel/The Novel as History.* New York: Signet-NAL, 1968.

—. *Barbary Shore.* New York: Signet-NAL, 1951.

—. "Superman Comes to the Supermart." *Esquire* Nov. 1960: 119–27. Rpt. as "Superman Comes to the Supermarket." *The Presidential Papers.* 1963. New York: Berkley Medallion, 1970. 25–61.

Marlan, Tori. "To Leap without Faith." *Chicago Reader* 10 June 2005, sec. 1: 1, 28–29.

Marsh, James, dir. *Man on Wire.* Magnolia, 2008.

Mather, Israel. "The Mystery of Israel's Salvation." 1667. *The Puritans in America: A Narrative Anthology.* Ed. Alan Heimert and Andrew Delbanco. Cambridge, MA: Harvard UP, 1985. 237–46.

McClure, John A. "DeLillo and Mystery." *The Cambridge Companion to Don DeLillo.* Ed. John N. Duvall. Cambridge: Cambridge UP, 2008. 166–78.

—. *Late Imperial Romance.* London: Verso, 1994.

—. *Partial Faiths: Postsecular Fiction in the Age of Pynchon and Morrison.* Athens, GA: U of Georgia P, 2007.

McMinn, Robert. "*Underworld*: Sin and Atonement." *UnderWords: Perspectives on DeLillo's Underworld.* Ed. Joseph Dewey, Steven G. Kellman, and Irving Malin. Newark, DE: U of Delaware P, 2002. 37–49.

Moraru, Christian. *Cosmodernism: American Narrative, Late Globalization, and the New Cultural Imaginary.* Ann Arbor, MI: U of Michigan P, 2010.

Moss, Maria. "'Writing as a Deeper Form of Concentration': An Interview with Don DeLillo." *Sources* (Spring 1999): 85–97. Rpt. in *Conversations with Don DeLillo.* Ed. Thomas DePietro. Jackson, MS: UP of Mississippi, 2005. 155–68.

Murakami, Haruki. *The Wind-Up Bird Chronicle.* Trans. Jay Rubin. New York: Knopf, 1997. Trans. of *Nejimaki-dori kuronikuru.* 1994, 1995.

Nabokov, Vladimir. "On a Book Entitled *Lolita.*" 12 Nov. 1956. Appendix. *Lolita.* 1955. New York: Berkley, 1977. 282–88.

Nadel, Ira. "The Baltimore Catechism; or Comedy in *Underworld.*" *UnderWords: Perspectives on Don DeLillo's Underworld.* Ed. Joseph Dewey, Steven G. Kellman, and Irving Malin. Newark, DE: U of Delaware P, 2002. 176–98.

Nadotti, Maria. "An Interview with Don DeLillo." *Salmagundi* 100 (1993): 86–97.

Nichols, Mike, dir. *The Graduate.* Embassy, 1967.

Norris, Frank. *The Octopus.* 1901. New York: Penguin, 1986.

O'Connor, Flannery. "Writing Short Stories." *Mystery and Manners: Occasional Prose*. Ed. Sally and Robert Fitzgerald. New York: Farrar, 1969. 87–106.

O'Donnell, Patrick. "*Underworld.*" *The Cambridge Companion to Don DeLillo*. Ed. John N. Duvall. Cambridge: Cambridge UP, 2008. 108–21.

O'Hara, Frank. "Meditations in an Emergency." *Poetry* 85 (Nov. 1954): 63. *Meditations in an Emergency*. 1957. New York: Grove, 1996. 38–40.

Osteen, Mark. *American Magic and Dread: Don DeLillo's Dialogue with Culture*. Philadelphia, PA: U of Pennsylvania P, 2000.

—. "DeLillo's Dedalian Artists." *The Cambridge Companion to Don DeLillo*. Ed. John N. Duvall. Cambridge: Cambridge UP, 2008. 137–50.

Palmer, David. "Last Days of Empire: DeLillo's America and Murakami's Japan." *Transnational Literature* 2.1 (2009): 1–13. <http://dspace.flinders.edu.au/dspace/bitstream/2328/7985/1/Palmer.pdf>.

Parrish, Timothy L. "Pynchon and DeLillo." *UnderWords: Perspectives on Don DeLillo's Underworld*. Ed. Joseph Dewey, Steven G. Kellman, and Irving Malin. Newark, DE: U of Delaware P, 2002. 79–92.

Passaro, Vince. "Dangerous Don DeLillo." *New York Times Magazine* 19 May 1991: 34–36, 38, 76–77.

Paz, Sharon. "Sharon Paz: *Falling*, 2002." 27 Aug. 2009 <http://www.sharonpaz.com/falling/index.html>.

Pike, Burton. *The Image of the City in Modern Literature*. Princeton, NJ: Princeton UP, 1981.

Pike, David L. *Metropolis on the Styx: The Underworlds of Modern Urban Culture, 1800–2001*. Ithaca, NY: Cornell UP, 2007.

—. *Passage through Hell: Modernist Descents, Medieval Underworlds*. Ithaca, NY: Cornell UP, 1997.

—. "Wall and Tunnel: The Spatial Metaphorics of Cold War Berlin." *New German Critique* 37.2 (2010): 73–94.

Platt, J. C., and J. Saunders. "Underground." *London*. Ed. Charles Knight. Vol. 1. London: Charles Knight and Co., 1841. 225–40. <http://books.google.com/books?id=iFMGAQAAIAAJ&printsec+frontcover&dq=charles+knights+london&source=>.

Podhoretz, Norman. "William Faulkner and the Problem of War." *Commentary* Sept. 1954: 227–32. Rpt. as "Faulkner in the 50's" ("I. The Problem of War"). *Doings and Undoings: The Fifties and After in American Writing*. New York: Farrar, 1964. 13–24.

Pound, Ezra. *Hugh Selwyn Mauberley*. 1920. *Pound: Poems and Translations*. Ed. Richard Sieburth. New York: Library of America, 2003. 547–63.

—. "The Teacher's Mission." *The English Journal* 23.8 (1934): 630–35.

Pynchon, Thomas. *The Crying of Lot 49*. 1966. New York: Bantam, 1967.

—. *Gravity's Rainbow*. New York: Viking, 1973.

—. *Mason & Dixon*. New York: Henry Holt, 1997.

—. *Slow Learner: Early Stories*. Boston, MA: Little, Brown, 1984.

—. *V*. Philadelphia, PA: J. B. Lippincott, 1963.

—. *Vineland*. Boston, MA: Little, Brown, 1990.

Rabb, Jane M., ed. *Literature and Photography: Interactions, 1840–1990*. Albuquerque, NM: U of New Mexico P, 1995.

Réage, Pauline. *Story of O.* Trans. Sabine d'Estrée. New York: Grove, 1965. Trans. of *Histoire d'O.* 1954.

Remnick, David. "Exile on Main Street: Don DeLillo's Undisclosed Underworld." *New Yorker* 15 Sept. 1997: 42–48.

Rogin, Michael Paul. *Ronald Reagan, the Movie and Other Episodes in Political Demonology.* Berkeley, CA: U of California P, 1987.

Rosen, Elizabeth K. *Apocalyptic Transformation: Apocalypse and the Postmodern Imagination.* Lanham, MD: Lexington-Rowman and Littlefield, 2008.

Ross, Rick. "The Ross Institute Internet Archives for the Study of Destructive Cults, Controversial Groups and Movements." <http://www.rickross.com/>.

Roth, Philip. "Writing American Fiction." *Commentary* Mar. 1961: 223–33.

Rowe, John Carlos. "Culture, US Imperialism, and Globalization." *Exceptional State: Contemporary U.S. Culture and the New Imperialism.* Ed. Ashley Dawson and Malini Johar Schueller. Durham, NC: Duke UP, 2007. 37–59.

—. "*Mao II* and the War on Terrorism." *South Atlantic Quarterly* 103 (2004): 21–43.

Rushdie, Salman. *Fury.* London: Jonathan Cape, 2001.

Salinger, J. D. "Down at the Dinghy." *Harper's* Apr. 1949: 87–91. *Nine Stories.* New York: Modern Library-Random, 1953. 111–30.

Sante, Luc. "Between Hell and History." *New York Review of Books* 6 Nov. 1997: 4, 6–7.

Sciorra, Joseph. "'Why a Man Make the Shoes?': Italian-American Art and Philosophy in Rodia's Watts Towers." Unpublished essay. Art and Migration: Sabato (Simon) Rodia and the Watts Towers of Los Angeles. Università di Genova. Genova, Italy. 2–5 Apr. 2009.

Shakespeare, William. *Hamlet. Shakespeare: The Complete Works.* Ed. G. B. Harrison. New York: Harcourt, 1968. 885–934.

Slade, Joseph W. "Thomas Pynchon, Postindustrial Humanist." *Technology and Culture* 23 (1982): 53–72.

Snow, C. P. "Science, Politics, and the Novelist: or, The Fish and the Net." *Kenyon Review* 23 (1961): 1–17.

Sontag, Susan. *Regarding the Pain of Others.* New York: Farrar, 2003.

Steiner, George. *Language and Silence: Essays on Language, Literature, and the Inhuman.* New York: Atheneum, 1967.

Stevens, Wallace. "Man Carrying Thing." 1947. *Collected Poetry and Prose.* Ed. Frank Kermode and Joan Richardson. New York: Library of America, 1997. 306.

Swartz, Anne K. "American Art after September 11: A Consideration of the Twin Towers." *symplokē* 14.1–2 (2006): 81–97.

Trotter, David. "The New Historicism and the Psychopathology of Everyday Modern Life." *Filth: Dirt, Disgust, and Modern Life.* Ed. William A. Cohen and Ryan Johnson. Minneapolis, MN: U of Minnesota P, 2005. 30–48.

Updike, John. *Rabbit at Rest.* New York: Knopf, 1990.

—. *Terrorist.* New York: Knopf, 2006.

Venturi, Robert, Denise Scott Brown, and Steven Izenour. *Learning from Las Vegas.* Cambridge, MA: MIT Press, 1972.

Versluys, Kristiaan. *Out of the Blue: September 11 and the Novel*. New York: Columbia UP, 2009.

Walford, Edward. *Old and New London: A Narrative of Its History, Its People, and Its Places*. Vol. 3 (*Westminster and the Western Suburbs*). London: Cassell, Petter, and Galpin, n.d. [1873]. <http://www.archive.org/details/oldnewlondonnarr03thor> .

West, Nathanael. *The Day of the Locust*. 1939. Rpt. in Miss Lonelyhearts *and* The Day of the Locust. New York: New Directions, 1962. 59–185.

White, Hayden. *Metahistory: The Historical Imagination in Nineteenth-Century Europe*. Baltimore, MD: Johns Hopkins UP, 1973.

Whitfield, Stephen J. *The Culture of the Cold War*. 2nd ed. Baltimore, MD: Johns Hopkins UP, 1996.

Wildermuth, John. "Going, Going—Gone!" *San Francisco Chronicle* 16 Sept. 2007: B1+.

Woolf, Virginia. *Mrs. Dalloway*. 1925. New York: Harvest-Harcourt, 1953.

Wright, Richard. "How 'Bigger' Was Born." New York: Harper, 1940. *Early Works: Lawd Today! Uncle Tom's Children, Native Son*. Ed. Arnold Rampersad. New York: Library of America, 1991. 851–81.

Yeats, W[illiam] B[utler]. "Meditations in Time of Civil War." 1923. *The Variorum Edition of the Poems of W. B. Yeats*. Ed. Peter Allt and Russell K. Alspach. New York: Macmillan, 1957. 417–27.

Further Reading

Books

All the works that follow, with the exception of the two published prior to 2000, extend their analyses of DeLillo's fiction through *Underworld* (1997) and the approach taken in each is indicated by its title. Of those two exceptions, Tom LeClair's study retains its importance as its consideration of contemporary systems theory in DeLillo's novels up to and including *White Noise* focuses on a theme that is central to both DeLillo's later work and the work of the three other novelists—Williams Gaddis, Thomas Pynchon, and Robert Coover—against which DeLillo's fiction is juxtaposed. Equally important are the studies by Mark Osteen and David Cowart. The former provides extensive analysis of the numerous cultural references, literary and extra-literary, that are embedded in DeLillo's fiction; the latter explores that fiction with respect to the numinous qualities that language continues to possess in the face of poststructuralist tenets. Three authors—Peter Boxall, Joseph Dewey, and David Cowart (in the revised edition of his text)—extend their examinations of DeLillo's work so as to include *Cosmopolis* (2003). In the case of Peter Boxall, that examination—while not including *Falling Man* (2007) specifically—is explicitly informed by the events of 9/11 and the phenomenon of globalization.

Boxall, Peter. *Don DeLillo: The Possibility of Fiction*. London: Routledge, 2006.

Cowart, David. *Don DeLillo: The Physics of Language*. Athens, GA: U of Georgia P, 2002. Rev. ed. 2003.

Dewey, Joseph. *Beyond Grief and Nothing: A Reading of Don DeLillo*. Columbia, SC: U of South Carolina P, 2006.

Duvall, John. *Don DeLillo's Underworld: A Reader's Guide*. New York: Continuum, 2002.

Kavadlo, Jesse. *Don DeLillo: Balance at the Edge of Belief*. New York: Peter Lang, 2004.

Kesey, Douglas. *Don DeLillo*. New York: Twayne, 1993.

Laist, Randy. *Technology and Postmodern Subjectivity in Don DeLillo's Novels*. New York: Peter Lang, 2010.

LeClair, Tom. *In the Loop: Don DeLillo and the Systems Novel*. Urbana, IL: U of Illinois P, 1987.

Martucci, Elise. *The Environmental Unconscious in the Fiction of Don DeLillo*. London: Routledge, 2009.

Osteen, Mark. *American Magic and Dread: Don DeLillo's Dialogue with Culture.* Philadelphia, PA: U of Pennsylvania P, 2000.

Schuster, Marc. *Don DeLillo, Jean Baudrillard, and the Consumer Conundrum.* Youngstown, NY: Cambria, 2008.

Essay Collections and Collected Interviews

Of the collections that follow, only *Under Words* and *The Cambridge Companion to Don DeLillo* provide new critical readings of DeLillo's fiction after 1990. The first includes essays that compare *Underworld* (1997) to the work of other writers (e.g., Thomas Pynchon, John Updike, F. Scott Fitzgerald, T. S. Eliot); the second includes essays that approach DeLillo with respect to topics that span most of his career (e.g., modernism, postmodernism, masculinity, artistry, language, mystery). Both *Don DeLillo* and *Critical Essays on Don DeLillo* consist of previously published material, the most noteworthy of which are articles on *Underworld* by Tony Tanner (in the Chelsea House collection), John N. Duvall, and Peter Knight (in the G. K. Hall collection). *Introducing Don DeLillo*, which stops short of addressing *Mao II* (1991), ends with Frank Lentricchia's seminal essay, "*Libra* as Postmodern Critique" (193–215).

Bloom, Harold, ed. *Don DeLillo*. Philadelphia, PA: Chelsea House, 2003.

DePietro, Thomas, ed. *Conversations with Don DeLillo*. Jackson, MI: UP of Mississippi, 2005.

Dewey, Joseph, Steven G. Kellman, and Irving Malin, eds. *Under Words: Perspectives on Don DeLillo's* Underworld. Newark, DE: U of Delaware P, 2002.

Duvall, John N., ed. *The Cambridge Companion to Don DeLillo*. Cambridge: Cambridge UP, 2008.

Lentricchia, Frank, ed. *Introducing Don DeLillo*. Durham, NC: Duke UP, 1991.

Ruppersburg, Hugh, and Tim Engles, eds. *Critical Essays on Don DeLillo*. New York: G. K. Hall, 2000.

Special Issues – Journals

Duvall, John N., ed. *Modern Fiction Studies* 45 (1999): 559–853.

Green, Geoffrey, Donald J. Greiner, and Larry McCaffery, eds. *Critique* 42 (2001): 339–436.

Journal Articles and Book Chapters

Mao II

Barrett, Laura. "'Here But Also There': Subjectivity and Postmodern Space in *Mao II*." *Modern Fiction Studies* 45 (1999): 788–810.

Caporale Bizzini, Silvia. "Can the Intellectual Still Speak? The Example of Don DeLillo's *Mao II*." *Critical Quarterly* 37.2 (1995): 104–17.

Green, Jeremy. "Last Days: Millennial Hysteria in Don DeLillo's *Mao II.*" *Essays and Studies* 48 (1995): 129–48.

Hardack, Richard. "Two's a Crowd: *Mao II*, Coke II, and the Politics of Terrorism in Don DeLillo." *Studies in the Novel* 36 (2004): 374–92.

Karnicky, Jeffrey. "Wallpaper Mao: Don DeLillo, Andy Warhol, and Seriality." *Critique* 42 (2001): 339–56.

Moran, Joe. "Don DeLillo and the Myth of the Author-Recluse." *Journal of American Studies* 34 (2000): 137–52.

Noland, William. "The Image World of *Mao II.*" *South Atlantic Quarterly* 103 (2004): 5–19.

Osteen, Mark. "Becoming Incorporated: Spectacular Authorship and DeLillo's *Mao II.*" *Modern Fiction Studies* 45 (1999): 643–74.

Rowe, John Carlos. "*Mao II* and the War on Terrorism." *South Atlantic Quarterly* 103 (2004): 21–43.

Scanlan, Margaret. "Writers among Terrorists: Don DeLillo's *Mao II* and the Rushdie Affair." *Modern Fiction Studies* 40 (1994): 229–52.

Simmons, Ryan. "What Is a Terrorist? Contemporary Authorship, the Unabomber, and *Mao II.*" *Modern Fiction Studies* 45 (1999): 675–95.

Velcic, Vlatka. "Reshaping Ideologies: Leftists as Terrorists/Terrorists as Leftists in DeLillo's Novels." *Studies in the Novel* 36 (2004): 405–18.

Wilcox, Leonard. "Terrorism and Art: Don DeLillo's *Mao II* and Jean Baudrillard's *The Spirit of Terrorism.*" *Mosaic* 39.2 (2006): 89–105.

Underworld

Annesley, James. "'Thigh Bone Connected to the Hip Bone': Don DeLillo's *Underworld* and the Fictions of Globalization." *Amerikastudien/American Studies* 47 (2002): 85–106.

Apter, Emily. "On Oneworldedness: Or Paranoia as a World System." *American Literary History* 18 (2006): 365–89.

Duvall, John N. "Baseball as Aesthetic Ideology: Cold War History, Race, and DeLillo's 'Pafko at the Wall.'" *Modern Fiction Studies* 41 (1995): 285–313.

Evans, David H. "Taking Out the Trash: Don DeLillo's *Underworld*, Liquid Modernity, and the End of Garbage." *Cambridge Quarterly* 35 (2006): 103–32.

Green, Jeremy. "Disaster Footage: Spectacles of Violence in DeLillo's Fiction." *Modern Fiction Studies* 45 (1999): 571–99.

Helyer, Ruth. "'Refuse Heaped Many Stories High': DeLillo, Dirt, and Disorder." *Modern Fiction Studies* 45 (1999): 987–1006.

Knight, Peter. "Beyond the Cold War in Don DeLillo's *Mao II* and *Underworld.*" *American Fiction of the 1990s: Reflections of History and Culture.* Ed. Jay Prosser. London: Routledge, 2008. 193–205.

—. "Everything Is Connected: *Underworld*'s Secret History of Paranoia." *Modern Fiction Studies* 45 (1999): 811–36.

McGowan, Todd. "The Obsolescence of Mystery and the Accumulation of Waste in Don DeLillo's *Underworld.*" *Critique* 46 (2005): 123–45.

Mexal, Stephen J. "Spectacularspectacular!: *Underworld* and the Production of Terror." *Studies in the Novel* 36 (2004): 318–35.

Mohr, Hans-Ulrich. "DeLillo's *Underworld*: Cold War History and Systemic Patterns." *European Journal of English Studies* 5 (2001): 349–65.

Morley, Catherine. "Don DeLillo's Transatlantic Dialogue with Sergei Eisenstein." *Journal of American Studies* 40 (2006): 17–34.

Nel, Philip. "'A Small Incisive Shock': Modern Forms, Postmodern Politics, and the Role of the Avant-Garde in *Underworld*." *Modern Fiction Studies* 45 (1999): 724–52.

Parrish, Timothy L. "From Hoover's FBI to Eisenstein's *Unterwelt*: DeLillo Directs the Postmodern Novel." *Modern Fiction Studies* 45 (1999): 696–723.

Rosen, Elizabeth. "Lenny Bruce and His Nuclear Shadow Marvin Lundy: Don DeLillo's Apocalyptists Extraordinaires." *Journal of American Studies* 40 (2006): 97–112.

Spencer, Nicholas. "Beyond the Mutations of Media and Military Technologies in Don DeLillo's *Underworld*." *Arizona Quarterly* 58.2 (2002): 89–112.

Tanner, Tony. "Afterthoughts on Don DeLillo's *Underworld*." *Raritan* 17.4 (1998): 48–71.

Walker, Joseph S. "Criminality, the Real, and the Story of America: The Case of Don DeLillo." *Centennial Review* 43 (1999): 433–66.

Wallace, Molly. "'Venerated Emblems': DeLillo's *Underworld* and the History-Commodity." *Critique* 42 (2001): 367–83.

Wegner, Phillip E. "October 3, 1951 to September 11, 2001: Periodizing the Cold War in Don DeLillo's *Underworld*." *Amerikastudien/American Studies* 49 (2004): 51–64.

Wilcox, Leonard. "Don DeLillo's *Underworld* and the Return of the Real." *Contemporary Literature* 43 (2002): 120–37.

"In the Ruins of the Future," *Falling Man*, and 9/11

Abel, Marco. "Don DeLillo's 'In the Ruins of the Future': Literature, Images, and the Rhetoric of *Seeing* 9/11." *PMLA* 118 (2003): 1236–50.

Conte, Joseph M. "Writing amid the Ruins: 9/11 and *Cosmopolis*." *The Cambridge Companion to Don DeLillo*. Ed. John N. Duvall. Cambridge: Cambridge UP, 2008. 179–92.

Kauffman, Linda S. "The Wake of Terror: Don DeLillo's 'In the Ruins of the Future,' 'Baader-Meinhof,' and *Falling Man*." *Modern Fiction Studies* 54 (2008): 353–77.

—. "World Trauma Center." *American Literary History* 21 (2009): 647–59.

Thurschwell, Adam. "Writing and Terror: Don DeLillo on the Task of Literature after 9/11." *Law and Literature* 19 (2007): 277–302.

Varsava, Jerry A. "The 'Saturated Self': Don DeLillo on the Problem of Rogue Capitalism." *Contemporary Literature* 46 (2005): 78–107.

Versluys, Kristiaan. "American Melancholia: Don DeLillo's *Falling Man*." *Out of the Blue: September 11 and the Novel*. New York: Columbia UP, 2009. 19–48.

Websites

Don DeLillo's America. Ed. Curt Gardner. www.perival.com.

The Don DeLillo Society. Ed. Philip Nel. www.k-state.edu/english/nelp/delillo/.

Notes on Contributors

Laura Barrett is currently Professor of English and Dean of the College of Liberal Arts at Armstrong Atlantic State University. Most of her work focuses on the relationship between images and words in twentieth-century American fiction, and her essays on Don DeLillo, E. L. Doctorow, F. Scott Fitzgerald, Paul Auster, Marilynne Robinson, and Wright Morris have appeared in *Modern Fiction Studies*, *Journal of Modern Literature*, *Literature and History*, *Studies in the Novel*, *Papers on Language and Literature*, *South Atlantic Review*, and *Western American Literature*.

David Cowart, Louise Fry Scudder Professor at the University of South Carolina (Columbia), is the author of *Don DeLillo: The Physics of Language* (2002), which won the SAMLA Literary Studies Award in 2003. A consulting editor for the journal *Critique*, Professor Cowart has been an NEH fellow and held Fulbright chairs at the University of Helsinki and at the Syddansk Universitet in Odense, Denmark. In 2005, he toured Japan as a Fulbright Distinguished Lecturer. He is also the author of *Thomas Pynchon: The Art of Allusion* (1980), *Arches and Light: The Fiction of John Gardner* (1983), *History and the Contemporary Novel* (1989), *Literary Symbiosis: The Reconfigured Text in Twentieth-Century Writing* (1993), and *Trailing Clouds: Immigrant Fiction in Contemporary America* (2006). He is working on a book about literary generations in the postmodern period.

John N. Duvall is Professor of English and editor of *MFS: Modern Fiction Studies* at Purdue University. He is the author of *Faulkner's Marginal Couple: Invisible, Outlaw, and Unspeakable Communities* (1990), *The Identifying Fictions of Toni Morrison: Modernist Authenticity and Postmodern Blackness* (2000), *Don DeLillo's Underworld: A Reader's Guide* (2002), and *Race and White Identity in Southern Fiction: From Faulkner to Morrison* (2008). He also has edited or co-edited several collections, including *Productive Postmodernism: Consuming Histories* *and Cultural Studies* (2002), *Approaches to Teaching DeLillo's* White Noise (2006; with Tim Engles), and *The Cambridge Companion to Don DeLillo* (2008).

Josephine Gattuso Hendin is Professor of English and Tiro A. Segno Professor of Italian American Studies at New York University. Her novel, *The Right Thing To Do* (1988), won an American Book Award from the Before Columbus Foundation. She is the author of *The World of Flannery O'Connor* (1970), *Vulnerable People: A View of American Fiction since 1945* (1978), and *HeartBreakers: Women and Violence in Contemporary Culture and Literature* (2004), and the editor of Blackwell's *A Concise Companion to Postwar American Literature and Culture* (2004). Her awards include a John Simon Guggenheim Fellowship in Literary Criticism and the Elena Lucrezia Cornaro Award for distinguished scholarship by an Italian American woman. Her essays have appeared in *The New Republic*, *Harper's Magazine*, *American Literary History*, *VIA*, and *MELUS*. She is currently President of the Italian American Historical Association.

Linda S. Kauffman is the author of *Discourses of Desire: Gender, Genre, and Epistolary Fictions* (1986), *Special Delivery: Epistolary Modes in Modern Fiction* (1992), and *Bad Girls and Sick Boys: Fantasies in Contemporary Art and Culture* (1998). She is the editor of three volumes, including *American Feminist Thought at Century's End* (1993). She is Professor of English and Distinguished Scholar-Teacher at the University of Maryland, College Park, and a former Senior Fulbright Scholar (the Netherlands).

Peter Knight is Senior Lecturer in American Studies at the University of Manchester, UK. He is the author of *Conspiracy Culture: From the Kennedy Assassination to* The X-Files (2000) and *The Kennedy Assassination* (2007), and the editor of *Conspiracy Nation: The Politics of Paranoia in Postwar America* (2002) and *Conspiracy Theories in American History: An Encyclopedia* (2003). His current research examines how non-experts learned to read the market in nineteenth-century America.

Stacey Olster is Professor of English at the State University of New York at Stony Brook and a former Fulbright Scholar (Belgium). She is the author of *Reminiscence and Re-Creation in Contemporary American Fiction* (1989) and *The Trash Phenomenon: Contemporary Literature, Popular Culture, and the Making of the American Century* (2003), and the editor of *The Cambridge Companion to John Updike* (2006).

David L. Pike is Professor of Literature at American University, where he also teaches film. His books include *Passage through Hell: Modernist Descents, Medieval Underworlds* (1997), *Subterranean Cities: The World beneath Paris and London, 1800–1945* (2005), and *Metropolis on the Styx: The Underworlds of Modern Urban Culture, 1800–2001* (2007), all published by Cornell University Press. He is co-editor of the *Longman Anthology of World Literature* (2008) and co-author of *Literature: A World of Writing* (2010), and has published widely on nineteenth- and twentieth-century urban literature, culture, and film. He is currently completing a history of Canadian cinema since the 1980s and a study of Cold War bunkers since the end of the Cold War.

John Carlos Rowe is USC Associates' Professor of the Humanities and Chair of the Department of American Studies and Ethnicity at the University of Southern California. He is the author of *Henry Adams and Henry James: The Emergence of a Modern Consciousness* (1976), *Through the Custom-House: Nineteenth-Century American Fiction and Modern Theory* (1982), *The Theoretical Dimensions of Henry James* (1984), *At Emerson's Tomb: The Politics of Classic American Literature* (1997), *The Other Henry James* (1998), *Literary Culture and U.S. Imperialism: From the Revolution to World War II* (2000), *The New American Studies* (2002), *The Cultural Politics of the New American Studies* (2010), as well as over one hundred scholarly essays and critical reviews. He is the editor of *The Vietnam War and American Culture* (1991), *New Essays on* The Education of Henry Adams (1996), *"Culture" and the Problem of the Disciplines* (1998), *Post-Nationalist American Studies* (2000), *Ralph Waldo Emerson and Margaret Fuller: Selected Works* (2002), *A Concise Companion to American Studies* (2010), and *A Historical Guide to Henry James* (2010). His current scholarly projects are *Culture and U.S. Imperialism since World War II* and *The Rediscovery of America: Multicultural Literature and the New Democracy*.

Thomas Hill Schaub is Professor of English at the University of Wisconsin-Madison. He is the author of *Pynchon: The Voice of Ambiguity* (1981) and *American Fiction in the Cold War* (1991), and the editor of *Approaches to Teaching Thomas Pynchon's* The Crying of Lot 49 *and Other Works* (2008). Since 1989 he has been editor of the journal *Contemporary Literature*.

Index

9/11 (11 September 2001) 2–3, 11–13, 22, 29, 31, 38, 47, 97, 118–19, 121–26, 128–30, 131, 132, 133, 134, 135–38, 139, 140, 141–43, 144, 145, 147–48, 149, 151, 152–53, 154, 155, 156–68

Aaron, Hank 22
Abdel-Rahman, Omar (Blind Sheik) 142, 148
Abu Nidal Organization 29
Abu Sayyaf Group 29
Adams, Henry 24
   The Degradation of the Democratic Dogma 77
   The Education of Henry Adams 15–16
Adorno, Theodor W.: "Cultural Criticism and Society" 12, 152, 158
Aeneid, The (Virgil) 94
aesthetics 3, 12–13, 119, 122, 132, 146–47, 148, 151, 152–54, 161, 165–68
   Aquinas, Thomas 102, 103–04, 109–10
   Dewey, John 102
   terrorism as aestheticism 155–59
      see also arte povera
   author
   commodification, aesthetic
   graffiti art
   outsider art
   performance art
   photography
   representation

Afghanistan, war in 29, 119, 130, 140, 151, 155
Agamben, Giorgio: *Homo Sacer* 124
Agent Orange 66, 81
Alighieri, Dante 84, 85, 89, 92–93
   Commedia 67, 87, 98
   Inferno 86–87
al-Qaeda 29, 123–24, 126, 132, 133, 140
Amazons (DeLillo) 21
Americana (DeLillo) 3–4, 5, 7–8, 12, 21, 26, 49–50, 88
"American Blood" (DeLillo) 2
Antonioni, Michelangelo 63
   Zabriskie Point 11
apocalypse 1–2, 15, 16–17, 19–22, 24, 46, 69–71, 97
Appiah, Kwame Anthony: *Cosmopolitanism* 121
Aquinas, Thomas 67, 73, 102, 103–05, 109–10
   Catena Aurea 107
   De Veritate 114
   Summa Contra Gentiles 110
   Summa Theologica 101, 106
Arendt, Hannah: *The Origins of Totalitarianism* 124
Armies of the Night, The (Mailer) 4
Arnold, Eve 59
Arnold, Matthew: *Culture and Anarchy* 28
Art as Experience (Dewey) 102
arte povera 67, 100, 102–03, 111–12
Ash, Timothy Garton 32
Asmodeus (halting devil) 85–89

atomic bomb 1, 5, 66–67, 69–70, 72, 74, 78, 82, 88, 93, 97, 105, 118
  in popular culture 69–70
  sexualized discourse of 67, 79–80
    see also weapons systems, nuclear
Atta, Mohamed 123, 124, 128–29, 130, 132
Auster, Paul 17, 42
  The Invention of Solitude 62–63, 64
  Leviathan 59–60
author: act of writing 45–46, 55
  decline of 12–13, 17, 25–26, 50, 51, 133–34, 155, 158–59
  omniscience of 85–89
Awlaki, Anwar al- 133

Baader-Meinhof Group (Red Army Faction) 127, 156
Ballard, J. G.: "Build-Up" 97
  "Concentration City" 97
Barbary Shore (Mailer) 1–2
Barrett, Laura 17
Barth, John 24
  The End of the Road 2
  The Floating Opera 2
  The Sot-Weed Factor 65
baseball 8, 22, 58, 66, 71, 72, 73–74, 75–76, 79, 82, 88, 92, 93, 98, 103–06
Baudelaire, Charles 96
Baudrillard, Jean 3, 10, 36–37, 38, 45, 157
"Beast in the Jungle, The" (James) 139–40
Beattie, Ann: *Chilly Scenes of Winter* 6
Beckett, Samuel 63, 119, 145
Begley, Adam 49, 61–62, 63
Beirut 11, 20, 26, 27, 28, 36, 37, 38–41, 43, 44, 46, 47, 48, 61, 122, 154
Benjamin, Walter 97
Bercovitch, Sacvan 4
Bergman, Ingmar 63
Berlin Wall 16, 24, 25, 28, 30, 34, 47, 70, 89–90, 94

"Big Two-Hearted River" (Hemingway) 77
Billen, Andrew 29
bin Laden, Osama 124, 143, 156
Blind Sheik *see* Abdel-Rahman, Omar
Bloomberg, Michael R. 160–61
Body Artist, The (DeLillo) 3, 26, 155, 167
Bonds, Barry 22
Book of Daniel, The (Doctorow) 65
Boxall, Peter 28–29, 34
Branca, Ralph 8, 66, 104, 106
Bremer, Arthur 10
Briley, Jonathan 163
Broch, Hermann: *The Death of Virgil* 15
Bruce, Lenny 12, 75, 78, 79, 87, 154
Bruegel, Pieter: *The Triumph of Death* 51, 71, 84, 88, 92, 98, 104
"Build-Up" (Ballard) 97
Burdick, Eugene, and Harvey Wheeler: *Fail Safe* 69
Bush, George H. W. 9, 17, 34, 105
  see also New World Order
Bush, George W. 140, 153, 154

Calvino, Italo: *Invisible Cities* 93
Campbell, Martin: *GoldenEye* 80
Campkin, Ben, and Rosie Cox 97
capitalism 69, 99, 118
  consumer 36, 47
  cyber- 11, 16, 47, 81–82
  global 37, 43–44, 47, 66, 124, 133, 157
  hyper- 123–24, 130–31
  late 16, 81, 132
  neoliberal 34, 39, 47
  urban 94
Castro, Fidel 121
Catch-22 (Heller) 70
Catena Aurea (Aquinas) 107
Chapman, Jake and Dinos:
  Fucking Hell 84
  Hell 84
Chilly Scenes of Winter (Beattie) 6
Christ in Concrete (Di Donato) 111

CIA (Central Intelligence Agency) 3, 9, 121, 154
Closing Circle, The (Commoner) 78
Cloud of Unknowing, The 76, 113, 115
Cocksucker Blues (Frank) 86
Cohen, William A. 96
Cohen, William A., and Ryan Johnson 97
Cold War 1–3, 5, 8, 12, 15, 34, 44, 47, 66–67, 69–71, 74–75, 78–80, 81–82, 87, 89, 90–91, 97–98, 105, 131, 154, 165
Colie, Rosalie L. 102–03
Commedia (Alighieri) 67, 87, 98
commodification, aesthetic 3, 16, 36–38, 52, 154–55, 157
Commoner, Barry: *The Closing Circle* 78
communism 2, 3–5, 11, 29, 69, 121
"Compensation" (Emerson) 106–07
"Concentration City" (Ballard) 97
"Concord Hymn" (Emerson) 105
"Constant Symbol, The" (Frost) 25
consumerism 2, 4–5, 9, 11, 16, 36, 46, 47, 51, 54, 56, 63, 138, 153
"Conversations on the Craft of Poetry" (Frost) 25
Coover, Robert 24
   The Public Burning 6
Coppola, Francis Ford: *The Godfather* 140
Corliss, Jeb 148
Cosmopolis (DeLillo) 2, 10, 11, 16, 26, 39, 118, 123–24
cosmopolitanism 121–22, 134
Cosmopolitanism (Appiah) 121
Cousins, Norman 1
Cowart, David 16–17, 73, 74, 77–78
Crowd (Warhol) 54
Crying of Lot 49, The (Pynchon) 58, 74, 77
"Cultural Criticism and Society" (Adorno) 12, 152, 158
Cultural Revolution, Chinese 16, 32, 47

Culture and Anarchy (Arnold) 28
cyberspace 57, 81–82, 89, 91–92, 113

D'Acierno, Pellegrino 100–01
Danielewski, Mark Z. 17
   House of Leaves 62
Dante *see* Alighieri, Dante
Day of Doom, The (Wigglesworth) 19
Day of the Locust, The (West) 19–20, 54
Death of Virgil, The (Broch) 15
Debord, Guy 3, 6
DeCurtis, Anthony 4, 63
Deer Park, The (Mailer) 2
Degradation of the Democratic Dogma, The (Adams) 77
DeLillo, Don: and the act of writing 21, 23, 32, 45–46, 55–56, 60, 63, 144–45, 158
   artistic influences 36, 49, 63
   artistic surrogates 3, 7, 13, 26, 27–28, 33, 42, 86–88, 102, 111–12, 154–55
   Bronx upbringing 91, 99, 101
   and Catholicism 30, 101, 102–03, 106–07, 108, 110–11, 130, 132, 143, 149–50, 151, 152
   interviews 4, 7, 15, 19, 21, 27, 29, 30, 36, 38, 42, 49, 50–51, 56, 63, 66, 83, 85, 89–90, 98
   and language 2, 7, 12–13, 45–46, 49, 55–58, 60–61, 63–64, 100, 141–42, 144–45, 152, 155
   and limitations of the novel 119, 133–34, 155, 158–59, 167
   prescience of 10, 16, 22, 97, 117, 124, 134, 154
   and religion 29–30, 31–32, 143–44, 149–50
   and transcendence 29–30, 32, 37, 45–47, 62, 64, 114, 118, 138, 143, 149–50, 167
   and U.S. paradigms 119, 134
   see also individual works
De Niro, Robert 140

De Palma, Brian: *The Untouchables* 140
Derrida, Jacques 100
    Specters of Marx 124
Desalm, Brigitte 27
De Veritate (Aquinas) 114
Dewey, John: *Art as Experience* 102
Dewey, Joseph 30, 42, 61
Didion, Joan: "The White Album" 62
Di Donato, Pietro: *Christ in Concrete* 111
dietrologia 23, 84, 103–04, 108
Doctorow, E. L.: *The Book of Daniel* 65
Dodgers, Brooklyn 8, 66, 72, 92, 104
    see also baseball
Dolce Vita, La (Fellini) 89
Dos Passos, John 1
    U.S.A. 65
Dostoevsky, Fyodor 30–31
    The Possessed 33
Douglas, Mary 98
"Down at the Dinghy" (Salinger) 143
Drew, Richard: "Falling Man" 118, 135, 148–49, 153, 162–67
Dr. Strangelove (Kubrick) 70, 79
Duchamp, Marcel 78, 156
Dutschke, Rudi 127
Duvall, John N. 61–62, 77, 119

Echlin, Kim 83
Eco, Umberto 102, 110, 114
Education of Henry Adams, The (Adams) 15–16
Eisenstein, Sergei 86, 154
Eliot, T[homas] S[tearns]: "The Love Song of J. Alfred Prufrock" 82
    "Tradition and the Individual Talent" 158
    The Waste Land 20, 77
Ellison, Ralph: *Invisible Man* 2, 78
Emerson, Ralph Waldo 67, 103
    "Compensation" 106–07
    "Concord Hymn" 105
Emmanuelle (Jaeckin) 79
End of the Road, The (Barth) 2
End Zone (DeLillo) 2, 5–6, 56, 61

"Entropy" (Pynchon) 78
Enzensberger, Hans Magnus 127
ethnicity 67, 99–104, 107–15, 125–26, 128, 140
Evans, David H. 96–97
existentialism 119, 122–23, 125, 129–30, 139
Extremely Loud and Incredibly Close (Foer) 62, 118

Fail Safe (Burdick and Wheeler) 69
Falling (Paz) 159
Falling Man (DeLillo) 2, 8, 12–13, 26, 29–30, 67, 88, 117–68
    and 9/11 (11 September 2001) 2, 12–13, 118–19, 121–26, 128–30, 131, 132, 133, 134, 135–38, 139, 140, 141–43, 144, 145, 147–48, 149, 151, 152–53, 154, 155, 156–68
    and aesthetics 119, 122, 132, 146–47, 148, 151, 152, 153, 156–59
    Alzheimer's disease in 143–45, 149, 151, 158, 167
    corporeality in 135–37, 141, 142, 144–45, 148
    and ethnicity 125–26, 128, 140
    and existentialism 119, 122–23, 125, 129–30, 139
    the fall and falling in 2, 131–32, 135, 140, 151, 158, 161–63, 167
    Falling Man in 13, 26, 131–32, 135, 140, 148–49, 151, 153, 156, 159, 161–63, 165, 167, 168
    the family in 122, 124, 132, 135–36, 139, 143, 147, 150–51, 152
    and global politics 8, 12, 118–19, 121–34
    and language 12, 141–42, 143, 144–45, 151
    masculinity in 139, 140, 147, 150–51
    and performance art 13, 67, 119, 131, 135, 140, 148–49, 151, 153, 156, 159
    and religious belief 29–30, 130, 132, 143–44, 149–50

trauma in 124–26, 132, 133, 137,
140, 142, 152–53, 167–68
and witnessing 161–62, 167
and women, portrayal of 88, 119,
125–26, 135, 137–39, 140–41,
144, 150–51
"Falling Man" (Drew) 118, 135,
148–49, 153, 162–67
"Falling Man, The" (Junod) 163,
165–66, 167
Farben, IG 66, 80
Farrell, James T. 77
Faulkner, William 1, 83, 119
The Wild Palms 145
Fellini, Federico 63
La Dolce Vita 89
Fiedler, Leslie A. 1
film 6–7, 36, 49–50, 52, 63, 67, 76,
155 *see also* individual films
Finnegans Wake (Joyce) 139, 145,
147
Fischl, Eric 161, 166
Tumbling Woman 159
Fitzgerald, F. Scott 83
The Great Gatsby 7, 74, 77
Fleming, Ian 69
Floating Opera, The (Barth) 2
Foer, Jonathan Safran 17, 167
*Extremely Loud and Incredibly
Close* 62, 118
Fordham University 101, 102, 108
Frank, Robert: *Cocksucker Blues* 86
Franzen, Jonathan 23
Freud, Sigmund 96
Frost, Robert: "The Constant
Symbol" 25
"Conversations on the Craft of
Poetry" 25
"Mending Wall" 25
Fucking Hell (Chapman) 84
Fukuyama, Francis 17, 28, 29, 32, 34
fundamentalism, religious 11–12, 44,
47, 123, 129, 154
Fury (Rushdie) 133, 134

Gehry, Frank 146
Get Smart (television series) 70

Giants, New York 8, 66, 72, 88, 104,
106 *see also* baseball
Giddens, Anthony 8, 10
Gillmore, Alison 159
Giuliani, Rudolph W. 149
Gleason, Jackie 104
Gleich, Lewis 148
globalization 3, 34–35, 38, 47, 99,
118–19, 121, 134, 141
as Americanization 39
erasure of national differences 8,
10, 16, 37, 38, 39–41, 43
globalized economy 8, 9, 40–41,
43–44, 124, 131, 132, 133, 157
Godard, Jean-Luc 63
Godfather, The (Coppola) 140
Godfather, The (Puzo) 78
Goldberg, Vicki 64
GoldenEye (Campbell) 80
Goldman, Eric F. 1
GoodFellas (Scorsese) 140
Gorbachev, Mikhail S. 32–33
Graduate, The (Nichols) 78
graffiti art 13, 17, 40–41, 90, 92, 102,
112, 154
Graham, Gordon 100
Gramsci, Antonio 99
Grass, Günter 127
Gravity's Rainbow (Pynchon) 4, 19,
66, 70, 78, 80
Great Gatsby, The (Fitzgerald) 7, 74,
77
Great Jones Street (DeLillo) 3, 7, 26,
65, 117–18

Haas, Robert: "Meditation at
Lagunitas" 19
Habermas, Jürgen 99–100
Hamas 129
Hamlet (Shakespeare) 21
Hardack, Richard 38
Hardt, Michael, and Antonio Negri 8
deterritorialization 9, 40, 47
Empire 9, 40, 47
possibilities of resistance 11, 128
Hardy, Arnold: "Winecoff
Hotel Fire" 164–65, 166

Hardy, Thomas: *Tess of the d'Urbervilles* 139
Hasan, Nidal Malik 133
Hassan, Steven Alan 21
Held, David 8
Hell (Chapman) 84
Heller, Joseph: *Catch-22* 70
Helyer, Ruth 139
Hemingway, Ernest 1, 23
  "Big Two-Hearted River" 77
Hendin, Josephine Gattuso 67
Hezbollah 129
Hillsborough Stadium 20, 33, 35, 54
Hinckley, John, Jr. 10
Hitler, Adolf 22, 36
Hodges, Russ 88
Holocaust 12, 124, 152, 158
homo faber 100, 109, 111
Homo Sacer (Agamben) 124
Honeymooners, The (television series) 104
Hoover, J. Edgar 9, 66, 79, 88, 91, 98, 104
House of Leaves (Danielewski) 62
Howard, Gerald 66, 85, 89–90, 98
"How 'Bigger' Was Born" (Wright) 122
"How It Feels to Be Colored Me" (Hurston) 126
Hugh Selwyn Mauberley (Pound) 29
Hugo, Victor: *Notre-Dame de Paris* 89
Human Use of Human Beings, The (Wiener) 78
Humphrey, Hubert H. 127
Hungerford, Amy 30, 64
Hurston, Zora Neale: "How It Feels to Be Colored Me" 126
Hutcheon, Linda 3

imperialism 8–9, 39, 47, 129, 131–33, 134, 154
Inferno (Alighieri) 86–87
Internet 9, 10, 57–58, 113, 163
interviews, DeLillo 4, 7, 15, 19, 21, 27, 29, 30, 36, 38, 42, 49, 50–51, 56, 63, 66, 83, 85, 89–90, 98

"In the Ruins of the Future" (DeLillo) 2–3, 12, 19, 29, 31, 47, 134, 139, 158
Invention of Solitude, The (Auster) 62–63, 64
Invisible Cities (Calvino) 93
Invisible Man (Ellison) 2, 78
Iraq: Abu Nidal Organization 29
  Iran-Iraq War 8, 123, 129
  Persian Gulf War 34
  war in 119, 140, 151, 153, 154, 155
Islam 29, 44, 123, 129, 132, 133, 141
Islamic Jihad 29

James, Henry: "The Beast in the Jungle" 139–40
  The Portrait of a Lady 147
Jameson, Fredric 3, 36–37
Jemaah Islamiah 29
Johnson, Uwe 127
Joyce, James 16, 26, 30, 63, 77, 119
  Finnegans Wake 139, 145, 147
  Stephen Hero 73
  Ulysses 1, 144
Junod, Tom: "The Falling Man" 163, 165–66, 167

Kaczynski, Theodore (Ted) 142
Kauffman, Linda S. 119, 126, 137, 145, 146, 148
Keats, John 119, 136, 145
  Negative Capability 119, 136, 149
Kelly, Walt: *The Pogo Papers* 121
Kennedy, John F. 2, 6, 7–8, 51, 65, 121–22, 134, 142
Kennedy, Robert F. 163–64
Kertész, André 83, 99, 118
Khomeini, Ayatollah Ruhollah 20, 33, 35
Kierkegaard, Søren 129–30, 140
  Philosophical Fragments or A Fragment of Philosophy 74
Kingston, Maxine Hong: *The Woman Warrior* 27–28
Knight, Peter 16–17, 71
Kommune 1 12, 127, 128, 132
Krementz, Jill 26

Kubrick, Stanley: *Dr. Strangelove* 70, 79
Kunzelmann, Dieter 127
Kusturica, Emir: *Underground* 84

Language and Silence (Steiner) 12
Lashkar-e-Taiba 132
Lawrence, Frederick G. 104
Learning from Las Vegas (Venturi,
     Brown and Izenour) 130
Le Carré, John: *The Spy Who Came in
     from the Cold* 69
LeClair, T[h]om[as] 30, 56, 84, 153
Leonardo da Vinci: *Mona Lisa* 156
Leviathan (Auster) 59–60
Libra (DeLillo) 2, 3, 5, 7, 8, 65, 119,
     121–22, 142
Life Goes On (Skarbakka) 160–61
Lolita (Nabokov) 135, 139, 151
Lonergan, Bernard 108
Love-Lies-Bleeding (DeLillo) 26
"Love Song of J. Alfred Prufrock,
     The" (Eliot) 82
"Low-lands" (Pynchon) 77
Lukács, Georg 65
Lyotard, Jean-François 16

Macdonald, Dwight 5, 36
Mailer, Norman: *The Armies of the
     Night* 4
     Barbary Shore 1–2
     The Deer Park 2
     "Superman Comes to the
          Supermart" 4, 78
"Man Carrying Thing" (Stevens) 23
Manifest Destiny 4
Man on Wire (Marsh) 131
Mao Tse-tung 26, 28, 32, 38, 39, 44,
     47, 50, 61 *see also* Cultural
     Revolution, Chinese
Mao II (DeLillo) 3, 8, 10, 11, 12, 13,
     15–64, 117, 119, 121–22, 124,
     136, 138, 149, 154–55, 156, 166
     and commodification,
          aesthetic 16, 36–38, 52
     and crowds 17, 20–22, 23–24, 26,
          32, 35, 38–39, 42, 43, 44–46,
          50–51, 53–54, 60, 61, 124, 138

doublings and echoes in 38–42, 61
erasure of national differences
     in 8, 10, 37, 38, 39–41, 43
globalized economy in 8, 34–35,
     37, 40–41, 43–44
and history, end of 15, 19, 21,
     28–29, 31, 34, 47, 55
and individuality 17, 21, 27, 32,
     34–36, 38–39, 42, 43, 44–46,
     50, 53, 55, 61
and language 55–58, 60–62, 64
and millennialism 15–17, 19–21,
     24, 28, 32, 33, 40
and the millennium 15, 20, 21, 23,
     30, 33
novelists versus terrorists in 16,
     26, 32, 37–38, 41, 43, 50, 52,
     60, 119, 121–22, 154–55, 156
and photography 12, 17, 26–27,
     35–36, 50, 51–53, 55–57,
     58–59, 60–62, 64, 166
and prophecy 21, 22–24, 46
and wall epistemology 25, 27–29
Marsh, James: *Man on Wire* 131
Marx, Karl 43, 124
Mason & Dixon (Pynchon) 9, 25
Mays, Willie 104
McClure, John A. 30, 46, 149–50
McEwan, Ian 167
     Saturday 118
Mean Streets (Scorsese) 140
"Meditation at Lagunitas" (Haas) 19
"Meditations in an Emergency"
     (O'Hara) 31
"Meditations in Time of Civil War"
     (Yeats) 24
"Mending Wall" (Frost) 25
Metahistory (White) 79
metaphor 17, 43, 56, 61, 63, 64,
     110, 145
     Alzheimer's disease as 145
     and metonymy 17, 42–43, 54
     underworld as 83–85
     waste as 67, 77–78, 84, 89, 96–97
"Midnight in Dostoevsky"
     (DeLillo) 30–31
Moawad, Rene 20

modernism 3, 5, 8, 17, 36, 42, 46, 51, 58, 67, 77, 85, 86, 87, 107, 122, 153, 155
   modernity 129–31
Mona Lisa (Leonardo) 156
Monroe, Marilyn 54
Montgolfier, Joseph-Michel and Jacques-Étienne 87
Moon, Sun Myung 15, 21, 24, 29, 32, 38, 46, 54 *see also* Unification Church
Morandi, Giorgio 132, 146–47, 149, 153, 157–58
Moraru, Christian 25
Moro, Aldo 127
Moss, Maria 7
Mrs. Dalloway (Woolf) 86, 87
Murakami, Haruki: *The Wind-Up Bird Chronicle* 84

Nabokov, Vladimir: *Lolita* 135, 139, 151
Nadel, Ira 86–87
Nadotti, Maria 36, 50–51
Names, The (DeLillo) 8–10, 12, 26, 30, 56, 60, 63–64, 118, 149, 154
nation-state: decline of 8, 10, 39–41, 122
   emergence of 5
Nausea (Sartre) 139
Negri, Antonio 127
Neverland (O'Neill) 118
New World Order 9, 17, 34, 39, 44
   see also Bush, George H. W.
Nichols, Mike: *The Graduate* 78
Nietzsche, Friedrich 96
1989, events of 20, 23–24, 30–31, 32, 70, 131 *see also* Berlin Wall
Norris, Frank: *The Octopus* 9
Notre-Dame de Paris (Hugo) 89

O'Connor, Flannery: "Writing Short Stories" 23
Octopus, The (Norris) 9
O'Donnell, Patrick 77
O'Hara, Frank: "Meditations in an Emergency" 31

O'Neill, Joseph: *Neverland* 118
On the Beach (Shute) 69
Origins of Totalitarianism, The (Arendt) 124
Osteen, Mark 39, 42, 62, 80–81
Oswald, Lee Harvey 5, 7, 10, 119, 121–22, 124, 127, 134
Outsider, The (Wright) 2
outsider art 67, 100, 101, 112, 119, 153, 154, 155, 156, 161
   see also arte povera
  graffiti art
  performance art

"Pafko at the Wall" (DeLillo) 92
Palmer, David 84
Parrish, Timothy L. 94
Passaro, Vince 19, 21, 36, 38, 42, 49, 63
Paz, Sharon 161, 166
   Falling 159
performance art 3, 13, 17, 67, 119, 131, 135, 148–49, 152, 153, 155, 156, 159–63, 165, 167–68
Petit, Philippe 131, 148
Philosophical Fragments or A Fragment of Philosophy (Kierkegaard) 74
photography 26–27, 35–36, 51–53, 64, 66, 119, 131, 153
  Arnold, Eve 59
  DeLillo, Don, on 27, 37
  Drew, Richard ("Falling Man") 118, 135, 148–49, 153, 162–67
  in *Extremely Loud and Incredibly Close* (Foer) 62
  Hardy, Arnold ("Winecoff Hotel Fire") 164–65, 166
  images and words 49–51, 55–57, 58–59, 60–64
  interpolated photographs in *Mao II* (DeLillo) 12, 17, 35, 50, 61
  in *The Invention of Solitude* (Auster) 62–63, 64

Junod, Tom, on 163, 165–66, 167
Kertész, André 83, 99, 118
Krementz, Jill 26
   in *Leviathan* (Auster) 59–60
   Skarbakka, Kerry (*Life Goes
      On*) 159–61, 165
   Sontag, Susan, on 163, 165–66
   in "The White Album"
      (Didion) 62
   Winogrand, Garry 58–59
Pike, Burton 94
Pike, David L. 67, 85, 87, 91
Platt, J. C., and J. Saunders 95
Players (DeLillo) 11, 22, 117, 118,
      149, 154
Podhoretz, Norman 1
Pogo Papers, The (Kelly) 121
Point Omega (DeLillo) 26
Polo Grounds 104
Portrait of a Lady, The (James) 147
Possessed, The (Dostoevsky) 33
postmodernism 3, 5, 8, 11, 17, 28, 35,
      36, 39, 40, 43, 46, 48, 58, 77,
      81, 85, 97, 101, 113, 121, 122,
      124, 130, 132, 153, 157
Pound, Ezra: *Hugh Selwyn
      Mauberley* 29
   "The Teacher's Mission" 23
"Power of History, The" (DeLillo) 1,
      2, 12
prophecy 21, 22–24, 46, 87, 97
Public Burning, The (Coover) 6
Puritanism 3–4, 15, 19–20
Puzo, Mario: *The Godfather* 78
Pynchon, Thomas 27, 94
   The Crying of Lot 49 58, 74, 77
   "Entropy" 78
   Gravity's Rainbow 4, 19, 66, 70,
      78, 80
   "Low-lands" 77
   Mason & Dixon 9, 25
   Slow Learner 70
   V. 19–20, 24, 80
   Vineland 6–7

Rabbit at Rest (Updike) 66, 70
Rabehl, Bernd 127

radicalism, 1960s–1970s 11–12, 119,
      126–29, 156
   Baader-Meinhof Group
      (Red Army Faction) 127, 156
   Kommune 1 12, 127, 128, 132
   Red Brigades 12, 127
   Weather Underground
      Organization
      (Weathermen) 78
Ray, James Earl 10
Reagan, Ronald 7, 70
Réage, Pauline: *Story of O* 79
Red Brigades 12, 127
Regarding the Pain of Others
      (Sontag) 163, 165–66
Remnick, David 15
representation 3, 11, 17, 54, 58, 60,
      63–64, 118, 119, 132–33, 158,
      161–62, 166, 167
reproduction, mechanical 35–36, 38,
      50, 53–54
Rodia, Sabato 113
   Watts Towers 77, 111–12, 118
Rogin, Michael 5
Rolling Stones 86
Rosen, Elizabeth K. 24
Ross, Rick 21
Roth, Philip 2, 77
   "Writing American Fiction" 78
Rowe, John Carlos 45, 118–19, 131
Running Dog (DeLillo) 9, 11, 22
Rushdie, Salman 20
   Fury 133, 134
   The Satanic Verses 42

Salinger, J. D. 42
   "Down at the Dinghy" 143
Sante, Luc 97
Sartre, Jean-Paul: *Nausea* 139
Satanic Verses, The (Rushdie) 42
Saturday (McEwan) 118
Schaub, Thomas Hill 67
Sciorra, Joseph 111–12
Scorsese, Martin: *GoodFellas* 140
   Mean Streets 140
Shreve, Anita: *A Wedding in
      December* 118

Shute, Nevil: *On the Beach* 69
Sinatra, Frank 104
Skarbakka, Kerry 159, 165
   Life Goes On 160–61
Slade, Joseph W. 77
Slow Learner (Pynchon) 70
Snow, C. P. 1
Sontag, Susan: *Regarding the Pain of
   Others* 163, 165–66
Sot-Weed Factor, The (Barth) 65
South Bronx 5, 67, 89–90, 91, 94–95,
   98, 99, 101, 102–03, 107, 108,
   109, 112, 114
Soviet Union 1, 5, 8, 32, 36, 66, 69, 72,
   80, 105, 121
"Spaghetti and Meatballs"
   (DeLillo) 99
spectacle 5, 45, 54, 154–55
Specters of Marx (Derrida) 124
*Spy Who Came in from the Cold,
   The* (Le Carré) 69
Stalin, Josef 36
Steiner, George: *Language and
   Silence* 12
Stephen Hero (Joyce) 73
Stevens, Wallace: "Man Carrying
   Thing" 23
Stockhausen, Karlheinz 156
Story of O (Réage) 79
Summa Contra Gentiles
   (Aquinas) 110
Summa Theologica (Aquinas) 101,
   106
"Superman Comes to the Supermart"
   (Mailer) 4, 78
Swartz, Anne K. 159

"Take the 'A' Train" (DeLillo) 99
"Teacher's Mission, The" (Pound) 23
television 6–7, 10, 20, 35, 38, 46, 49,
   52, 54, 55, 124, 132, 136, 147
   Get Smart 70
   The Honeymooners 104
terrorism 8, 9–10, 11–12, 16, 26, 32,
   34–35, 37–39, 41, 43–44, 45,
   47–48, 50, 51–52, 60, 61, 121,
   128, 132–33, 154–55, 156

9/11 (11 September 2001) 2–3,
   11–13, 22, 29, 31, 38, 47, 97,
   118–19, 121–26, 128–30, 131,
   132, 133, 134, 135–38, 139,
   140, 141–43, 144, 145, 147–48,
   149, 151, 152–53, 154, 155,
   156–68
   Abu Nidal Organization 29
   Abu Sayyaf Group 29
   al-Qaeda 29, 123–24, 126, 132,
   133, 140
   Baader-Meinhof Group (Red
   Army Faction) 127, 156
   Dar es Salaam and Nairobi
   (1998) 22
   Ford Hood, Texas (2009) 119, 133
   Hamas 129
   Hezbollah 129
   Islamic Jihad 29
   Jemaah Islamiah 29
   Lashkar-e-Taiba 132
   in literature 45, 59–60, 118, 133, 134
   Moro, Aldo, murder of (1978) 127
   Oklahoma City (1995) 11
   Pam Am 103 (1988) 11, 22
   Red Brigades 12, 127
   Shining Path 12
   Taj Mahal Palace and Tower Hotel
   (2008) 119, 132
   Unabomber (Theodore
   Kaczynski) 142
   USS *Cole* (2000) 22
   Weather Underground
   Organization
   (Weathermen) 78
   World Trade Center (1993) 119,
   142, 148
Terrorist (Updike) 133
Tess of the d'Urbervilles (Hardy) 139
Thomson, Bobby 8, 66, 71, 75, 82, 88,
   104, 105, 106
Tiananmen Square 10, 33, 35
Times Square 6, 10, 57
Tompkins Square Park 39–40,
   41, 46
totalitarianism 2, 5–6, 21, 36, 39, 61,
   124

"Tradition and the Individual Talent" (Eliot) 158
Trafalgar Square 10, 37
trauma 124–26, 132, 133, 137, 140, 142, 152–53, 155, 158, 167–68
Triumph of Death, The (Bruegel) 51, 71, 84, 88, 92, 98, 104
Trotter, David 96
Tumbling Woman (Fischl) 159
Tunick, Spencer 26
twin towers *see* World Trade Center

Ulysses (Joyce) 1, 144
Underground (Kusturica) 84
Underworld (DeLillo) 2, 8, 9–10, 11, 12, 13, 22, 23, 26, 29–30, 35, 37, 39, 51, 56, 65–115, 118, 123, 131, 149, 154, 155
  analogy in 82, 103–04
  and baseball 8, 22, 66, 71, 72, 73–74, 75–76, 79, 82, 88, 92, 93, 98, 103–06
  the city, representations of 67, 85, 87–88, 92–93, 94–98
  and Cold War narrative 66–67, 69–71
  connections in 9, 10, 66, 73–74, 78, 79, 81, 82, 89–90, 94–95, 97–98
  and ethnicity 67, 99–104, 107–15
  the family in 101, 107–12, 113–14
  globalization in 8, 37, 39, 99
  and language 56, 74, 100, 108, 113
  memory in 67, 71–74, 75–78, 81
  narrative perspective of 86–89
  and outsider art 13, 67, 77, 90, 92, 100, 101, 102, 111–12, 118, 154
  reconciliation of opposites in 100–01, 102–07, 110, 113–14
  repetition and parataxis in 74–81, 84–85, 92–93
  reverse chronology of 66, 67, 71–74, 75, 81, 89, 94
  spatial representation in 83–98
  spirituality in 29–30, 99, 101, 113–15, 149–50
  underworlds in 67, 71, 76–77, 83–85, 86, 90, 91–92, 93, 102
  verticality in 83, 85–89
  walls and bunkers in 89–93
  and waste 67, 74, 76, 77–78, 84, 89, 91, 93, 94–97, 99, 100, 102
  wasteland in 94–95, 97
Unification Church 20–21, 31, 33, 35, 40, 43, 46, 53, 60 *see also* Moon, Sun Myung
United Nations 47
United States: apocalyptic historicism 15, 19–20
  binarism 2–3, 5, 8, 34, 66, 69, 105–07, 154
  citizenship 5–7
  Exceptionalism 5, 8, 134
  fall of 119, 131–32
  and global supremacy 101, 105, 165
  irrelevance of 8, 10, 40, 128
  isolationist paradigm of 119, 134
  neoliberal triumph of 3, 4, 34, 39, 47
  origins of 3–4
  popular culture 6–7
  susceptibility to terror 123–26, 128
  violence 4–5, 7–8, 9–10, 19
Untouchables, The (De Palma) 140
Updike, John 2, 167
  Rabbit at Rest 66, 70
  Terrorist 133
U.S.A. (Dos Passos) 65

V. (Pynchon) 19–20, 24, 80
Velvet Revolution 23–24
Velvet Underground 78
Venturi, Robert, Denise Scott Brown, and Steven Izenour: *Learning from Las Vegas* 130
Versluys, Kristiaan 118
Vidal, Gore 2
Vietnam War 4, 5, 66, 79, 80, 88, 91
Vineland (Pynchon) 6–7

Virgil: *The Aeneid* 94
Vonnegut, Kurt, Jr. 24

Walford, Edward 96
Wallerstein, Immanuel 8
Warhol, Andy 17, 26, 28, 32, 36, 37,
    53–54, 55, 58
    Crowd 54
Warren Commission *Report* 65
waste 67, 74, 76, 77–78, 84, 89, 91, 93,
    94–97, 99, 100, 102, 153
Waste Land, The (Eliot) 20, 77
Watts Towers (Rodia) 77, 111–12,
    118
weapons systems, nuclear 32, 66–67,
    70, 86, 90, 91, 107, 112
    see also atomic bomb
Weather Underground Organization
    (Weathermen) 78
Weber, Max 99–100
Wedding in December, A
    (Shreve) 118
West, Nathanael: *The Day of the
    Locust* 19–20, 54
White, Hayden 24
    Metahistory 79
"White Album, The" (Didion) 62
White Noise (DeLillo) 3–4, 6, 8, 12,
    22, 24, 31, 60, 63, 149, 155
Whitfield, Stephen J. 70
Wiener, Norbert: *The Human Use of
    Human Beings* 78
Wigglesworth, Michael: *The Day of
    Doom* 19

Wild Palms, The (Faulkner) 145
Wind-Up Bird Chronicle, The
    (Murakami) 84
"Winecoff Hotel Fire"
    (Hardy) 164–65, 166
Winogrand, Garry 58–59
Woman Warrior, The
    (Kingston) 27–28
Woolf, Virginia: *Mrs. Dalloway* 86, 87
World Trade Center 16, 22, 31, 83,
    86, 99, 117–19, 122, 123, 124,
    129, 130, 131, 132, 135, 136,
    137, 138, 140, 142, 146, 148,
    149, 152, 153, 155, 156–59,
    161, 162–63, 165
Wright, Richard: "How 'Bigger' Was
    Born" 122
    The Outsider 2
"Writing American Fiction"
    (Roth) 78
"Writing Short Stories"
    (O'Connor) 23

Yamasaki, Minoru 157
Yankees, New York 106
Yankee Stadium 15, 21, 22, 35, 38,
    53, 61
Yeats, W[illiam] B[utler]:
    "Meditations in Time of
    Civil War" 24

Zabriskie Point (Antonioni) 11
Zapruder film 51, 78
Zurbarán, Francisco de 31